The Transforming Power of Grace

Thomas C. Oden

ABINGDON PRESS / NASHVILLE

THE TRANSFORMING POWER OF GRACE

Library of Congress Cataloging-in-Publication Data

Oden, Thomas C.
   The transforming power of grace / Thomas C. Oden.
      p. cm.
   Includes bibliographical references.
   ISBN 0-687-42260-4 (alk. paper)
   1. Grace (Theology)   I. Title.
BT761.2.025   1993
234—dc20   92-36839
                                                                              CIP

94 95 96 97 98 99 00 01 02—10 9 8 7 6 5 4 3 2

MANUFACTURED IN THE UNITED STATES OF AMERICA

In appreciation for the hospitality of Catholic colleagues at Casa Santa Maria and the North American College of the Gregorian University of Rome, and for valued dialogue with Evangelical colleagues at Christianity Today and Zondervan, and Orthodox colleagues at St. Vladimir's Seminary of New York. These communities of discourse contributed consequentially to this evangelical-catholic charismology.

Work out your own salvation with fear and trembling;
for it is God who is at work in you, enabling you
both to will and to work for his good pleasure.
(Phil. 2:12-13 NRSV)

CONTENTS

ABBREVIATIONS

ACE   Stephen M. Merrill, *Aspects of Christian Experience*. Cincinnati: Walden & Stowe, 1882.

ACW   *Ancient Christian Writers: The Works of the Fathers in Translation*. Ed. J. Quasten, J. C. Plumpe, and W. Burghardt. 44 vols. New York: Paulist Press, 1946–.

AEG   *Ante-Nicene Exegesis of the Gospels*. Ed. Harold D. Smith. 6 vols. London: S.P.C.K., 1925.

Ag.   against.

AMW   Thomas C. Oden, *After Modernity . . . What? Agenda for Theology*. Grand Rapids: Zondervan, 1989.

ANF   *The Ante-Nicene Fathers*. Ed. A. Roberts and J. Donaldson. 10 vols. 1885–1896. Repr. Grand Rapids: Wm. B. Eerdmans Publishing Co., 1979. Book and chapter or section number (in arabic numerals) of patristic source, followed by volume and page number in ANF trans.

Aspects   Frank Gavin, *Some Aspects of Contemporary Greek Orthodox Thought*. Milwaukee: Morehouse, 1923.

Bk.   book.

BOC   *The Book of Concord* (1580). Ed. T. G. Tappert. Philadelphia: Muhlenberg Press, 1959.

BOCJ   *Book of Concord*, annotated by Henry E. Jacobs. 2 vols. Philadelphia: G. W. Frederick, 1893.

BW   *St. Anselm: Basic Writings*. Trans. S. N. Deane. LaSalle, Ill.: Open Court, 1962.

Catech.   catechism or catechetical.

CC   *Creeds of the Churches*. Ed. John Leith. Richmond, Va.: John Knox Press, 1979.

CD   Karl Barth, *Church Dogmatics*. Ed. G. W. Bromiley, T. F. Torrance, et al. 4 vols. Edinburgh: T. & T. Clark, 1936–1969.

CDG G. H. Joyce, *The Catholic Doctrine of Grace*. London: Burns & Oates, 1920.

CF 1) *The Christian Faith*. Ed. J. Neuner and J. Dupuis. New York: Alba House, 1982.

2) Moss, *The Christian Faith*.

CG Augustine, *City of God*.

CH Eusebius of Caesarea, *Church History*.

Chr. Christian.

CLA Luis de Molina, *Concordia liberi arbitrii cum gratiae donis*. London: n.p., 1588.

COC *Creeds of Christendom*. Ed. P. Schaff. 3 vols. New York: Harper and Bros., 1919.

Comm. 1) commentary.

2) *Commonitory*. Vincent of Lérins.

Compend. 1) compendium.

2) Thomas Aquinas, *Compendium of Theology*. New York: Herder, 1947.

3) William Burt Pope, *Compendium of Christian Theology*. 3 vols. New York: Phillips and Hunt, n.d.

Conf. Augustine, *Confessions*.

CR *Corpus reformatorum: Huldreich Zwinglis sämmtliche Werke; Johannis Calvini opera; Philippi Melanchthonis opera*. Ed. C. G. Bretschneider and H. E. Bindseil. Halle: Halis Saxonium, 1834–1860.

CSEL *Corpus scriptorum ecclesiasticorum latinorum*. Vienna: Hoelder-Pichler-Tempsky, 1866–.

CT 1) Emery H. Bancroft, *Christian Theology*. Ed. Ronald B. Majors. Grand Rapids: Zondervan, 1976.

2) Millard Erickson, *Christian Theology*. 3 vols. Grand Rapids: Baker, 1983.

CTC *Christianae theologiae compendium*. Johannes Wollebius. Ed. Ernst Bizer. Neukirchen: n. p., 1935. (English trans. by John Beardslee, in RDB).

CUP Søren Kierkegaard, *Concluding Unscientific Postscript*. Trans. H. and E. Hong. Princeton: Princeton University Press, 1991.

CWI	Charles Journet, *The Church of the Word Incarnate.* London: Sheed and Ward, 1954 (vol. 1 unless otherwise noted).
CWS	*Classics of Western Spirituality.* Ed. Richard J. Payne, et al. 30 vols. to date. Mahwah, N.J.: Paulist Press, 1978–.
DF	Johannes Braun, *Doctrina foederum sive systema theologiae didacticae et elencticae.* Amsterdam: n.p., 1588.
DI	Lactantius, *Divine Institutes,* ANF.
Doc. Vat. II	*Documents of Vatican II.* Ed. W. M. Abbott. New York: America Press, 1966.
Dogm.	dogmatic, dogmatics.
DT (Hall)	Francis Hall, *Dogmatic Theology.* 9 vols. New York: Longmans, Green, and Co., 1907–1922.
DT (Pohle)	Joseph Pohle, *Dogmatic Theology.* 12 vols. Ed. Arthur Preuss. St. Louis: B. Herder, 1922.
DT (Schmid)	Heinrich Schmid, *Doctrinal Theology of the Evangelical Lutheran Church,* 3rd ed. Minneapolis, Minn.: Augsburg, 1899.
EA	*Dr. Martin Luther's sämmtliche Werke* (Erlangen Ausgabe). Erlangen and Frankfurt: Heyder & Zimmer, 1826–1857.
East. Orth. Catech.	Eastern Orthodox Catechism. Trans. F. S. Noli. Boston: Albanian Orthodox Church of America, 1954.
EC	*The Economy of the Covenants.* 3 vols. New York: Lee and Stokes, 1798.
ECF	*Early Christian Fathers.* Ed. H. Bettenson. London: Oxford University Press, 1969.
ECW	*Early Christian Writers: The Apostolic Fathers.* Trans. Maxwell Staniforth. London: Penguin Books, 1968.
Epist.	epistle.
ETA	David Hollaz, *Examen theologicum acroamaticum.* Leipzig: B. C. Brietkopf, 1763.
Evang.	evangelical.
Expos.	exposition.

F&T   Søren Kierkegaard, *Fear and Trembling and Sickness Unto Death*. Trans. W. Lowrie. Princeton: Princeton University Press, 1968.

FC   *The Fathers of the Church: A New Translation*. Ed. R. J. Deferrari. 74 vols. to date. Washington, D.C.: Catholic University Press, 1947–.

FEF   William Jurgens, *The Faith of the Early Fathers*. 3 vols. Collegeville, Minn.: Liturgical Press.

FGG   *From Glory to Glory: Texts from Gregory of Nyssa's Mystical Writings*. Trans. H. Musurillo. Crestwood, N.Y.: St. Vladimir's Seminary Press, 1979.

Gk.   Greek.

Her.   heresies.

Hom.   homilies or homily.

HPEC   Hymnal, The Protestant Episcopal Church. New York: Church Pension Fund, 1916.

HS   Alasdair Heron, *The Holy Spirit*. Philadelphia: Westminster Press, 1983.

Inst.   John Calvin, *Institutes of the Christian Religion*. In LCC, vols. 20, 21 (references by book and chapter number, at times followed by section number).

ital. ad.   italics added.

ITLC   Guelielmus Bucanus, *Institutiones theologicae seu locorum communium Christiane religionis*. Geneva: Torunes, 1658.

Lat.   Latin.

LCC   *The Library of Christian Classics*. Ed. J. Baillie, J. T. McNiell, and H. P. Van Dusen. 26 vols. Philadelphia: Westminster Press, 1953–1961.

Lect.   lectures.

LG   Thomas C. Oden, *The Living God: Systematic Theology*, vol. 1. San Francisco: Harper & Row, 1987.

Loci   Philip Melanchthon, *Loci communes theologici*, LCC 19:18-154.

LW   *Luther's Works*. 54 vols. St. Louis: Concordia, 1953–.

LXX   Septuagint.

MHD   B. J. Otten, *A Manual of the History of Dogma*. 2 vols. London: Herder, 1917–18.

MLS   *Martin Luther: Selections from His Writings*. Ed. John Dillenberger. New York: Doubleday, 1961.

MPG   *Patrologia Graeca*. Ed. J. B. Migne. 162 vols. Paris: Migne, 1857–1876 (vol. number followed by column number). General Index, Paris, 1912.

MPL   *Patrologia Latina*. Ed. J. B. Migne. 221 vols. Paris: Migne, 1841–1865 (vol. number followed by column number). General Index, Paris, 1912.

NDM   Reinhold Niebuhr, *The Nature and Destiny of Man*. 2 vols. New York: Scribner's, 1941, 1943.

NPNF   *A Select Library of the Nicene and Post-Nicene Fathers of the Christian Church*. First Series, 14 vols.; Second series, 14 vols. Ed. H. Wace and P. Schaff (references by title and book or chapter, and subsection, and NPNF series no., vol., and page number). New York: Christian Literature Co., 1887–1900.

NT   New Testament.

OCD   Darwell Stone, *Outlines of Christian Dogma*. New York: Longmans, Green and Co., 1900.

OED   *Oxford English Dictionary*.

OF   John of Damascus, *On the Orthodox Faith*.

OFD   Herman Witsius, *De oeconomia foederum Dei*. Utrecht: n.p., 1694.

OFP   Origen, *On First Principles*.

OOT   Archibald Alexander Hodge, *Outlines of Theology*. Grand Rapids: Wm. B. Eerdmans Publishing Co., 1928.

Or. or Orat.   oration or orations.

OT   Old Testament.

PF   Søren Kierkegaard, *Philosophical Fragments*. Princeton, N.J.: Princeton University Press, 1962.

PS   Wilbur Tillett, *Personal Salvation*. Nashville: Barbee and Smith, 1902.

PW   Richard Baxter, *Practical Works*. 23 vols. London: James Duncan, 1830.

RD   Heinrich Heppe, *Reformed Dogmatics*. Trans. G. T. Thomson. London: George Allen and Unwin, 1950.

RDB   *Reformed Dogmatics: Seventeenth-Century Reformed Theology Through the Writings of Wollebius, Voetius, and Turretin*. Ed. John W. Beardslee III. Grand Rapids: Baker, 1965.

RDL   Juliana of Norwich, *Revelations of Divine Love*. New York: Doubleday, 1977.

SCD   *Sources of Christian Dogma (Enchiridion symbolorum)*. Ed. Henry Denzinger. Trans. Roy Deferrari. New York: Herder, 1954.

SCF   1) A *Summary of the Christian Faith*. Henry E. Jacobs. Philadelphia: General Council of Publications, 1905.

2) Hugh of St. Victor, *On the Sacraments of the Christian Faith*. Cambridge, Mass.: Medieval Academy of America, 1951.

SDF   Johannes Cocceius, *Summa doctrinae de foedere et testamento Dei*, in *Opera* 6. Amsterdam: n.p., 1673.

Sent.   Peter Lombard, *Sentences* (as contained in Bonaventure, *Commentaria in quator libros sententiarum*).

SHD   Reinhold Seeberg, *Textbook of the History of Doctrines*. Grand Rapids: Baker, 1952.

SML   *Sermons of Martin Luther*. Ed. J. N. Lenker. 8 vols. Grand Rapids: Baker, 1988.

ST   Thomas Aquinas, *Summa theologica*. Ed. English Dominican Fathers. 3 vols. New York: Benziger, 1947 (references include part, subpart, question number, vol., and page number of Benziger ed.).

Syst.   systematic.

Syst. Theol.   1) C. Hodge, *Systematic Theology*. 3 vols. Grand Rapids: Wm. B. Eerdmans Publishing Co., 1986 repr.

2) John Miley, *Systematic Theology*. 2 vols. New York: Eaton and Mains, 1892.

3) Miner Raymond, *Systematic Theology*. 2 vols. Cincinnati: Hitchcock and Walden, 1877–79.

4) Lewis Chafer Sperry, *Systematic Theology*. 8 vols. Dallas: Dallas Seminary Press, 1947.

5) A. H. Strong, *Systematic Theology*. 3 vols. in one. Old Tappan, N.J.: Fleming H. Revell, 1907.

6) Thomas O. Summers, *Systematic Theology*. 2 vols. Nashville: Publishing House of the Methodist Episcopal Church South, 1888.

TC   Søren Kierkegaard, *Training in Christianity*. Princeton: Princeton University Press, 1941.

TDP   Freidrich Quenstedt, *Theologia didactico-polemica*. Four parts in 1 vol. Wittenberg: J. L. Quenstedt, 1691.

Th.   theology.

Tho. Aq.   Thomas Aquinas.

TI   1) Karl Rahner, *Theological Investigations*. London: Helicon Press, 1961.

2) Richard Watson, *Theological Institutes*. 2 vols. Ed. John M'Clintock. New York: Carlton & Porter, 1850.

Tr.   tractate.

Trent   *The Canons and Decrees of the Council of Trent*. Ed. H. J. Schroeder. Rockford, Ill.: TAN, 1978.

v., vv.   verse, verses.

Vat.   Vatican.

WA   *Dr. Martin Luther's Werke, Kritische Gesamtausgabe* (Weimar Ausgabe). Weimar: Hermann Böhlau, 1883–.

Werke   *Huldreich Zwingli's Werke*. Ed. M. Schuler and J. Schulthess. 8 vols. Zürich: Schulthess, 1828.

WJW   *Works of the Rev. John Wesley*. Ed. Thomas Jackson. 14 vols. London: Wesleyan Conference Office, 1872.

WJWB   *The Works of John Wesley*. Frank Baker, ed. Bicentennial ed. Nashville: Abingdon Press, 1984–.

WL   Thomas C. Oden, *The Word of Life: Systematic Theology*, vol. 2. San Francisco: Harper & Row, 1989.

WLS   *What Luther Says*. Ed. E. Plass. 3 vols. St. Louis, Mo.: Concordia, 1959.

WML   *Works of Martin Luther: An Anthology* (Philadelphia ed.). 6 vols. Philadelphia: Muhlenberg Press, 1943.

Works   1) *The Works of Jacobus Arminius*. 3 vols. Auburn, N.Y.: Derby and Miller, 1853.

        2) *The Works of Bonaventure*. Trans. Jose de Vinck. 5 vols. Patterson, N.J.: St. Anthony Guild Press, 1960–70.

        3) *The Works of Jonathan Edwards*. 2 vols. Carlisle, Pa.: Banner of Truth Trust, 1984.

        4) *The Works of John Fletcher*. 4 vols. Salem, Ohio: Schmul, 1974.

        5) *The Works of Thomas Goodwin*. 12 vols. Edinburgh: J. Nichol, 1861–1866.

        6) *The Works of John Owen*. 16 vols. Carlisle, Pa.: Banner of Truth, 1965 repr.

WZ   Huldreich Zwingli, *Works of Zwingli*. Trans. and ed. J. Furcha and Wayne Furcha. 2 vols. Allison Park, Pa.: Pickwick Press, 1984.

THE ROOT OF CHRISTIAN SPIRITUALITY

Neither caregiving, interpersonal meeting, teaching, nor social responsibility can live long by bread alone. The caregiver, friend, teacher, and proactive change agent remain hungry for liberating grace. This book reaches out for hungry listeners.

I do not assume that my reading partner already affirms the classic Christian teaching of grace. Those who have been most denied the refreshment of grace are most apt to be quietly yearning for it.

This is why there is a special need for a book such as this, and why it is urgently needed today. These pages take the premise of personal growth back to square one to ask how renewing grace is actively working to resurrect the broken life.

THE NEED FOR THIS STUDY

Grace is God's way of empowering the bound will and healing the suffering spirit. The grace offered in the Christian community is intended for all. The unmerited blessing of God is being offered to all who are alienated from their true selves.

There is a hole in the standard shelf of books on self-help. That hole is waiting to be filled by classical Christian reasoning on grace. The spiritual formation popularizers have offered us centering without a center, meditating without a divine Thou, individual fulfillment without a history. We are now armed with a small bookshelf of strategies for personal growth controlled by ideas of human planning and convenience, but lacking plausible empowerment. My task is to show how grace seeks out the lost soul, reawakens the spiritually demoralized, and elicits spiritual growth.

Grace is the unheard note in the strident chorus of literature on spirituality and moral development. Christian spirituality quietly thrives on grace. The empowerment of the languid human spirit comes by grace. A new will is being offered to the old life trapped in sin.

Think of this as a short course on grace in pastoral care, grace in spiritual formation, and grace in evangelical witness. In staking out this path, I unapologetically ask a lot of the reader, because the subject demands a lot, but not without giving much more in return. It is the intent of the Word of God to be clearly heard, and not to return empty.

The purpose of caregiving is to make the truth of grace plausible and appropriable in the inner life of the individual. The purpose of preaching is to attest the history of grace effectively at work amid the history of sin.

I am seeking an audience that includes not only my own tradition of mainline Protestants but also Catholics, Orthodox, charismatics, and evangelicals. This book is best understood not merely as a potential textual resource for courses in theology, pastoral care, spiritual formation, and spirituality, but more so as a resource for personal spiritual formation. Here the need is the greatest.

There is a vast, scattered lay readership earnestly on the outlook for that rare treatment of spirituality and personal moral development that elicits personal change from the center. I hope to serve that readership by offering a basic doctrine of grace in plain language. I want to show how the classical Christian teaching of grace undergirds and empowers the daily walk of faith. I reach out for the serious reader who is working thoughtfully on the sanctification of time, rigorous spiritual formation, the holy life, and the dynamics of sanctifying grace.

THE SPECIAL CULTURAL SITUATION IN WHICH GRACE SEEKS A HEARING

When sex is reduced to orgasm, spirituality to numbers, and politics to power, grace has been squandered and neglected. We treat spiritual formation as the baseball fan treats the statistics page or a broker treats computer readouts of stock averages, or television treats sweeps week, or educators treat grade averages. Spiritual growth is reduced by some to a spreadsheet operation. Bean counters and number crunchers pretend to measure personal maturation, focusing on technique and quantification at the expense of spiritual empowerment.

Much in our cultural environment goes directly against the stream of the Christian teaching of grace. In an era of performance-oriented religion, the rediscovery of grace presents a profoundly subtle challenge. Teaching a religionist grace is like teaching a workaholic to relax. In a fast-paced, lonely culture of self-congratulatory striving, the Good News of grace is like a fresh breeze of relief. It is like gaining an unexpected helping partner in a colossal struggle whose outcome had remained doubtful. Unearthing the ancient teaching of grace is more like being discovered than discovering.

This generation has tried to grasp moral responsibility without that which empowers it. The more we try autonomously to ignite a moral imperative within, the more it turns to dust and ashes in our hands. Were we able to tell the story of grace entering each of our lives personally, Christianity would find vital empowerment.

American society is the advancing storm front of a narcissistic individualism thundering around the world. Those who imagine that this is a wonderful, historic achievement have not noticed the social devastations left in the path of the storm. By disenchantment, the acids of modernity have eaten away at mystery, viewing wonder as unnecessary.

Protestant Christianity, whether in its liberal or conservative garb, finds itself waking up each morning in bed with a deteriorating modern culture, between sheets with a raunchy sexual reductionism, despairing scientism, morally normless cultural relativism, and self-assertive individualism. We remain resident aliens, *of* the world but not profoundly *in* it, dining at the banquet table of waning modernity without a whisper of table grace. We all wear biblical name tags (Joseph, David, and Sarah), but have forgotten what our Christian names mean.

While some Christians have learned a graceless accommodation to the spirit of the age, others seem to know only how to hurl biblical invectives at its idolatries. Most lack a sense of the history of how the Holy Spirit is ceaselessly, actively, quietly working to elicit communities awakened by grace. The world modernity has let loose upon us must be taken with calm seriousness, but always penultimately in the light of the long and continuing history of grace, which is remembered in specific ways by Jews and Christians.

Christians who remain ignorant of this history of grace are not apt to take deep root spiritually. Christian spiritual formation must once again be shaped by its own character and calling, not by assumptions alien to itself.

In an era of sound bites, advertising-induced needs, the professionalization of need-identification, and market engineering, the community set aside by God for the reception of grace is trapped in a trendy syndrome of sweat and burnout. Therapeutic and managerial strategems have swamped the process of listening attentively for grace.

Against all odds, Protestant pietists and evangelicals have become quintessential modernizers with respect to using technology and harnessing microchip power. Piety has found ways of turning off the neighbor's suffering whimper by turning on cathode ray tubes, semiconductors, fast-track menus, and market research. When evangelical pietists lead the field in worldliness, and where social idealists have become the leading slave traders in the human market for bound souls, grace has been turned on its head. Liberal idealists insist on being duped by Marxist historical fantasies even when Marxism is everywhere else dead.

Christian presence in the world has moved from idolatrous compromise to accommodation to adjustment to surrender to moral capitulation. When the gospel of grace is abandoned, there ensues a gradual adaptation of other values to the abandonment of the gospel, ending with the assimilation of Christianity into despairing modernity.

The notion that the world must set the agenda for the worshiping community was a preemptive capitulation, once advertised as a lofty principle, but now being recognized as a massive loss of Christian identity. In civil religion the apostolate has become domesticated. Through existentialist narrowing and privatistic psychologizing, grace is robbed of its concrete history. By logical analysis the language of truth is made to seem trivial. By process philosophy the Almighty is naturalized, domesticated. By situation ethics moral judgment is turned into private sentiment. By liberation theology the care for the poor has become a political instrument and ideologized in ways completely out of touch with actual history.

When the church exists to satisfy immediately felt needs, it has lost the grace that makes it whole. When the Bible is treated as a vending machine and evangelization as a marketing plan, grace is tamed and reduced to routine. When preachers look to polls more than to prophets, hoping to guess what the public next wants to hear, grace comes cheap. In all these ways the word of grace has in our time become conventional, trivial, prosaic, uninteresting, and predictable.

In a time when user-friendly religious communities have lost their distinct identity amid a maze of relativisms, the study of grace takes on new urgency and decisive meaning. We are the generation that has tried to massage worshiping communities into existence by using organizational finesse. We have sought to induce spirituality through strategies, to coax spiritual growth by design. Spiritual formation has been thought of like painting by the numbers, as if all it takes is five fingers, twelve steps, and three colors of paint.

The acquisitive spirit works by advertising and publicity. Grace works silently, inwardly, without publicity, like seeds underground.

The modern pragmatic spirit lusts to find quick solutions that can be plotted on a pie chart and shown to be measurably workable. Grace works in its own time in hidden ways that seem too slow or too quick for human time schemes.

Lacking grace, the task of personal growth turns into a frantic search for innovative strategies. Grace works to find that very person who is desperately searching for a strategy. We have tried to manufacture spiritual growth while missing the very grace that would enable it. We have wanted to produce results without a readiness to receive help through the available means of grace—prayer, scripture study, sacrament, and actively serving love.

Church growth has been conceived as measurable numerical increase, using advertising technologies to draw in a hungry clientele as would a fast food franchise. No matter how big the numbers or how impressive the quantities, all such efforts, lacking grace, in time amount to a digression or a retrogression. Only that which is enabled by divine grace will endure in the church. All ploys and maneuvers circumventing grace will atrophy.

Our generation has tried to devise a democratic design for liberation of the poor while missing the grace that could have enabled it. Liberation theology has fitfully dreamed of revolutionary strategies for social change that could reorder unjust political power, while the grace of personal charity was becoming a lost art. Insofar as social activism has lived without grace it has pathetically become a politics of empowerment bewildered by its lack of power.

In our time we have tried to grasp and hold the elusive secret of pastoral care by means of psychological analysis, while missing the grace that would truly embody interpersonal caring. Insofar as pastoral care has lived without grace it has pathetically become a ministry in search of a motive.

Having experimented frenetically with sexuality in hopes of physical satisfaction, this generation has tended to misplace the grace of enduring covenant sexuality. Sex without the grace of covenant accountability is more akin to a jungle than to a human habitat.

Among those to whom I am most deeply indebted in developing this argument are George Lawless of the Augustinianum in Rome, Gerald O'Collins of the Gregorian University of Rome, Robert Buchiarelli of the Roman Athenaeum, and dear friends at Casa Santa Maria in Rome. I am indebted to my insightful graduate assistant, Paul Sparacio, who facilitated my work in innumerable ways.

I am grateful for critical feedback from varied audiences of students and faculty of Wyclif College (Episcopal), Toronto, Canadian Theological (Alliance) Seminary in Regina, Saskatchewan, and the Assembly of God Theological Seminary in Springfield, Missouri, where various parts of the following were presented as lectures. These pages were offered as the Simeon Lectures at Trinity Episcopal School of Ministry of Ambridge, Pennsylvania, and the Kirschner Lectures at Emmanuel School of Religion in Johnson City, Tennessee, where I benefited greatly from thoughtful responses.

—T. C. O.

Drew Forest,
Madison, New Jersey
Epiphany, 1992

INTRODUCTION

WHETHER GRACE CAN BE STUDIED

That grace is at work amid human follies is less an argument than a merciful historical fact. I seek not to establish by argument that God is gracious, but rather to show that this has indeed been believed by Christians of innumerable cultures, historical eras, and social locations.

Grace is requisite to the study of grace. Cyril of Jerusalem taught that grace is working constantly to enable its witnesses to "speak without deficiency" and its hearers to "hear with discretion."[1] There is sufficient grace for me to speak rightly of grace if I am duly attentive to the means of grace. There is sufficient grace for you to hear and discern rightly, provided you are attentive to the means of grace through scripture, prayer, historical reasoning, and dialogue.

Whatever grasp one may have of God's freeing address is enabled by grace. Whatever one may do in response to it is empowered by grace. Historically, Christianity has not thought of the teaching of grace as incidental or ancillary, for here the work of God enters deeply into the sphere of personal choices to meet and redeem ordinary struggling persons. The study of grace illumines friendships, relationships, truth-telling, and inward spirituality. Neglect of this central Christian teaching results in forgetfulness of how God accomplishes the salvation of humanity.

Many perennial distortions of faith might have been prevented had more sustained attention been given to the biblical teaching of grace. I speak of excessive emotivism, nativistic spiritualism, pantheisms of many hues, and crude views of faith healing. These misjudgments would have sewn fewer weeds in the human garden had the teaching of grace been rightly grounded, studied, and taught.[2]

The study of grace is the study of the empowerment of freedom. The freedom to which I refer is not political or economic freedom, but the more fundamental human freedom which secondarily expresses itself in

---

1. *Catechetical Lectures* 16.1, NPNF 2:7:115.
2. Augustine, *On Faith and the Creed* 9.19, FEF 3:1561:44.

political and economic life. The freedom we are most interested in enabling is classically called freedom from bondage to sin, freedom for living a life that is blessed.

In asking whether grace can or should be made an object of inquiry, *three preliminary questions* require our attention: whether grace has a history that itself can become an object of study, whether a classical consensual Christian teaching of grace is identifiable, and whether sexist premises undercut the plausibility of speaking classically of the history of grace.

WHETHER GRACE HAS A HISTORY

Revealed grace is known through the history of its disclosure. This is why there is such a close connection in Jewish and Christian thinking between grace and history (the primary focus of the last part of this study). This is why the best Christian preaching speaks of grace narratively, as story; not speculatively, but simply by telling the true, unvarnished story of God's own gracious coming among us as that singular history has been attested in scripture and human experience.[3]

Grace has a history. It is a history of human communities, not merely of individuals. The faithful do not reason toward grace independently, separated from an actual historical community of memory and testimony. We respond to grace only from within a palpable community of belief, not out of a vacuum. It is unthinkable that grace could be adequately considered abstractly, apart from the actual history in which grace is made known.[4] The biblical teaching of grace resists the opinion that individual faith chronologically precedes grace, or that conversion or church responsibilities or the means of grace may be grasped without considering the nature and history of grace.

The modern tendency is to reduce grace to a feeling or to depersonalize it into an idea or political movement so as to miss God's own self-giving in history. Augustine understood that "God does not give a Gift

---

3. Cyril of Jerusalem, *Catechetical Lectures* 16.2, 17.1, NPNF 2:7:115, 124.
4. Irenaeus, *Ag. Her.* 3.21-25, ANF 1:451-60; cf. Pannenberg, *Revelation as History* (New York: Macmillan, 1968); H. R. Niebuhr, *The Meaning of Revelation* (New York: Macmillan, 1970).

inferior to Himself."[5] Having once been given the indwelling Gift at Pentecost, the believing community has never been left without this incomparable Comforter.[6]

In studying grace the classical Christian tradition has sought not to be wise above scripture, not to pretend to exceed the ways in which grace has become self-attested through holy writ (1 Cor. 1:18-31). Irenaeus wrote: "It is not our duty to indulge in conjecture,"[7] but tell the story accurately as it occurred. With the New Testament it has become a matter of historical record that grace has come personally to humanity, and become meaningfully revealed. That the church exists at all is itself multigenerational proof of the history of grace, as Eusebius argued.[8]

Arrogant talk of competencies and achievements instantly disqualifies anyone who would speak of grace. Grace solicits the meekness of plain speech. Proud speech instantly betrays a misunderstanding of grace. The slightest whiff of grace-talk that lacks humility smells of self-deception. Faith knows that its grasp of the story of grace is always limited, for faith "sees *something* of that which it does *not see entire*, nor is it permitted to *ignore* what it is *not allowed to comprehend*."[9] God "gives grace to the humble" (Prov. 3:34).

WHETHER A CLASSICAL CONSENSUAL TEACHING OF GOD'S SELF-GIVING IS IDENTIFIABLE

Although the study of grace lives out of the narrative of the events of grace, we are not limited simply to anecdotal reports. Each of these reports points beyond itself to the truth embodied in grace-revealing events. The story is told in order that others in other times and places may grasp something of the way grace is perennially working in human affairs.

It is the task of biblical study to ensure that the story is accurately told. It is the task of preaching to seek out the meaning of the story for today. It is the task of pastoral care to mediate grace interpersonally.

5. Augustine, *On Faith and the Creed* 9.19, FEF 3:1561:44.
6. John 14:18; cf. John Chrysostom, *Hom. on John* 75, NPNF 1:14:274-75.
7. *Ag. Her.* 2.28.6, ECF 75; cf. ANF 1:401.
8. CH 9, NPNF 2:1:357-68; cf. CH 1.1, 2.1.
9. Hugh of St. Victor, SCF 53, ital. ad.

It is the task of theology to provide biblical study, preaching, and caregiving with a cohesive understanding of how the various stories of grace connect with one another meaningfully and form a plausible understanding of the world. Theology looks for a balanced, reasonable organization of Christian teaching of the events of grace. The orderly study of grace proceeds economically, listening irenically for consensual, ecumenical voices, seeking a coherent account of a varied history.

Grace is hardly a popular subject in theology today. We look in vain for a recent definitive treatment of charismology—the systematic analysis of texts of scripture and tradition that deal with the Giver and workings of grace. Yet the study of grace remains a crucial premise of spiritual formation and of every phase of Christian living and learning. The reality of grace precedes and conditions every discrete Christian inquiry into the meanings of creation, redemption, and consummation. Grace is presupposed in every serious call to repentance, faith, new birth, and holy living.

My personal resolve in kindling this inquiry is not to make any new contribution to the traditional Christian teaching of grace, but merely to attest accurately what believers have to say about the grace they have received. I would ask the reader not to discount this as a pious aside. I seek quite simply to express the one mind of the believing church which has been ever attentive to that apostolic teaching to which consent has been given by Christian believers everywhere (*ubique*), always (*semper*), and by all (*omnibus*). This is what is meant by the Vincentian method, after Vincent of Lérins, who offered this rule for judging any claim to ecumenical teaching: By the threefold test of ecumenicity, antiquity, and general lay consent, the believing community may distinguish between true and false teaching.[10]

My aim is not to catalog the protean forms of *dissent* to the ecumenic teaching of grace, but to identify and plausibly set forth the cohesive central tradition of general Christian *consent* to apostolic teaching on grace. My focus is on stating the most reliable layers of argument traditionally employed in presenting in connected order the commonly held points of the evangelical and ecumenical teaching of grace, especially as classically shared by the leading teachers of its first five centuries.

---

10. *Comm.*, LCC 7:37-39; cf. 65-74. For an accounting of this method, see *LG* 1.322-25, 341-51.

I am pledged not to become fixated on the fruit fly pace of mutating species of current critical opinion. I am bent on resisting the temptation to quote modern writers less schooled in the whole counsel of God than the best ancient classical exegetes. Rather, I focus singlemindedly on early consensual assent to the apostolic teaching of God's own self-giving.

I am not looking for a clever ruse by which the narrow way of discipleship is made conveniently acceptable to the prejudices of modernity. I will not eviscerate traditional language or seek constantly to substitute diluted terms congenial to modernity. The tested language of the church speaks in its own unrelenting ways to modern minds struggling with the absurdities and limits of modernity. Deteriorating modern ideologies must now work hard to stay abreast with the creativity of classical Christianity, not the other way around.

I do not assume that all potential partners in dialogue must have already assented to classical Christian teaching or language. Rather I ask only that the reader be willing to hear me out as to how I understand how Christians have most often reasoned about their own grounding and empowerment.

In this historical-traditional way of inquiring into grace, my own story of how grace has influenced me personally is less consequential than the church's multigenerational story of how grace is being revealed in history. This history is capable of ever-extending repercussions upon each of our personal histories. Grace shapes autobiography, but the biblical teaching of grace cannot be reduced to autobiography.

This is why I prefer consent-expressing ancient exegetes to those whose thoughts are characterized more by individual creativity, controversial brilliance, stunning rhetoric, or speculative genius. The weighting of references may be compared to a pyramid of sources, with canonical scripture as the firm foundation. The stable center of the pyramid is the consensual Christian writers of the first five centuries. Atop these are the best of medieval writers followed by consensual teachers of the Reformation and Counter-Reformation at the narrowing heights, and more recent interpreters at the tapering apex, but only those few who best grasp and express the one mind of the believing historical church of all cultures and times.

I am pledged not to try to flip that pyramid upside-down, as have guild theologians, who tend to value only what is most recent. Earlier rather than later sources are cited where pertinent, not because of an antiquarian nostalgia for that which is older, but because antiquity is a criterion of authentic memory in any historical testimony, and because the most ancient attesters have had longer to shape the ecumenical tradition of general lay consent.

Those who belittle proof-texting must watch carefully that they do not end in ignoring the very canonical textuary upon which the formative power of grace thrives. Some modern forms of historical criticism that sincerely intend at every step to place every scripture reference in its historical circumstances risk becoming a long string of esoteric critical remarks on modern commentators that inadvertently forgets the sacred text itself. In this way the well-motivated attempt at historical critical exegesis has taken a heavy toll on both religious instruction and moral practice.

My purpose is to delineate points of substantial agreement between traditions of East and West—Catholic, Protestant, and Orthodox—on the power of grace in spiritual formation. I will be listening intently for the historical ecumenical consensus received by believers of widely varied languages, social locations, and cultures, whether the consensus is of African, pre-European, or European Christian traditions, whether it is expressed by women or men of the second or first Christian millennium, whether it is post- or pre-Constantinian.

I reach out for traditional evangelical Protestants, hoping not to miss the vital questions being raised by traditional Catholics, and vice versa. I reach out actively for charismatics hoping not to lose touch with Eastern rite communicants, for liturgical renewalists without offense to low church Protestants, for social liberationists without demeaning pietists. How? By seeking the shared roots out of which each has grown.

Who are the principal consensual exegetes to whom this argument constantly appeals? Above all they are the ecumenical councils and early synods that have come to be so often quoted as representing the mind of the believing church; the four preeminent ecumenical teachers of the eastern Christian tradition (Athanasius, Basil, Gregory of Nazianzus, John Chrysostom), as well as the western (Ambrose, Jerome, Augustine, and Gregory the Great); and others whom the church has perennially valued for accurately stating broad points of ecumenical consensus: Cyril of Jerusalem, Cyril of Alexandria, Hilary, Leo, and John of Damascus. These people spent their lives not in academic retreats, but on the firing line of the daily practice of soul care.

"Classical" in this definition includes consensus-bearing medieval and Protestant formularies consistent with ancient consensual exegesis. In this way the traditions from Anselm, Thomas Aquinas, Luther, Melanchthon, Calvin, Cranmer, Hooker, Chemnitz, and Ursinus, through Wesley and Edwards to Barth and Pannenberg are referenced where congruous with patristic teaching. I do not hesitate to quote at times relatively nonconsensual writers like Origen, Tertullian, and Novatian, but I do so only on those points at which they have generally confirmed or articulated or refined consensual views, not on points where they diverge into idiosyncratic thinking.[11]

WHETHER SEXIST PREMISES UNDERMINE CLASSICAL UNDERSTANDINGS OF THE HISTORY OF GRACE

The life of faith is never motherless (*amētōr*, Heb. 7:3). The spiritually reborn do not utter the name of God as Father (*Abba*, Papa) without the community of faith as mothering matrix (*mētēr*).[12] The work of grace is often compared to maternal, nurturing actions: "As a mother comforts her child, so will I comfort you" (Isa. 66:13; cf. Ps. 22:9, 10; Isa. 49:14-15).

Gregory of Nazianzus was long ago amused by those who foolishly held "God to be a male," which he regarded as a misplaced analogy. Just as one cannot say that God because Father is therefore male, so one cannot conclude that "Deity is feminine from the gender of the word, and the Spirit neuter," since the designation "has nothing to do with generation. But if you would be silly enough to say, with the old myths and fables, that God begat the Son by a [physical] marriage with His own Will, we should be introduced to the Hermaphrodite god of Marcion and Valentinus who imagined these newfangled Aeons."[13]

---

11. Vincent of Lérins, *Comm.* 17, 18, NPNF 2:11:143-45.
12. Cyprian, *Letters* 39, ANF 5:316-19.
13. Gregory of Nazianzus, *Or.* 31.7 (*On the Holy Spirit*), NPNF 2:7:320, amended.

It is because grace comes to us personally that gender has become a decisive theological issue. Gender is not a recent issue, but a question lodged already in the nativity event.

Whenever we speak *personally*, whether of ourselves or of God, we are pressed to use personal language with personal pronouns (he and she), rather than impersonal pronouns (it). It is ironic that today when we speak personally of God we seem to be trapped in categories of gender. Yet this has historically been preferred to the flat depersonalization of all language about God.

The Giver of grace is less a depersonalized "it" than One who addresses us personally as responsible, free individuals. It is only through a particular personal Thou, God the Son, that the love of the Father is offered up, and only through a particular personal Thou, God the Spirit, that the Father's love incarnated in the Son is made plausible inwardly. One is sorely tempted to rewrite scripture to gain a more advantageous posture with some modern audiences. But no well-instructed believer thinks of grace as "it" or prays to an "it," even if steeped in modernity.

Neither male nor female language adequately grasps the fullness of grace coming personally.[14] Both sexes are honored and blessed in the incarnation: The one giving birth must be female, the one receiving birth is male.[15] Do not hasten over this point. Linger. Meditate. Savor a delicious classical inference: *If the mother of Grace Incarnate must of necessity be female, since only females are mothers, the Savior is more likely to be male if both sexes are to be equitably and evenhandedly involved in the singularly gracious nativity event.* The only alternative would be to have a female mother of the Savior and a female Savior. For one cannot have a *male mother* of the Savior. Further, an androgynous or hermaphroditic Savior would fail entirely to share in the specific *either-or* nature of our human sexual condition. This is why the female birth-enabler is traditionally regarded as no less an intrinsic part of the divine nativity drama than the maleness of the Messiah in the male line of David as promised.[16]

Augustine summed up that God "was not ashamed of the male nature, for He took it upon Himself; or of the female, for He was born of

14. Gregory of Nazianzus, *Or.* 27, NPNF 2:7:284-88; cf. John of Damascus, OF 1.4-8; FC 37:170-85.
15. Augustine, *Eighty-three Different Questions* 11, FC 70:42.
16. Cf. LG 7-9, 222-23; WL 117-18, 148.

a woman." Hence we are *"liberated by the agency of both sexes."*[17] God's "temporal plan ennobled each sex, both male and female. By possessing a male nature and being born of a woman He further showed by this plan that God has concern not only for the sex He represented but also for the one through which He took upon Himself our nature."[18]

To divest language of all gender reference is ideological bias reflecting an anti-historical prejudice. This is quintessential modern chauvinism. This exclusion tends toward an implicit denial of our very createdness as sexual beings. No woman or man I know wishes to be called an "it." If so, how can one finally rest easy with "it" language addressed to God? God is not rightly viewed as even less personal than ourselves.

The scandal of particularity remains. God meets us in specific times and places among people with specific names and genders—ordinary people with particular parents, of a particular race, an unduplicable time, and a distinctive culture. To back away wholly from gender reference is to stand offended at the gospel of a man born of woman, and the Spirit who utterly transcends the lingual gender differences between *ruach* and *pneuma*.

Elizabeth Achtemeier has astutely shown that the prophets did not suffer from a lack of imagination in conceiving of God as female, for they were already surrounded by cultures dominated by feminine deities. Rather they deliberately chose not to apply feminine language uncritically to God, she says, "because they knew and had ample evidence from the religions surrounding them that the female language for the deity results in a basic distortion of the nature of God and of his relation to his creation"[19]—namely, the deification of nature, pantheism, and immanental religion. Even as male terms for God are subject to distortion, so are female. "When you have a Goddess as the creator, it's her own body that is the universe. She is identical with the universe."[20] This the prophets called idolatry and classical Christianity defined as pantheism. These dangers call us to make a sustained effort to use language fairly and without sexist bias, according to the incarnate mission of God, which redeems and embraces both sexes.

---

17. *The Christian Combat* 22, FC 21:338-39, ital. ad.
18. *On Faith and the Creed* 4.9, FC 27:326.
19. D. Miller, ed., *The Hermeneutical Quest* (Allison Park, Pa.: Pickwick, 1986), p. 109.
20. J. Campbell, *The Power of Myth* (New York: Doubleday, 1991), p. 167.

PART ONE

GRACE IN SPIRITUAL FORMATION

CHAPTER 1

THE NURTURE OF GRACIOUS ABILITY

Grace is an overarching term for all of God's gifts to humanity, all the blessings of salvation, all events through which are manifested God's own self-giving. Grace is a divine attribute revealing the heart of the one God, the premise of all spiritual blessing.

DEFINING GRACE

Grace is the favor shown by God to sinners. It is the divine goodwill offered to those who neither inherently deserve nor can ever hope to earn it. It is the divine disposition to work in our hearts, wills, and actions, so as actively to communicate God's self-giving love for humanity (Rom. 3:24; 6:1; Eph. 1:7; 2:5-8).

Charis

By grace, God freely moves toward sinners to offer reconciling forgiveness, a new birth of freedom, sonship and daughterhood in the family of God. The disposition of God is most clearly revealed as sheer grace, unmerited goodwill, unearned favor toward the ungodly (Rom. 5:15-21). This disposition is mirrored in the ministry of Word and Sacrament whose care of souls offers grace to all.

The Greek word for grace is *charis* (from *charizesthai*, to favor or gratify by showing favor), from which our words "charisma" and "charismatic" derive. The Latin parallel is *gratia*, from which our English word "grace" derives.

Charis is quintessentially a gift, not an achievement. Its plural, the gifts (*charismata*) of the Spirit, are freely given, divinely enabled, and effectively offered through historical and concrete means, being received in faith.

The Hebrew words that anticipate and attest this unmerited divine disposition are *chen* (gracious, *channun*) and *chesed* (mercy, steadfast love). The Lord is gracious and merciful (2 Chron. 30:9; Neh. 9:17), slow to anger, full of compassion, and gracious (Ps. 86:15; 111:4; 112:2).

Grace may be used in the objective sense to speak of a favor or privilege. When one freely receives a favor out of the goodwill or benevolence of another, that unmerited gift is called *charis*. The same root word may also point to a subjective disposition to grant something readily, freely, liberally. When goodwill is shown by one who is not indebted and who has no objective need to show benevolence, the subjective attitude of the benevolent party is called *charis*. Both the divine disposition to work good in us and the spiritual gift or blessing that ensues from the unmerited favor of God are viewed as grace.

The aesthetic dimension of grace is seen in the fact that one may be said to be gracious when personal gifts make one's behavior beautiful or desirable. The idea of wooing and giving gifts is an intrinsic aspect of the demeanor of grace. The Spirit actively seeks out the beloved and offers gifts. Thus grace has rightly come to be associated with attractive aesthetic qualities. To receive a blow with grace is to do so with good spirit or charm or style. To catch a ball or dance ungracefully is to do so clumsily, ineptly, awkwardly. God woos humanity with beautiful, not ugly acts. Even the cross is made beautiful by grace.

The way of grace is sharply contrasted with the way of works, by which we are prone to seek to achieve merit: "And if by grace, then it is no longer by works; if it were, grace would no longer be grace" (Rom. 11:6). The deep motive of God's saving action is simply stated: "He saved us, not because of righteous things we had done, but because of his mercy" (Titus 3:5). It is simply because God "is rich in mercy" that the faithful have been made "alive with Christ even when we were dead in transgressions—it is by grace you have been saved" (Eph. 2:4, 5).

The entire plan of redemption is called a covenant of grace, which in time embraces, fulfills, and recasts the Mosaic covenant of works. Christ is the incarnate embodiment of grace to humanity, the Word become flesh, "full of grace and truth" (John 1:14). "For the law was given through Moses; grace and truth came through Jesus Christ" (John 1:17; cf. Eph. 2:7).

The classical exegetes pondered whether a gracious act is precisely the same as a loving act. If so, grace is finally nothing more or less than love. Some medieval and scholastic writers have theorized that grace, whether God is sole agent or the human person is cooperating agent, is wholly indistinguishable from love (stated classically by Duns Scotus, Robert Bellarmine, and Leonard Lessius).

Closer to ecumenical consent is the subtler view of Augustine that grace and love, though inseparable, are distinguishable. For grace imparts to the soul a new spiritual being, while love confers upon that being a renewing spiritual power. Hence the grace of God precedes the engendering of a loving spirit in us.[1] Such a distinction seems embedded in the thought that "the *grace* of our Lord was poured out on me abundantly, *along with the faith and love* that are in Christ Jesus" (1 Tim. 1:14).[2]

In gracious actions a blessing is bestowed. The active mercy of God has become expressed in time and space through touchable, tasteable, visible means of the grace of God the Life-giver and Helper. Such acts are freely given, not earned. By these gifts we are blessed.[3] When one "says grace" before meals, the one who is receiving splendid gifts feels "graced" or blessed and hence "grateful."[4]

Readers of scripture find the thought of God's grace appearing abundantly with extremely variable flexibility and numerous complementary levels of meaning. As the unmerited favor of God, grace may point to an era of history in which God's mercy is shown to transcend the law, or point to an encompassing relation of reconciliation of humanity with God, or point to a special gift that enables one to perform a distinctive service by God's help.

God's Own Self-giving

So intimately connected are the terms "grace" and "Spirit" that they flow together as if virtually interchangeable (Acts 6:5, 8). God's Spirit is called "the Spirit of grace" (Heb. 10:29) since it is through the Spirit that the Father confers the grace of the Son upon the celebrating community. From the fullness of this saving event we continue to receive

---

1. Augustine, *On the Gift of Perseverance* 14-19, NPNF 1:5:530-31.
2. Ital. ad.; cf. Tho. Aq., *ST* 1-2.Q110.3-4, 1:1134-35.
3. Augustine, *Comm. on John* Tr. 3.9, NPNF 1:7:21.
4. Tho. Aq., *ST* 1-2.Q110.1, 1:132.

grace upon grace in a persevering series of divine gifts to humanity (John 1:15, 16).

Grace flows from the Father's goodwill, as it has become mediated to us through the active life and obedient death of the Son, whose mission is completed and made effective in our hearts by the work of the Holy Spirit. The Spirit, in turn, proceeds from the Father and the Son, and comes to convict, convert, regenerate, justify, transform, and sanctify us, and bring to complete fruition the mission of the Son.[5]

The Spirit is called simply the Gift[6] because in it God not only gives himself, but actively *enables* the Gift to be received.

The Gift is given with the precise intent of being fully and freely received. God by self-giving seeks to transform our human habits and behavioral responses. Human responsiveness is called for at every step.[7] The Spirit is sent precisely to nurture faith, hope, love, and the fruits of the Spirit, so that persons can grow through prayer and dialogue to be as fully reflective as possible of the incomparable goodness of God.

The Gift-giver and Gift are one (John 14:26; 20:22; Acts 1:16; 11:15; 19:2-6). "As the Son is both Priest and Sacrifice, so the Spirit is both Gift and Giver."[8] As "there are different kinds of gifts, but the same Spirit," so "there are different kinds of working, but the same God works all of them in all men. Now to each one the manifestation of the Spirit is given for the common good" (1 Cor. 12:4, 6-7).

The triune premise helps the believer to behold that the grace of God the Father is the grace of God the Son, and the grace of the Son is the grace of God the Spirit, not three graces but the unifying grace of the one God—uncreated, begotten in the Son, and proceeding in the Spirit. The grace of the Father is for all creatures, enabling all life, and prior to all choice and all sin. The grace of the Son is particularly given for sinners (Rom. 5:8). The grace of the Spirit administers the finished work of the Son.[9] Although all grace as such is the work of the triune God, the enabling and appropriation of grace is primarily the constant work of God the Spirit.[10]

---

5. Calvin, *Inst.* 2.2-3; cf. Barth, *CD* 4:4:143ff.
6. Tho. Aq., *ST* 1-1.Q38, 1:191-93.
7. Prosper of Aquitaine, *On Grace and Free Will* 4ff., FC 7:352ff.
8. Pope, *Compend.* 2:334.
9. Novatian, *Treatise Concerning the Trinity* 16, ANF 5:625-26.
10. Ambrose, *On the Holy Spirit* 1.12, NPNF 2:10:110; cf. Calvin, *Inst.* 2.2.

Life as Unearned Gift

Life can only be received; it is offered as sheer gift. No one has ever come into being by writing a letter to parents and asking them for life, because there is no one yet there to do the asking. Precisely nothing exists before the zygote receives nascent life in conception. Think of it: Before your conception, there was not even a hint or glimpse or preliminary fantasy of the gift of life by which you might have imagined that you desired or even vaguely hoped for life.[11]

Similarly, in new birth from above, there is no way for those already dead in their sins to give themselves life (Rom. 8:10, 11; Eph. 2:1-5). One cannot apart from grace even pray for or hope for, much less initiate or design, a reborn relationship to God. One cannot simply grasp, claim, or seize faith, hope, or love.[12] They are gifts of the Spirit, which, until given, the unawakened sinner cannot cajole or manipulate into birth or possession.

God's own Spirit remains sovereignly free, coming and going, working when and where God pleases. The Christian life comes to us on God's own initiative, not our own. We can choose by God's grace to put ourselves in those places and times where God promises to be present. We can avail ourselves of the means of grace, but not so as to control them. They remain precisely grace—sheer gift. The teaching of grace stands as a penetrating challenge to all pretensions of self-sufficiency.[13]

God's grace is freely offered to but not unilaterally intruded upon human freedom. God treats us as self-determining persons, not mud-balls to be thrown. Grace appeals to our freedom, seeking to engender free responsiveness. The Spirit works to awaken the cooperation of human willing with God's own goodwill. "Through Christ Jesus the law of the Spirit of life set me free from the law of sin and death" (Rom. 8:2). Although justification is imputed, wholly as a gift, an answer is required: For *what is imputed seeks to be imparted*, given in such a way that spiritual gifts can be appropriated as acts of freedom.

---

11. John 3:3-8; cf. John Chrysostom, *Hom. on John* 24, 25, FC 33:232-50.
12. Wesley, "The New Birth," WJW 6:65ff. (WJWB 1:186-201, Sermon 45); cf. "The Imperfection of Human Knowledge," WJW 6:337-50 (WJWB 1:568-86, Sermon 69).
13. Augustine, *On Nature and Grace*, NPNF 1:5:121ff.

THE GRACE THAT PREPARES THE WAY

Preaching attests grace to the worshiping community; pastoral care seeks to make it real for the individual; sacramental life embodies it. Grace is also present in the preparation leading to readiness to respond to each of these ministries.

The Grace of Praying for Openings to Grace

Rather than entering at some point in a process of natural spiritual formation already begun, grace is there from the beginning, calling that process forth from nothing. It is grace which awakens the very desire to pray, and which enables one to say in prayer: "Open my eyes that I may see/wonderful things in your law./I am a stranger on earth;/do not hide your commands from me./My soul is consumed with longing / for your laws at all times" (Ps. 119:18-20).

The humble prayer for readiness for grace is modeled in Psalm 51: "Create in me a pure heart, O God, / and renew a steadfast spirit within me./Do not cast me from your presence/or take your Holy Spirit from me./Restore to me the joy of your salvation/and grant me a willing spirit, to sustain me" (vv. 10-12).

The Second Council of Orange (A.D. 529) refused to reverse the priority of grace over prayer: "If anyone says that the grace of God can be conferred as a result of human prayer, but that it is not grace itself which makes us pray," that is inconsistent with the scripture that says "I revealed myself to those who did not ask for me" (Rom. 10:20, quoting Isa. 65:1).[14]

As the travelers walked to Emmaus, the risen Lord "opened their minds so they could understand the Scriptures" (Luke 24:45). Luke reported that the Lord opened Lydia's "heart to respond to Paul's message" (Acts 16:14). Their eyes became open not because they sought God, but because God sought them (John 9; Acts 9:18). Seeing is not a human given, but a divine gift. Pastoral care relentlessly searches for some responsive circumstantial opening up of the soul to God's gracious presence. The caregiver does not elicit grace but seeks to discover and name the grace already there.

---

14. CC 38.

Why Grace First Illumines the Darkness of Sin

The condition in which passion-driven humanity typically exists was carefully described by Paul: "They are darkened in their understanding and separated from the life of God because of the ignorance that is in them due to the hardening of their hearts. Having lost all sensitivity, they have given themselves over to sensuality so as to indulge in every kind of impurity, with a continual lust for more" (Eph. 4:18-19).[15] This sounds like our own culture of narcissism, with its hedonists' "Madonna," crack babies, and sexually transmitted diseases. Willfully we give ourselves over to the world, the flesh, and the adversary.

Neurotic anxiety, self-deception, overdependency, and compulsive behaviors require the grace that first uncovers the depths of the bondage of the will, before one can pray for wholeness. Lacking God's own costly outreaching love for fallen persons, humanity would have remained blinded and trapped in decaying syndromes of the history of sin. Lacking grace, "There is no one righteous, not even one; / there is no one who understands, / no one who seeks God. / All have turned away" (Rom. 3:10-12). "The man without the Spirit does not accept the things that come from the Spirit of God, for they are foolishness to him, and he cannot understand them, because they are spiritually discerned" (1 Cor. 2:14). "The sinful mind is hostile to God. It does not submit to God's law, nor can it do so. Those controlled by the sinful nature cannot please God" (Rom. 8:7-8). This condition requires a radical illumination enabling those in darkness to begin to awaken to the light, and to come themselves to be "light in the Lord."[16]

The grace of illumination seeks out and addresses fallen humanity precisely amid its utter inability to behold, discern, or respond to God. The toxic syndrome of sin is described by the Formula of Concord: "Although man's reason or natural intellect still has a dim spark of the knowledge that there is a God, as well as of the teaching of the law," nevertheless the fallen will has become so perversely blinded "that when even the most gifted and the most educated people on earth read or hear the Gospel of the Son of God and the promise of eternal salvation, they cannot by their own powers perceive this, comprehend it, understand it, or believe and accept it as the truth. On the contrary,

15. Cf. Second Helvetic Confession, CC 133.
16. Eph. 5:8; cf. Barth, CD 4:3:508ff.

the more zealously and diligently they want to comprehend these spiritual things with their reason, the less they understand or believe, and until the Holy Spirit enlightens and teaches them they consider it all mere foolishness and fables" (cf. Rom. 1:19-21, 28, 32).[17]

It is into this utter darkness that the light of illuminating grace comes shining through. Even while the light is shining through the darkness which lacks the grace of recognition, "the darkness has not understood it" (John 1:5). No one can "assent to the Gospel teaching" apart from "the illumination of the Holy Spirit," by which one "yields voluntary obedience to God himself, by assenting to and co-operating with his grace, which he is able to resist."[18] Far more than simply one step in the call to repentance, illumination is better conceived in a more extensive sense as embracing the whole sequence of the saving acts of grace.[19]

The Continuing Need to Petition for Illumination

Aware of the knotty depth of self-deception, the faithful of all generations have continued daily to pray for the ability to see, for illumination, for awakening from spiritual and moral stupor.[20] In Psalm 119, the psalmist prayed ten times that God would grant him understanding. Paul prayed often for illuminating grace (Eph. 1:17, 18; Col. 1:9, 11; Phil. 1:9, 10).[21] By petition for illumination, believers are implicitly acknowledging "that what they ask of God they cannot obtain by their own natural powers."[22]

The unregenerate heart is compared to a stone; it is so hard, it so lacks responsiveness that it is practically impenetrable (Ezek. 36:26; Jer. 5:3). It is like a wild, unbroken beast that requires austere taming (Ps. 73:22), or rough timber that needs extensive trimming, that grace cuts and shapes for use (Hos. 6:5).

---

17. Formula of Concord, "Solid Declaration" 2, BOC 521, 522.
18. Vat. I, COC 2:244.
19. John Chrysostom, *To the Fallen Theodore*, NPNF 1:9:97-99; cf. Ilias the Presbyter, *Gnomic Anthology* 2, in *Philokalia*, compiled by Nikodimos of the Holy Mountain and Makarios of Corinth (London: Faber and Faber, 1979–84), 3:43-46; Martin Chemnitz, *Harmony* (Hamburg: Herteli and G. Libernickelii, 1704), commenting on John 1:9; Jacobs, SCF 228, 229.
20. Charles Wesley, "Awake Thou That Sleepest," WJWB 1:142-58; cf. WJW 5:17-25; Barth, CD 4:3:511ff.
21. Formula of Concord, "Solid Declaration" 2, BOC 523.
22. Ibid.

In matters relating to the physical world of causes and effects, fallen humanity remains capable of practical intelligence. But when it comes to grasping matters of the spirit, human beings are more like

> a pillar of salt, like Lot's wife, yes, like a log or a stone, like a lifeless statue which uses neither mouth nor eyes nor senses nor heart, inasmuch as man does not see or recognize the dreadful. . . . All pleas, all appeals, all admonitions are in vain. It is useless to threaten, to scold, or even to teach or preach until the Holy Spirit enlightens, converts, regenerates.[23]

Everything that one "lives and does without and outside of faith" is encompassed in one word: sin.[24] Humanity without grace remains a fallen heap of ruin (*massa perditionis*),[25] the self-alienated will being free only to blunder toward corruption, and incapable of its own power to repent.[26] Without the grace of the Spirit, even "the message of the cross is foolishness to those who are perishing, but to us who are being saved it is the power of God" (1 Cor. 1:18).

> No man can truly say
>   That Jesus is the Lord,
> Unless thou take the veil away,
>   And breathe the living Word.
> Then, only then, we feel
>   Our interest in his blood,
> And cry, with joy unspeakable,
>   "Thou art my Lord, my God!"[27]

HOW GRACE WORKS THROUGH COMPLEMENTARY FACULTIES OF CONSCIOUSNESS: KNOWING, WILLING, AND THE SENSES

Grace offers care for souls by descending to the level of awareness fit for ministry to a particular soul at a particular moment.[28] The strata of

---

23. Formula of Concord, "Solid Declaration" 2, BOC 525; cf. Luther's exposition of Psalm 90, LW 13:75-141.
24. Luther, EA 12:111.
25. Luther, WA 1:427.
26. Ibid., 1:359; cf. 2:362, 702; EA 7:239.
27. Charles Wesley, "Spirit of Faith Come Down," as found in *PS* 139.
28. Gregory the Great, Pastoral Care 3, NPNF 2:12:24-71.

the workings of grace in the soul may be viewed in terms of three discrete faculties of human consciousness: intellect, will, and the sensory
capacities. In brief, grace penetrates consciousness so as to *illumine the
intellect, strengthen the will, and discipline the senses.*[29]

Grace Illumines the Intellect

Illumination is the act of God the Spirit by which the power to
apprehend the truth is communicated to the petitioner. The Spirit
must render human consciousness receptive to the gospel call before it
can have any effect.[30]

By illumination the Spirit challenges our prejudices, disarms our resistances, reveals our egocentricity for what it is, and enables us to hear
the Word.[31] By these means the Spirit cultivates a frame of mind and
readiness to hear of which the corrupted will is incapable.[32] In this way
the Spirit not only "rids of ignorance," but "invests with knowledge."[33]

Precisely through the limitations of his suffering thorn, Paul was graciously illumined so as to recognize that "my grace is sufficient for you,
for my power is made perfect in weakness" (2 Cor. 12:9). The illumination Paul experienced on the road to Damascus was peculiar to Paul's
history. Similarly, the process by which each person is illumined by
grace is specific to that person's own story.

Illumining grace *(gratia illuminationis)* enlightens the eyes: "The commands of the Lord are radiant, / giving light to the eyes" (Ps. 19:8).
Normally the discernment which results from illuminating grace takes
time, requiring an unfolding process of discovery by which deceptions
and idolatries are gradually identified and weeded out. At every layer of
growth God gives the increase. "I planted the seed, Apollos watered it,
but God made it grow" (1 Cor. 3:6).

Grace Strengthens the Will

To know the good is not always to do it, or will to do it, or have the
strength of will to do it. In order to receive grace we must not only

---

29. Augustine, *The Spirit and the Letter* 52-61, NPNF 1:5:106-11; cf. *On the Trinity* 11,
    NPNF 1:3:144-54; DT (Pohle) 7:19-48.
30. Augustine, *On the Grace of Christ*, NPNF 1:5:217ff.; cf. Kierkegaard, PF, "A
    Project of Thought."
31. Calvin, *Inst.* 3.24.
32. John Chrysostom, *Baptismal Instructions*, ACW 31:88-90.
33. Cyril of Jerusalem, *Catech. Lect.* 16.17, NPNF 2:7:120.

"*know* what we ought to strive after," but we must also be free to "*love* to do it."[34]

The work of grace encourages the will to desire (and so to do) that truth one is coming to know. The greater good we once thought we ought to do we now want to do. A transformation is taking place in the will. What this grace transforms in its work of enabling is not simply our understanding of truth, but more so our disposition to embody the truth. The willingness and desire of the seeker behaviorally to embody the truth is made increasingly possible. This is especially so since the deeper resistances to grace are less in knowing than in willing. Life under grace is not merely a matter of intellect (*cogitatio, suasio, scientia, cognitio*), but also a matter of will and desire (*delectatio, desiderium, caritas, bona voluntas, cupiditas*).[35]

This renewing of the will is not a disabling or temporary abrogation of freedom, but a deeper enabling of it. "Therefore if God moves man's will, this is evidently not opposed to freedom of choice, just as God's activity in natural things is not contrary to their nature," Thomas reasoned. "God moves things in a way that is consonant with their nature."[36] God moves in the will in ways consonant with willing, not coercively against the will, a point we will treat more fully later.

Grace Guides the Senses

Grace, while illumining the intellect and strengthening the will, goes even further to guide the appetites, passions, and affective states, so as to draw the emotive life toward saving faith. Grace works differently on the appetitive level than when it works through intellect or will. Its task is gently to guide and shape the passions and appetites toward greater responsiveness to God's incomparable goodness.

Grace guides the senses negatively by restraining the lusts and libidinal energies and impulses of concupiscence that would prevent one from responding to the now revealed good. On this ground, grace moves positively by helping to offer the soul an appetite for heavenly food, a desire to reach the celestial city, a joy that exceeds the joys of

---

34. Council of Carthage 14.4, SCD §104, p. 45.
35. DT (Pohle) 7:27:28.
36. *Compend.* (Tho. Aq.) 129, p. 137.

the senses, a hunger for eternal blessedness as distinguished from the satiable dregs of sensory pleasure.[37]

Love is the key affection that gives contour to all other affections.[38] If what one loves becomes radically redirected toward the love of God, then one's mind, will, emotions, and behavior will be consequently converted and redirected. Among emotions met and influenced by grace are joy and sorrow, desire and aversion, hope and despair. Grace is in the business of refashioning what sinners love. Grace works not only to bring us to "believe what ought to be loved," wrote Augustine, but also to "love what we have believed."[39]

Amid these emotive processes, grace works through natural agencies—neural systems, synapses, brains, hormonal mechanisms—to draw persons preveniently and cooperatively toward the salvation God desires to give to all. By grace working through the intellect, will, emotions, and behavioral patterns, God addresses our innermost thoughts and feelings.[40] "Who can see or tell by what affections God visits and guides the human soul?"[41]

ATONEMENT AND GRACIOUS ABILITY

How could it be that one spiritually lost and dead could be "yet possessed of moral ability that makes him responsible for his lost condition"?[42] The Pelagian view that the freedom of the natural moral will has suffered no disability must be rejected.[43] The deterministic view that natural man is utterly incapable of exercising free will leads to opposite excesses.

The classical consensual answer lies in a balanced distinction between created nature as good, and fallen nature as relatively incapable of exercising free will so as to move toward saving faith. No one

37. *The Martyrdom of Polycarp*, ANF 1:127ff.; cf. Kierkegaard, *The Gospel of Suffering* (Minneapolis: Augsburg, 1948).
38. Augustine, *Conf.* 4, NPNF 1:1:68-78; cf. Tho. Aq., *ST* 1-2.Q25.2.
39. *On the Grace of Christ* 12, NPNF 1:5:222.
40. Augustine, *Comm. on Psalms* 102.16, NPNF 1:7:368; cf. *Comm. on John* 16.7, in DT (Pohle) 7:27:28.
41. Fulgentius, *Contra Collator.* 7.2, DT (Pohle) 7:26.
42. Tillett, *PS* 115.
43. Augustine, *Letters*, FC 32:120-38.

remains merely in an utterly ungraced, fallen state, as if fallen human-ity can be imagined without any hints or tinges whatever of preparing grace.[44]

The good that is to be found in the unregenerate fallen human will is not due to nature, as the semi-Pelagians would have it, but grace. This explains why "all men are not as bad as they can be."[45] "Grace arrested man in his fall, and placed him in a salvable state, and endowed him with the *gracious ability* to meet all the conditions of per-sonal salvation. Fallen man has never been without the benefits and influences of the atonement," wrote Tillett. "The benefits of Christ's righteousness and atoning death are coextensive with the effects of Adam's sin."[46]

No human being has been condemned for Adam's sin alone, but insofar as anyone is subject to condemnation and judgment, it is due to one's own freely collusive cooperation with the conditions of sin result-ing from the history of sin following Adam.[47] The principle of free moral agency is preserved in and through the doctrine of sufficient grace.[48] Sin is never unilaterally imputed, but chosen, rechosen, and transmitted historically and intergenerationally by repeated social choice.

All sin presupposes some preliminary intuition of moral law and eth-ical awareness. Sin is not committed out of invincible ignorance, but out of personal will.[49] Conversely, no human being has been coercively forced to be redeemed by Christ's atoning work.[50] Rather, the redemp-tion that God intends for all must be cooperatively chosen by freedom cooperating with the conditions of grace enabled by the history of grace in Christ. Those "weary of wandering" are "now made willing to return," learning that God is "more full of grace than I of sin."[51] God's love enables precisely that response in the sinner which God's holiness demands: trust in God's own self-giving.

44. Nemesius, *On the Nature of Man*, LCC 4:397-420.
45. G. B. Stevens, quoted in *PS* 119.
46. *PS* 117, 120; Rom. 5:12-21.
47. Justin Martyr, *First Apology* 28, 61, ANF 1:172; cf. *Second Apology* 14, ANF 1:93; *Dialogue with Trypho* 141, ANF 1:269-70.
48. Nemesius, *On the Nature of Man*, LCC 4:397-420.
49. Lateran Council 5, SCD §775, p. 242.
50. Ephraim Syrus, *Nisibene Hymns* 16, NPNF 2:13:185.
51. Charles Wesley, "Weary of Wandering from My God" (1749), HPEC 119.

The gracious ability enabled through Christ is not inferior to the moral disability suffered through Adam (Rom. 5:12-17). In the renewal of gracious ability, righteousness and grace are fully as "original" as sin is. In Christ, original sin has been arrested and "changed into a conditional sentence."[52]

Overview: Grace Prevening, Convicting, Operating, Cooperating, and Persevering

Among the stages or kinds of grace the church has customarily differentiated are: (1) *prevening* grace, which works to remove the barriers in natural reason and conscience to faith, hope, and love, so that persons may respond in penitence and trust; (2) *convicting* grace, which restrains the natural resistance to unmerited justification and disposes the will to faith in God's justifying action; (3) *operating* or *justifying* grace, which confers the power of faithful response to God's saving substitutionary sacrificial action on the cross; (4) *cooperating* grace, following after justification to elicit a faith that is active in love; and (5) *persevering* grace, by which faith and the life of holiness are conserved, strengthened, and confirmed.[53]

Human freedom is thereby assisted from beginning to end to become awakened to sin and unfeignedly aware of divine mercy. The work of salvation at every step remains God's own act, leading first to repentance, then to forgiveness and justification, adoption, union with Christ, and sanctification of the whole of one's life.[54]

---

52. Tillett, *PS* 122.
53. Tho. Aq., *ST* 1-2.Q111, 1:1135-40; cf. Pope, *Compend.* 2:358.
54. Second Council of Orange, CC 38; cf. Tho. Aq., *ST* 2-1.Q112, 3:1140-43.

CHAPTER 2

Preparing and Cooperating Grace

Grace prepares the will and coworks with the prepared will. Insofar as grace precedes and prepares free will it is called prevenient. Insofar as grace accompanies and enables human willing to work with divine willing, it is called cooperating grace.

PREVENIENT GRACE

Prevening grace antecedes human responsiveness so as to prepare the soul for the effective hearing of the redeeming Word.[1] This preceding grace draws persons closer to God, lessens their blindness to divine remedies, strengthens their will to accept revealed truth, and enables repentance. Only when sinners are assisted by prevenient grace can they begin to yield their hearts to cooperation with subsequent forms of grace.[2]

The Grace That Precedes Human Responsiveness

It was "while we were still sinners" that grace came to meet us (Rom. 5:8). Such grace is attested in the faith of the thief on the cross, of Cornelius the centurion, and of Zacchaeus whom grace made worthy to receive the Lord. The need for grace to prevene is great, for it was precisely when "you were dead in your transgressions and sins" (Eph. 2:1) that "by grace you have been saved" (Eph. 2:8).

The classical conciliar reception of the teaching of prevening grace is clear and textually well-established:

---

1. Augustine, *Conf.* 1, NPNF 1:1:45-55; cf. Tho. Aq., *ST* 2-1.Q111, 3:1135-39.
2. Tertullian, *On Baptism* 20, ANF 3:678-79.

God is the author of all good dispositions of mind, and also of works, and of all zeal and of all virtues by which from the beginning of faith we tend towards God; and we do not doubt that all the merits of man are *preceded* by His grace, through whom it is brought to pass, that we begin both *to will* and *to do* anything good.[3]

The sin of the first man has so impaired and weakened free will that no one thereafter can either love God as he ought or believe in God or do good for God's sake, unless the grace of divine mercy has *preceded* him.[4]

However viable the seed, it cannot sprout without sun and moisture. However active or assertive is human freedom, it cannot bear salutary fruit without being stimulated by the heat and gentle rain of prevenient grace.[5]

Offered to and for All

To every human creature, grace seeks to manifest God's saving intent in ways circumstantially fitting to that individual: "For the grace of God that brings salvation has appeared *to all* men. It teaches us to say 'No' to ungodliness and worldly passions, and to live self-controlled, upright and godly lives in this present age, while we wait for the blessed hope" (Titus 2:11-13, ital. ad.). To no one, not even the recalcitrant unfaithful, does God deny grace sufficient for salvation.[6] Prevening grace precedes each discrete human act.

The hard case of the Judas text on "better for him if he had not been born" (Mark 14:21) was brilliantly interpreted by the Damascene in this way:

Had God kept from being made those who through His goodness were to have existence, but who by their own choice were to become evil, then evil would have prevailed over the goodness of God. Thus, *all things which God makes He makes good, but each one becomes good or evil by his own choice.* So, even if the Lord did say: "It were better for him if that

---

3. Third Ecumenical Council at Ephesus, SCD §141, p. 57, ital. ad.; cf. Phil. 2:13.
4. Second Council of Orange, CC, 43, ital. ad.
5. Cf. John 15:4; DT (Pohle) 7:114.
6. Clement of Rome, *First Epistle to the Corinthians* 7:4, FC 1:15; cf. Prosper of Aquitaine, *The Call of All Nations* 2, ACW 14:118ff.

man had not been born," He did not say so in deprecation of His own creature, but in deprecation of that creature's choice and rashness.[7]

God did not allow evil to frustrate the very purpose of creation, which was to allow freedom to determine itself toward the greater good. This permission could not be given without giving each sapient person some possibility of turning away from the greater good. The good one receives and makes actual by one's own choice is only possible by grace. The good which is negated by one's own choice is emptied without any assistance from God. God does not assist the will to fall.

The Grace of Calling and Hearing

Prevenient grace is so closely related to God's calling of persons to salvation that it is sometimes referred to as the grace of calling (*gratia vocans*) or summoning grace. Although the invitation is offered in principle to all, it is answered only by some: "I stand at the door and knock. If anyone hears my voice and opens the door, I will come in and eat with him, and he with me" (Rev. 3:20). The grace of calling and hearing is always a prevening grace, which invites those buried in sin to awaken and rise to new life: "Wake up, O sleeper, / rise from the dead, / and Christ will shine on you" (Eph. 5:14).

The freedom to hear implies also the freedom not to hear, or to hear and to decline the invitation. Some who are called "did not listen or pay attention; they were stiff-necked and would not listen or respond to discipline" (Jer. 17:23). Hence the imperative: "Today, if you hear his voice, / do not harden your hearts" (Ps. 95:7-8).

To the extent that we fall from grace, it is our own act of diminishing the sufficient grace given. To the extent that we turn to receive grace, it is God's own act enabling our act. We cannot turn to God except as God arouses and helps us to a good will. Yet when we turn away from God, we do so without the help of God, by our own absurd willfulness. For, except evil, "What have we that we have not received" from God?[8]

---

7. John of Damascus, OF 4.21, FC 37:387-88, ital. ad.
8. Augustine, *On the Forgiveness of Sins and Baptism* 2.28, NPNF 1:5:56; cf. DT (Pohle) 7:33.

Prevenience and the Grace of Baptism

Sacramentally viewed, prevenient grace is that grace that leads to baptism and the solemn voluntary reaffirmation of baptism. Baptism bestows saving grace upon those who have been readied to respond to it in faith, either by one's own faith or the anticipatory faith of the worshiping and parenting community. Holy Communion augments and deepens the sanctifying grace of those who have received baptismal grace.[9]

The Second Council of Orange taught that

> the choice of the will, weakened in the first man, cannot be repaired except through the grace of baptism.[10]

> After grace has been received through baptism, all baptized persons have the ability and responsibility, if they desire to labor faithfully, to perform with the aid and cooperation of Christ what is of essential importance in regard to the salvation of their soul.[11]

The efficacy of baptism does not depend on the moral worthiness of the one who administers it.[12] The legitimacy of no one's baptism hinges on the fragile thread of the moral merit of the administering clergy: "Both the sacraments and the Word are effectual by reason of the institution and commandment of Christ even if they are administered by evil men" (cf. Matt. 23:2).[13] The sacraments confer grace on those who do not place an obstacle in the way.

Medieval scholastic teaching held that grace is being conferred sacramentally merely by virtue of the passive reception of the sacrament, by its own working which it works of itself (*ex opere operato*). This notion, whose original intent was to stress prevening grace, seemed to Protestant scholastics to imply that the efficacy of grace had to come from human initiative, which they rejected. Subsequent Catholic teaching has clarified that this notion does not imply either human merit or

---

9. Hugh of St. Victor, SCF 2.6-8, 282ff.
10. SHD 1:381; cf. CC 41.
11. Second Council of Orange, canon 13, CC 44.
12. See Augustine's writings on the Donatist controversy, *On Baptism, Ag. the Donatists* 4.14-26, NPNF 2:4:456-58; *Answer to the Letters to Petilian* 2.1-15, NPNF 2:4:530-32.
13. Augsburg Conf. 8, BOCJ 1:108; cf. CC 70.

cooperation apart from prevening grace, but that grace elicits coopera-tion, and thereby God sees to it that his Word does not return empty but surely delivers the promised benefit to the faithful recipient.[14]

COOPERATING AND SUBSEQUENT GRACE

While prevenient grace enables the will to do good, concomitant grace cooperates with the will thus enabled. Prevenient grace awakens responsiveness; concomitant (cooperating and subsequent) grace works in, with, through, and following human responsiveness.[15]

Prevenient grace is, from the viewpoint of its bounty and plenitude, intrinsically linked with *sufficient* grace because it suffices to make pos-sible all salutary actions. Concomitant or cooperating grace is, from the point of view of its effect, structurally correlated with *efficacious* grace because it works to make effective the free use of divine assistance even against willful resistances.[16] Grace is effective as it elicits willing coop-eration and sufficient insofar as it does what is necessary to lead the will to cooperate, even when the deficient will is resistant.

Grace Working and Coworking

Prevenient grace first operates before the will can cooperate. Pre-venient grace is therefore the grace that *works without us because it works before us (gratia operans)*, but cooperating grace is the grace that *works with us as it works through us (gratia cooperans)*. "The divine goodness first effects something in us without our cooperation," wrote Gregory the Great, "and then as the will freely consents, cooperates with us in performing the good which we desire."[17] "God thus oper-ates in the hearts of men and in the free will itself, so that a holy thought, a pious plan, and every motion of good will is from God."[18]

---

14. Rahner, *TI* 4:274; cf. H. Schwartz, *Divine Communication* (Philadelphia: Fortress Press, 1989), p. 56.
15. Trent 6, SCD §§797ff., pp. 806-13, 248ff.
16. Council of Orange; cf. Tho. Aq., *ST* 1-2.Q109, 1:1124; cf. *DT* (Hall) 3:255; Eras-mus, *Freedom of the Will.*
17. Gregory the Great, *Moralia in Job* 16.10, in *A Library of the Fathers of the Holy Catholic Church* (Oxford: J. Parker, 1844–1850), vol. 3; cf. *DT* (Pohle) 7:38.
18. Council of Ephesus 6, SCD §136, p. 55.

Augustine drew the point to a taut summary: God "*begins* His influence by working *in* us *that we may have* the will [prevenient grace], and He *completes* it by working *with* us *when we have* the will [cooperating grace]." The Holy Spirit thus "*operates without us,* in order that we may become willing; but when we once will so as to act, He *cooperates with us.*"[19]

Presented schematically, grace is viewed in complementary modes:

GRACE

Operates	Cooperates
Begins	Completes
Gratia Operans	*Gratia Cooperans*
Simply Works in Us Without Us	Dialogically Works with Us
Ergon	*Sunergos*
Before We Can Will	While We Are Willing
To Allow Willing	Lest One Will in Vain
Going Before	Accompanying
Gratia Vocans	*Gratia Adiuvans*
Calling Grace	Assisting Grace

The notion of cooperation translates the Greek *sun* + *ergeia,* from which we get our word "synergy," a controversial word in the scholastic tradition, because without due qualification the notion of our cooperating with God carries definite dangers of hubris and self-deception.

Consensual Christian teaching follows the apostolic testimony in speaking of the cooperation of freedom with grace, but carefully so as to avoid the perennial dual hazards of antinomianism and legalism. "God does many good things in one which one does not initiate; but one does nothing which God does not enable one to do."[20]

God first establishes in us the disposition toward the reception of grace.[21] Thus we speak of *operating grace* regarded from the viewpoint of God as its unassisted initiating cause, as distinguished from *cooperating*

---

19. Augustine, *On Grace and Free Will* 17.33, NPNF 1:5:458, ital. ad.; cf. Tho. Aq., *ST* 1-2.Q111.2, 1:1137.
20. Augustine, *Two Epistles Ag. Pelagius* 2.9, 21, DT (Pohle) 7:37, translation slightly amended.
21. Tho. Aq., *ST* 1-2.Q113.7, 1:1149-50.

grace regarded concretely and subjectively as the resulting movements of the consenting will enabled by divine grace.[22]

The Dynamics of Cooperating Grace

It is from the *locus classicus* text of cooperating grace, Philippians 2:12-13, that we derive the leitmotif of this study: "Work out your own salvation with fear and trembling; for it is God who is at work in you, enabling you both to will and to work for his good pleasure" (NRSV). "They are acted upon that they may act, not that they may themselves do nothing."[23]

Cooperating grace allows the will to give its own free consent to the divine will. In this cooperation, human willing does not cease, for

> it is we that *will* when we will, but it is He who makes us will what is good, of whom it is said . . . "The will is prepared by the Lord" [Prov. 8:35]. . . . It is certain that it is we that act when we act; but it is He who makes us act by applying efficacious powers to our will, who has said, "I will make you walk in my statutes" [Ezek. 36:27]. It does not, therefore, depend on the man's desire or effort, but on God's mercy [Rom. 9:16].[24]

Leo the Great expressed this point precisely: "For it was necessary that those who are to be saved should also do something on their part [in response to grace], and by the turning of their hearts to the Redeemer should quit the dominion of the enemy."[25] Grace has remained throughout human history as "a light to those in darkness, by the Divine goodness imparted to all, to those that are willing to obey this—for it is of use only to the willing, not to the unwilling—and co-operate with it, in what it requireth as necessary to salvation," according to Dositheus, "making us perseverant in the love of God."[26] "Keep with all diligence the remission which you have received as a gift, in order that, while the remission comes *from God*,

---

22. Council of Quiersy, SCD §317, p. 126; cf. Tho. Aq., *ST* 1-2.Q111.2, 1:1137; cf. Calvin, *Inst.* 2.2.6; 2.3.7.
23. Augustine, *On Rebuke and Grace* 4, NPNF 1:5:473.
24. Augustine, *On Grace and Free Will* 32, NPNF, 1:5:457.
25. Leo the Great, *Sermons* 77, NPNF 2:12:192.
26. Confession of Dositheus 3, CC 487, 488.

the preservation of it may come *from yourself also.*"[27] The salient word here for Gregory of Nazianzus is "also," for it is never a self-initiated preservation.

Subsequent Grace: How Each Form Taken by Prevenient, Cooperating, and Persevering Grace Is Followed by a Succeeding Form

God prepares one to will the good (by prevenient grace), to do the good (by concomitant or cooperating grace), preserves the will in doing good (by persevering grace), and finally works to complete and perfect whatever might have remained incomplete in previous receptions of grace (by consummating grace).[28] Subsequent grace is the grace that follows each succeeding stage of grace, brought finally to fulfillment by consummating grace.

The psalmist taught both that "God will go before me" (Ps. 59:10), and that God's "mercy shall follow me" (Ps. 23:6 KJV). The grace that follows any earlier work of grace is called subsequent grace. At each stage there is a different set of circumstances for the grace that comes before and the grace that accompanies or follows:

GRACE

Heals the Soul	Moves the Will	Enables Salutary Action	Perseveres in Resolve	Consummates in Glory
prevenient-subsequent				
	prevenient-subsequent			
		prevenient-subsequent		
			prevenient-subsequent	

Hence the grace that was subsequent at one stage becomes prevenient to a later stage. "As each effect is posterior to one and prior to another, so grace may be called prevenient or subsequent according as we regard

---

27. Gregory of Nazianzus, *Orat.* 40.34, NPNF 2:7:373, ital. ad.
28. "The Symbol of Faith" of Leo 9, SCD §348, p. 142; cf. Pieter Fransen, *Divine Grace and Man* (Paris: Desclee, 1962), pp. 40ff.

it in its relations to its different effects."[29] Whether grace is viewed as prevenient or subsequent thus depends on the particular stage of the sequence from which one is viewing the developing process. Yet in all these differences, "The work is one, the judgment one, the temple one, the life-giving one, the sanctification one."[30]

The Council fathers of Ephesus knew that each and every stage of heresy regarding grace lacked the criteria of apostolicity and antiquity: "The most pious Fathers, after casting aside the pride of pernicious novelty, have taught us to refer to Christ's grace both the *beginning* of good will, and the *advances* in commendable devotions and the *perseverance* in these unto the end."[31] "The whole work belongs to God, who both prepares the good will that is to be helped, and assists it when it is prepared."[32]

Analogy with the Incarnation

The affinity of divine and human willing is finally a mystery, but one that continues to command attentive reflection. This is seen by analogy with the incarnation. The monothelitic heresy attempted prematurely to reduce the divine will and human will of the Mediator to a unilateral action of only one will, tending to negate the human will and circumvent any hint of cooperation.

Similarly, in the mysterious confluence of grace and human freedom it remains as ill-advised to obliterate freedom as to obliterate grace. Divine agency and human agency cowork to do God's will and thus express an integral salutary act. Actual grace enables this concurrence of divine and human willing by empowering the human will to perform.[33] "Without the constant aid of God," remarked Jerome, "even my own act will not be mine."[34]

---

29. Tho. Aq., *ST* 1-2.Q111.5, 1:1140; cf. DT (Pohle) 7:35.
30. Ambrose, *Of the Holy Spirit* 2.2.25, NPNF 2:10:118; cf. Henri Rondete, *Gratia Christi* (Paris: Beauchesne, 1948), pp. 265ff.
31. Council of Ephesus, SCD §139, p. 56, ital. ad.
32. Augustine, *Enchiridion* 32.
33. Council of Constantinople 3, NPNF 2:14:342; cf. DT (Pohle) 7, 40.
34. Jerome, *Letters* 133, NPNF 2:6:272ff.; cf. DT (Pohle) 7, 109. The worshiping community prays for both prevenient and cooperating grace: "Precede, we beseech Thee, O Lord, our actions by Thy holy inspiration, and carry them on by Thy gracious assistance, that every prayer and work of ours may begin always from Thee, and through Thee be happily ended" (Roman Missal).

THE MEANS OF GRACE

Grace Works Outwardly Through Means

The Spirit uses varied means to illumine hearts: by reading of the Word, which is a "lamp to my feet / and a light for my path" (Ps. 119:105); by self-examination in the light of the moral requirement embodied in the law, for "through the law we become conscious of sin" (Rom. 3:20); by the proclamation of the gospel inviting all to repent and believe.[35]

Grace works *outwardly* through an ordered ministry of the Word, which proclaims the spoken word grounded in the written Word, and which becomes embodied in the visible Word of the sacraments. The triune God who becomes incarnate in the Son does not hesitate to use historical, tangible, fleshly, bodily means to reach out to sinners through the Spirit.[36] Grace works *mediately* through such varied means as common worship, the hearing of scripture, preaching, music, ascetic discipline, the influence of teachers, friends, and parental care.

Grace works corporately, through a worshiping *communio sanctorum*. The "means of grace" include the reading of scripture, prayer, attendance upon common worship, and sacramental life. There are visible means of invisible grace and dialogical means of inaudible grace. Through Word, sacrament, and ministry, the Holy Spirit "works faith, when and where he pleases, in those who hear the Gospel."[37]

Grace Works Inwardly with or without Means

These outward means prepare the soul for the reception of grace internally so as to empower the daily walk in the way of holiness. Grace working internally (*gratia interna*) transforms the soul *inwardly*, not by circumventing but by using outward means (*gratia externa*), which operate through heard language and duly administered sacraments to draw the soul effectively toward saving grace.[38] Meanwhile it

---

35. Melanchthon, *Loci*, LCC 19:70-86; cf. John Bunyan, *The Doctrine of the Law and Grace Unfolded* (n.p.: Manning and Loring, 1806).
36. Leo the Great, *Sermons on the Feast of the Nativity* 21-27, NPNF 2:12:128-39; Calvin, *Inst.* 4.14.
37. Augsburg Conf. 5, CC 69.
38. Hugh of St. Victor, SCF 2.2, 253-59; cf. A. Poulain, *The Graces of Interior Prayer* (London: Routledge and Kegan Paul, 1950).

is not beyond the ability of God the Spirit also to work *immediately* (straightaway, without mediation) through the direct, uninterrupted testimony of the Spirit in the heart.[39] Talk of God strikes the external ear in vain unless God by a spiritual gift opens the hearing of the inward person.[40] "God Himself co-operates in the production of fruit in good trees, when He both externally waters and tends them by the agency of His servants, and internally by Himself also gives the increase."[41] In this way grace works verbally and nonverbally, visibly and invisibly, to become adapted to our composite nature.[42]

THE DISTINCTION BETWEEN GRACE ENABLING DISCRETE ACTS AND ENGENDERING HABITUAL RESPONSES

Actual Grace

Actual grace is the help of God by which one is made fit to act in a way accountable to God.[43] All actual grace (whether antecedent or consequent to human willing) is grounded in the atoning merit of Christ's completed gift to humanity on the cross.

Actual grace is to be distinguished both from ordinary providence (the ordering of causality by which God sustains all creation), and from natural talent, since it is specifically defined as supernatural gift— unmerited internal divine assistance which enables the performance of salutary acts (the Greek fathers spoke of *theou energeia, ē tou logou cheir, theia kinēsis*, the Latin fathers of *Dei auxilium, subsidium adiutorium, motio divina*).[44]

Actual grace both removes the obstacles to salvation and enables the will to act in a salutary way. Grace works negatively to remedy the infirmity resulting from sin, and positively to elevate the soul to salutary acts, so that the soul may be enabled to receive God's own justify-

---

39. Rom. 8:12-17; cf. Augustine, *On the Spirit and the Letter* 34, 56, NPNF 1:5:97-108.
40. Augustine, *On the Profit of Believing* 22, NPNF 1:3:357; cf. *Comm. on John* 3, NPNF 1:7:19-25.
41. Augustine, *On the Grace of Christ and Original Sin* 1.20, NPNF 1:5:225.
42. Nemesius, *On the Nature of Man*, LCC 4:224ff.; cf. John Bunyan, *Grace Abounding to the Chief of Sinners*.
43. Council of Mileum 2, SCD §§103-5, p. 45.
44. Augustine, *On Grace and Free Will*, NPNF 1:5:443ff.; DT (Pohle) 7:14, 15.

ing action manifested on the cross and persevere in this reception.[45] Actual grace is not merely the bare absence of sin, but a divine gift palpably offered by God the Father through the merits of the Son by the power of the Spirit for our salvation.

Whether Grace Enters into Habit Formation

When gracious acts become habituated into recurrent patterns of behavior, then it is said that grace is being received in the form of a continuing *habitus*, a proximately sustained yet still vulnerable state of grace, a grace that points toward the reception of further grace (*gratia gratis data*), and continues to pray for eliciting grace.[46] Grace in this way becomes a continuing gift within the fragile arena of ripening, maturing finite freedom, by which the disciplined spiritual athlete's behavior may be to some extent *habitually* rendered pleasing to God, and not merely a transient gift of a momentary *act* of grace-enabled faith active in love.[47]

To summarize the distinction, according to scholastic theology: *Actual grace* is God's gift of help to enable salutary discrete actions, by which one is made fit to act as one should to obtain eternal life, operating in us without us, yet not without eliciting our willing,[48] healing the nature vitiated by original sin and restoring the liberty of the children of God.[49]

Actual grace tends toward and intends to further elicit regular patterns of response to sanctifying grace, or *habituating grace*, so as to become embedded in habitual actions.[50] By habituating grace, God's unmerited self-giving favor becomes woven and knitted and blended into the warp and woof of human behavior in one who, having been justified, puts on the new man, and is made heir of eternal life. Elicited

---

45. Tho. Aq., *ST* 1-2.Q109-14; cf. DT (Pohle) 7:18; Matthias Joseph Wilhelm, *A Manual of Catholic Theology*, ed. T. B. Scannell (New York: Benzinger, 1908–9), 2:227ff.; *DT* (Hall) 7:248ff.
46. John Chrysostom, *Hom. on the Statues*, NPNF 1:9:363, 388, 420; Trent 6, SCD §§792-801, pp. 248ff.; Pius 5, "Errors of Michael duBay," SCD §§1063-65, pp. 307-11.
47. Tho. Aq., *ST* 1-2.Q111.5.
48. Council of Orange 2, SCD §193, p. 79.
49. Council of Ephesus, SCD §§130-34, pp. 53-54.
50. Ambrose, *Duties* 1.10, NPNF 2:10:6ff., 35ff.; Pius 11, SCD §2237, pp. 584ff.

by preaching and conferred sacramentally in the grace of baptism,[51] grace may grow through the continued reception of the Word and sacraments and by works of mercy, and may be lost by neglect of the Word and sacraments and works of mercy, yet may be regained through repentance.[52]

51. SCD §130, p. 53; Council of Orange 2, SCD §186, p. 78.
52. Trent 6, SCD §§792-808, pp. 248ff.

PART TWO

THE REACH AND DEPTH OF THE FORMING WORK OF GRACE

CHAPTER 3

THE EXTENT OF COMMON GRACE

The Christian teaching of how far grace reaches is called common grace. The teaching that deals with the adequacy of grace to work steadily and thoroughly to transform each soul inwardly and fully is called sufficient grace.

The extent of grace is common human history. The intent of grace is complete transformation of each despairing will. The reach of grace is farther than any eye can see or heart imagine, its gravity as deep as is necessary for the Spirit to save effectively and transform utterly.

COMMON GRACE IN HUMAN HISTORY

That grace is called *common* which is shared by all humanity even amid all conceivable forms of fallenness. The gifts offered by God are never common in the sense of ordinary, profane, and petty, but in the sense of being universally offered to all. Common grace focuses on the global extent of sufficient and prevening grace, rather than on its source or motive.

The Universal Embrace of Common Grace

We may be thankful that by common grace God "upholds the universe by his word of power" (Heb. 1:3 RSV), "causes his sun to rise on the evil and the good" (Matt. 5:45), restrains social sin from becoming ungovernable (Rom. 13:1-4), enables society to live together in a proximately just and orderly manner, and enables it to cultivate scientific, rational, and economic pursuits of civilization.

The ancient Christian writers understood that "grace is supplied" sufficiently, not to believers only, "but also to all peoples in this world," "to each and all individually, in season and out, every day, every minute, and at every smallest moment of time."[1] If the saving work of God is to be communicated (either anticipatively or actually) to every fallen creature, then God the Spirit must be working at some primordial level throughout history to prepare the heart of every potential believer for Good News. "Every rational creature, without any distinction, receives a share of Him [the Holy Spirit] in the same way as of the Wisdom and of the Word of God."[2]

Calvin set forth the teaching of common grace that would be generally received in the Reformed tradition:

> Meanwhile, we ought not to forget those most excellent benefits of the divine Spirit, which he distributes to whomever he wills, for the common good of mankind. The understanding and knowledge of Bezalel and Oholiab, needed to construct the Tabernacle, had to be instilled in them by the Spirit of God [Exod. 31:2-11; 35:30-35]. It is no wonder, then, that the knowledge of all that is most excellent in human life is said to be communicated to us through the Spirit of God, [for] if the Lord has willed that we be helped in physics, dialectic, mathematics, and other like disciplines, by the work and ministry of the ungodly, let us use this assistance.[3]

The Ministry of the Spirit in Times of Unusual Historical Crisis

Though steadily present in every ordinary stretch of history, common grace appears more evidently in times of unusual historical crisis. This is not to deny that grace is also present in times of historical stability and equilibrium. But it is characteristic of the Spirit to minister specially to the human predicament at those times when it reaches precarious historical turning points.[4]

Noah and Samson offer biblical prototypes: When the sins of Noah's generation were finally brought to a critical self-destructive phase, the Spirit was prepared to constrain them (Gen. 6:3). When the sins of Samson's generation resulted in Philistine oppression, Samson was set

---

1. Orosius, *Apology* 19, FEF 3:186.
2. Origen, *OFP* 2.7, ANF 4:285.
3. Calvin, *Inst.* 2.2.16.
4. Leo the Great, *Sermons* 49, NPNF 2:12:161.

apart as a Nazirite empowered by the Spirit to confound the oppressors (Judg. 13:1-7; 14:19).

That God allows human freedom the proximate power to distort human history remains a mystery of the divine economy not disclosed even to those most faithful (Job 16:2-21). However deceptive or distortable, the power of freedom to destroy God's plan is always being hedged in the long run. The Spirit is determined to bring history through periods of cataclysm so that God's promises may be fulfilled. Grace may be temporarily rejected in certain periods of history but never ultimately nullified by human willing. The mercy of God can neither be finally earned by the supposed good works of sinners nor voided by the evil works of sinners.

The prototypical patristic example of common grace amid historical crisis is the observation that divine providence had "made ready the Roman empire, whose growth has reached such limits that the whole multitude of nations are brought into close connection. For the Divinely-planned work particularly required that many kingdoms should be leagued together under one empire, so that the preaching of the world might quickly reach to all people."[5]

The notion that the study of conflict in history itself was intrinsically related to the work of the Spirit received its most complete modern statement in Hegel, with the idea that the history of *Geist* (Spirit, Mind, historical reasoning) is a process of constant struggle and resolution—thesis, antithesis, and synthesis—in which all human culture, psychology, politics, art, and religion may be illumined by historical dialectical reasoning. Hegel considered his thought a philosophical refinement of the dialectical meaning of the history of religions, especially Judaism and Christianity, whereby Spirit brought forth nature as its antithesis, through which it moved to realize itself in a higher synthesis as Absolute Spirit. The Spirit reconciles opposites (subject/object, mind/matter, ideal/real) through historical process.[6] Critics of Hegel point to his attempted taming of God the Spirit by a process of logic that is forever unable to catch up with the eventful history it is trying to describe.[7]

---

5. Ibid., 82, NPNF 2:12:195.
6. Hegel, *Reason in History* (New York: Bobbs-Merrill, 1953); cf. John Chrysostom, *Hom. on the Statues*, NPNF 1:9:404-8; Heron, *HS* 114, 115.
7. Kierkegaard, *CUP* part 1; cf. Reinhold Niebuhr, *NDM* 1.

The Political Work of the Holy Spirit as Restrainer of Sin
in the Civil Order

The teaching of common grace does not soften or romanticize the harsh reality of sin. In the fallen world, the mystery of iniquity remains always at work, hidden in the depths of freedom.

The Spirit of God acts in a timely way to put this lawlessness under divine restraint (Ps. 76:10).[8] The Spirit's striving against sin is not to be viewed as a hopeless or despairing struggle. The Spirit wrestles effectively against historical evil, yet without ever undermining the premise of freedom. Ultimate victory is beheld only in the form of hope. It is a purposeful strife that occurs within the bounds of God's ultimate purpose amid the proximate histories of sin, to be finally concluded by victory over sin (Gen. 6:3; 1 Cor. 15:54-57). The sufferings of Israel were permitted by God, but only within bounds fixed by divine mercy, and with the purpose of testing the deeper layers of faith.

Paul expected a future apostasy of the church (2 Thess. 2:3; 2 Tim. 3:1-8), followed at some point by the dreaded temporary removal of the common grace that restrains the mystery of lawlessness, which was destined finally to be bound. It would ultimately require only a word from the Son by the power of the Spirit to restrain the worst that evil can do in the world. "One little word shall fell him," wrote Luther in "A Mighty Fortress."

Meanwhile the present age is protected by the restraining ministry of the Spirit, who works through the civil order to limit evil (Romans 13). Without these hedgings, the power of evil would surge to self-destructive heights. The Spirit works in the political order to continue in the present age to place merciful constraints on the self-destructiveness of sin (2 Thess. 2:7, 8).

Human governments are allowed by God to have proximate coercive power within history to restrain evil and permit justice to seek relative peace and concord by orderly and rational means. Proximate order and reasoned law are steadily being empowered by God, even though they remain blunt and imperfect instruments of justice within the ambiguities of history (Gen. 9:5, 6; Ps. 75:5-7; John 19:11; Rom. 13:1-7). Human governments are never to be directly equated with the will of God, but are freely and graciously permitted by God the Spirit to

---

8. Calvin, *Inst.* 2.3.3.

restrain evil and seek proximate justice. The political process thereby indirectly attests God's own incomparable righteousness, even though it is always prone to corruption.

How Common Grace Works to Prepare the Nations

The general preparation of the nations and the special preparation of Israel worked together in a complementary manner. The work of common grace was thought by early Christian writers to be a matter of historical record. Eusebius wrote a series of histories to establish the evidences for common grace in human history prior to Christ's coming.[9]

Even amid the Muslim conquest, John of Damascus could write of the signs of Christ's power in history:

Indeed, the worship of demons has ceased. Creation has been sanctified with divine blood. Altars and temples of idols have been overthrown. Knowledge of God has been implanted. The consubstantial Trinity, the uncreated Godhead is worshiped, one true God, Creator and Lord of all. Virtue is practiced. Hope of the resurrection has been granted through the resurrection of Christ. The demons tremble. . . . The Gospel of the knowledge of God has been preached to the whole world and has put the adversaries to flight not by war and arms and camps. Rather, it was a few unarmed, poor, unlettered, persecuted, tormented, done-to-death men, who, by preaching One who had died crucified in the flesh, prevailed over the wise and powerful, because the almighty power of the Crucified was with them. . . . These are the successes consequent upon the advent of the Christ; these are the signs of His power. . . . Well done, O Christ, O Wisdom and Power and Word of God, and God almighty! What should we resourceless people give Thee in return for all things? For all things are Thine and Thou askest nothing of us but that we be saved.[10]

The Peace of Rome and the Jewish Diaspora

The general preparation of all humanity provided distinct and diverse contributions that no particular nation or ethnic community

9. Eusebius, *Proof of the Gospel* 10, trans. W. J. Ferrar (New York: Macmillan, 1920), 190ff.; CH 9, 10, NPNF 2:1:357-87.
10. John of Damascus, OF 4.4, FC 37:338, 339.

could of itself fully provide: concepts of universality, of the rational ordering of life, alternative systems of justice, advances in commerce, art, architecture, engineering, and ethics.[11]

At the time of Christ's coming, the worldly empire that most fully exemplified this preparatory activity of God and human achievement was Rome, with its communication system, roads, aqueducts, unified rule, relatively universal culture (compared to earlier empires), stability, and relative peace. All of these elements contributed to the possibility of the rapid transmission and propagation of the gospel of salvation. The world into which Christianity appeared had been unified in the east by Alexander and in the west by Julius Caesar. These and similar facts were taken by Eusebius and other early Christian historical interpreters to be reliable evidences of providence.[12]

Meanwhile the diaspora of the Jews throughout the Roman Empire became a powerful instrument for the propagation of the gospel to the whole known world. The synagogue system was in place throughout much of the empire as an available network for the early communication of the Good News of Jesus Christ. Many of the great cities of the Mediterranean world had a Jewish synagogue that provided a monotheistic starting point, a communal memory of salvation history, Torah, and prophetic tradition for the proclamation of the gospel.[13]

The Prototypical Work of Common Grace Through Jewish and Greek Culture, Language, and Symbols

The moral language of Christianity had been nurtured by Mosaic law in readiness for its encounter with Stoic virtues and Roman traditions of law and justice. The spiritual vocabulary of Christianity was fed by the prophets and psalms, and was soon to enter into significant dialogue with Hellenistic, Gnostic, neo-Platonic, Manichaean, and other world views. Yet all such achievements proved ambiguous. One should remember that it was Roman power that put Jesus to death. It was

---

11. Augustine, CG 5.21, NPNF 1:2:103.
12. Eusebius, *Proof of the Gospel* 3.7, 160-62; Lactantius, *Of the Manner in Which the Persecutors Died*, ANF 7:301-22; cf. church histories by Socrates, Sozomen, and Theodoret.
13. Joseph Butler, *The Analogy of Religion* (Chicago: F. Ungar Publishing Co., 1961), pp. 228-38; J. Edwards, *History of Redemption*, Works 1:297-395; H. L. Martensen, *Christian Dogmatics* (Edinburgh: T & T Clark, 1898), 224-36.

Greek wisdom that thought of Christ as foolishness (1 Cor. 1:18-25).

It is an inadequate generalization, however, to say that only Hebraic history contributed positively to this preparation for salvation as if the rest of general human history were merely a negative preparation by way of deficit. In no place to which the Christian mission spread did it find that it had not been preceded by the Holy Spirit in the formation of culture.

The Greek language had long before the first century become the most universally received literary language of the ancient world. It served as a fitting and available linguistic medium through which the gospel could be communicated to distant parts. Where Greek was not understood, the gospel was presented in indigenous languages and cultural systems. In these ways the world had become prepared by providential politics for the "fullness of time" (Gal. 4:4).

THE HOLY SPIRIT AS GUIDE OF REASON AND MORAL AWARENESS

The common grace of the Holy Spirit is active throughout human history to engender critical reasoning and kindle informed moral awareness. At this juncture we shift our attention from common grace in human history to common grace in human rational processes.

Reasoning Through and Beyond Apostasy and Heresy

By reason one assesses arguments, hypotheses, and assertions. Christians pray for the Spirit constantly to illumine this assessment.[14] The worshiping community prays, hopes, and works for the sound and guileless use of reasoning.[15]

The church does well to listen carefully to its critics, yet not uncritically. It is to the church's interest to hear the best reasons for and against any given motive or contemplated action or proposed policy, and not to cut off debate prematurely or self-righteously. The truth is harder to find when undebated than debated.

---

14. Augustine, *Conf.* 1, NPNF 1:1:45ff.; cf. Tho. Aq., *ST* 1-2.Q79, 90, 1:396-408, 993-95.
15. Tertullian, *Prescription Ag. Heretics* 1-12, ANF 3:243-49.

A deeper faith is engendered by the balanced employment of doubt, critical debate, and measured skepticism, than by abruptly pretending to settle all moral ambiguities by narrow preemptive authoritarian appeals. Respect for the authority of scripture and tradition is not opposed to the power of critical reasoning, but rather invites its critique in order better to strengthen its modes of argument. Scriptural authority enables a deeper kind of reasoning, without which natural reason would be even more crippled and blind than it is.[16]

Finally, all reasonings of those called out to be the church are best judged in relation to the historically grounded reasoning of the apostles' testimony to God's living Word to humanity.[17] Thinking critically is a requirement of faith. Faith cannot be pursued without self-criticism, which is repentance in the mode of reflection. Faith best walks through life with a modest awareness of its own limitations and social location and of the self-interest that functions within all modes of reasoning.[18]

It is an ill-considered modern habit to pit reason and authority as simple opposites. Far from being intrinsically against all authority, valid reasoning characteristically honors legitimate authority, seeking rightly to assess and value its legitimacy. The authority of those who have special, hard won experience and moral insight is especially valuable to reason. The Soviet church oppression, the black church, the Armenian holocaust, and the Korean *minjung* offer especially poignant lessons not only for the sufferers but also for all in our time.

In proper perspective even heresy can be seen as providentially meaningful. Even the most ill-disposed and deluded heretics have inadvertently served as an indirect blessing to faith by challenging unclear teaching, which has been only partly grasped or inadequately defined. Heresy requires the faithful to clarify the biblical grounding of Christian teaching more carefully against specific challenges. Had not the Ebionites denied the divinity of Christ, or the Docetists his humanity, the unchallenged church would not have gone through the strengthening discipline of consensually defining the doctrine of the Incarnation as apostolic teaching at the Council of Chalcedon.[19] There is nothing

---

16. See Anselm, *Proslogion* 1, BW 3-7.
17. Justin Martyr, *Second Apology* 13, ANF 1:193.
18. See R. Niebuhr, *Moral Man and Immoral Society* (New York: Scribner's, 1932), NDM.
19. "The Definition of Faith of the Council of Chalcedon," NPNF 2:14:262.

to prevent persons today from entertaining Docetic or Ebionitic hypotheses again, but every time this has been attempted since the first three centuries it has repeatedly been rejected by ecumenical consent. It is unlikely that a fresh look at Docetism is going to persuade the whole church catholic that it should start all over with a prejudice against the flesh. Critical reasoning is intrinsic to the teaching function of the ministry of the Word.

It may become necessary at times for the daughters and sons of the church in a given period to oppose the parenting church of a previous backslidden generation. When this occurs they do well to pray for grace to see through their own limitations of experience and misdirected passions, that they may not harshly destroy tender social organisms that they have limited power to re-create. For *hairesis* (heresy, arbitrary self-choice) flows not only out of false teaching, but more so out of the determination to assert in an adolescent fashion one's own opinion as absolute over against the historical parenting wisdom of the church that follows and is blessed by apostolic teaching. Heresy essentially is the illusion that one's own independent opinion is more reliable and should override the consensual wisdom of historical experience of Christians of all other ages and times. Structural church reformation, while at times urgently required, never comes without hazards greater than the reformers imagine. Reform is best undertaken only when reforming agents have laid aside personal ambition, pride, and pretenses to omnicompetence.

How Common Grace Works Through Conscience

The worshiping community prays that the Spirit will illumine conscience, the inward moral awareness of the rightness or wrongness of specifically recalled behaviors. Conscience is a universal human experience of awareness that accompanies consciousness in every action, seeking to assess whether that action is consistent with what one knows is the best of one's moral self (Rom. 2:15; Heb. 10:2).[20]

One must distinguish conscience from human willfulness, from emotivity, and from God's will. Three caveats preface any serious Christian examination of conscience:

---

20. Tho. Aq., ST 1.Q79.13, 1:408; cf. Calvin, *Inst.* 3.2, 4.10; Wesley, "On Conscience," WJWB 3:479ff.; cf. WJW 7:186-95.

First, conscience is not reducible to merely an act of *will*, for one may be morally aware that something should be done and still will to do nothing.[21]

Second, conscience is not itself an *emotion*, though it may powerfully affect the emotive life, for it is possible to know one has done something wrong and still feel temporarily pleased by it, yet such temporary self-knowing is always subject to further searchings of conscience.

Finally, conscience itself is not the direct voice or absolute *will of God;* rather God speaks indirectly through conscience, which is the moral self-awareness that accompanies consciousness even amid myriad variables of cultural conditioning. Whatever one's acculturation, God the Spirit meets each one in the depths of moral self-awareness and there alone challenges each individually to truthful disclosures.[22] Conscience can be led astray by misperceptions, but does not itself mislead when listened to humbly, honestly, and intently.[23]

Except when a desensitized conscience appears at times to oppose God's revealed Word in scripture, Christians are called by scripture earnestly to follow a good, clear, and sincere conscience (1 Tim. 1:5; 1 Pet. 3:16, 21). Conscience seeks to lead each one silently toward one's best self, and in doing so becomes one of the common means by which God's Spirit addresses the human spirit.

Among those baptized into the believing, worshiping community, conscience is presumed to be in greater degree daily formed by the revealed Word made known in scripture. To the extent that this is not occurring, one can assume that there has been a failure of Christian education, preaching, sacramental life, and pastoral care.

The examination of conscience remains, for Christians, a matter closely enmeshed in the life of prayer (Heb. 9:9, 10:22). The deepest moral self-examination takes place in habitual dialogue with God, while we listen intently for the address of God and ask God for the grace to hear and behold rightly (Psalms 51, 86).

Deficiencies of conscience are due to the corrosive, pervasive history of sin, not the insufficiency of common grace. Regenerating grace offers new life amid the devastations of sin and the consequent impotence of conscience under the conditions of fallenness. Faith active in love

---

21. Barth, *CD* 2/1.518ff.; cf. 2/2.667ff.
22. Calvin, *Inst.* 3.2; 3.19, 20.
23. Lactantius, *DI* 6.24-25, FC 49:465-67.

seeks to change the fallen natural conscience to a redeemed, good, clear, holy conscience captive to the will of Christ (1 Cor. 10:25-29).[24]

Christians have learned by long experience that the social, experiential, and historical wisdom of the Christian community is more likely to have grasped the truth of scripture than the individual experience of one person living amid the special entanglements, passions, and fleeting political interests of history. Though not an infallible guide to conscience, it is ultimately promised that the community shaped by the Holy Spirit will by grace ultimately prevail against all challenges and distortions (Matt. 16:18). If an ambivalent or confused conscience seems to direct that one do something that apostolic teaching prohibits, such an inner conflict becomes for a believer a time for serious, probing self-examination, prayer, and disciplined search for the truth, and waiting upon the Lord.[25]

No law or church teaching is beyond criticism. On rare occasions it may be necessary for individual Christian conscience, having made every possible attempt to become reconciled to a particular church teaching or law, to say no to that teaching or law on behalf of a clear mandate of conscience. The best-known instance of this is Luther's statement before the Diet of Worms in 1521. When asked by Eck why his opinion should supersede that of so many teachers and councils of the church that had gone before him, Luther made the famous reply, "My conscience is captive to the word of God." In such an instance one had best be prepared spiritually to suffer if necessary for conscience' sake. Those persecuted for righteousness' sake are especially blessed by God (Matt. 5:10).

Jesus as remembered in John's Gospel set forth a profound practical moral insight when he pointed out that it is only when one actively *"chooses to do God's will,"* that one in due course *"will find out* whether my teaching comes from God" (John 7:17).[26] Hence the Christian's conscience is forever being tested in moral experience.

Fallen Humanity Is Never Left Without Sufficient Witness

Having conscience, scripture, consensual church teaching, reason, and experience to guide faith and action, few can plausibly plead an

24. T. Goodwin, *Works* 6:231-319.
25. Luther, WML 5:58-60.
26. John Chrysostom, *Hom. on John*, FC 41:16.

uninstructed moral sense. In each of these strata of guidance, we meet the same active work of the one God. Humanity is never left without grace sufficient to make a way proximately through moral ambiguities, though under the conditions of the history of sin we continue to "see through a glass, darkly."[27]

Even while God has been willing to "let all nations go their own way" in order not to undermine human freedom, God has never "left himself without testimony," as Paul and Barnabas told the Lycaonians. "He has shown kindness by giving you rain from heaven and crops in their seasons" (Acts 14:16, 17; cf. 1 Kings 19:4-6). Immediately after this Paul was stoned almost to death by those whom God had not left without witness.

Whether the Seed of Faith Abides in Honest Truth-seekers

The Spirit is not unwilling to work through the sound thinking of conscientious philosophers, "the Spirit using them as a flute-player plays his flute."[28] Ever vulnerable to misperceptions, the most proficient philosophers "knock at the gates of truth."[29] Too much philosophy, however, resembles a sword with silver hilt and leaden blade.[30] Plato's teachings were not wholly alien to Christ, or wholly the same.[31] Insofar as Socrates and Heraclitus, as well as Abraham, lived according to the whole Logos-nature that was revealed in Christ, they may be called implicit or proleptic Christians.[32] Zwingli embraced as elect not only these but also Cato, Scipio, Aristides, Antigonus, Numa, Camillus, and Theseus.[33] The early Christian apologists attempted to show that the best of heathen philosophy had in some fragmented sense looked anticipatively toward the coming justice and mercy of God, even though it was looking through the broken lens of self-assertive reasoning. The Word was present

---

27. 1 Cor. 13:12 KJV; cf. C. S. Lewis, *The Abolition of Man* (New York: Macmillan, 1947); Moss, CF 236-42.

28. Athenagoras, *A Plea for the Christians* 9, ANF 2:133; cf. SHD 1:112.

29. Tertullian, *Testimony of the Soul* 1, FC 10:131-32.

30. John Chrysostom, *Hom. on the Statues*, NPNF 1:9:465.

31. Justin Martyr, *Second Apology* 13, ANF 1:192; cf. Lactantius, *DI*, FC 49:491ff.

32. Justin Martyr, *First Apology* 46, ANF 1:178; cf. Minucius Felix, *Octavius* 20, ANF 5:184.

33. Zwingli, WZ 1:74; cf. *Werke*, 4:65; 6:1:242; 6:2:69; 7:550, 8:179; SHD 2:315.

among them in seminal form, engendering some refractions of the coming truth, just as it worked in Abraham anticipatively through his faith.[34]

Justin, who suffered martyrdom under the Roman emperor Marcus Aurelius, made this plea in his address to the Roman Senate: "For whatever either lawgivers or philosophers uttered well, they elaborated by finding and contemplating some part of the Word. But since they did not know the whole of the Word, which is Christ, they often contradicted themselves." Christ was "partially known even by Socrates, for He was and is the Word who is in every man."[35] Justin argued that the whole of human history, through reason and conscience, participated anticipatively in the Logos, who became in due time revealed in Jesus Christ.[36] Those who live according to reason have shared in this Logos insofar as their natural capacities were enabled by a common grace. "For all the writers [of antiquity] were able to see realities darkly through the sowing of the implanted Word."[37] Tertullian thought of Socrates as "almost one of us" (*paene noster*),[38] as one who "had a glimpse of the truth."[39]

Clement of Alexandria was also convinced that the best of philosophy had pointed the Hellenic mind toward Christ just as the law had pointed the Hebraic mind toward Christ.[40] Clement thought that "God the Creator was in a roundabout way worshiped by the Greeks. . . . By reflection and direct vision, those among the Greeks who have philosophized accurately, see God" in some dim way.[41] "The same God that furnished both the covenants was the giver of Greek philosophy to the Greeks, by which the Almighty is glorified among the Greeks."[42] It is on this basis that early Christian apologists argued that the human soul is at its deepest level persistently a

---

34. Origen, *Against Celsus*, 3.26, 8.12, ANF 4:474, 643; cf. Justin Martyr *First Apology* 8-11, ANF 1:165-66; Athenagoras, *Plea* 7, 9, ANF 2:132-33; Theophilis, *To Autolycus* 2.9, ANF 2:97.
35. *Second Apology* 10, ANF 1:191.
36. *First Apology* 45-46, ANF 1:178; *Second Apology* 10-13, ANF 1:191-93.
37. *Second Apology* 13, ANF 1:193.
38. Strong, *Syst. Theol.* 666.
39. Tertullian, *Apology* 46, ANF 3:51.
40. *Stromata* 1.5, ANF 2:305; cf. 6.17.
41. Ibid., 1.19, ANF 2:321-22.
42. Ibid., 2.5, ANF 2:489.

reflection of the image of God, and in a sense naturally Christian (*anima naturaliter Christiana est*).[43]

Whatever the Corruption, It Remains Incomplete

Human nature has not been so absolutely corrupted by sin as to eliminate the good creation of God out of which sin emerges as a distortion. Even in their fallen condition, the descendants of Eve and Adam remain capable of planting vineyards, building houses, and constructing governments and courts of law, "just as a sick man may of himself have some motion, but cannot be perfectly moved with the motion of a whole man unless he be made whole."[44]

In the state of fallen nature, sufficient grace was not lacking or withheld from humanity. "Through the regular succession of the centuries some have been saved by the law of grace, others by the law of Moses, others by the law of nature, which God has written in the hearts of all, in the expectation of the coming of Christ."[45] From before the flood, and even in the midst of Sodom, and notably among the Egyptians, "God, being a God of mercy from the beginning, called every generation to repentance by righteous men and prophets."[46] Yet in this state, fallen humanity could not desire grace simply by willing it of their own independent power.[47] Some were saved through the indistinct hope of the ultimate coming of God (Heb. 11:1-7).

---

43. Rahner, *TI* 6:390ff.
44. Tho. Aq., *ST* 1-2.Q109.2, 1:1124.
45. Lucidus, "Letter of Submission," Council of Arles, SCD §160*b*, p. 66; cf. Clement 11, "Errors of Paschasius Quesnel," SCD §§1356ff., pp. 348ff.
46. *Apostolic Constitutions* 2.55, ANF 7:420.
47. Augustine, *On the Grace of Christ and Original Sin*, NPNF 1:5:237ff.; cf. Pius 6, SCD §1518, pp. 370ff.

CHAPTER 4

THE INTENT OF SUFFICIENT GRACE

What God gives is never ineptly given or wanting in sufficiency. God antecedently wills that all should be saved, but not without their own free acceptance of salvation. Consequent to that exercise of freedom, God promises unmerited saving mercies to the faithful and fairness to the unfaithful.

THE SUFFICIENCY OF GRACE

God's offer of saving grace is always sufficient. Any deficiency always lies within the fallen will and its distorted receptivity, not in an intrinsic inadequacy of the gift. Sufficiency is intrinsic to the nature of grace. Any insinuation of deficiency must be traced to the inadequate acceptance of grace.

Whoever develops beyond infancy grows gradually in the exercise of responsible freedom, which remains ever vulnerable to corruption. Yet at each step of the way, God provides sufficient grace to every soul for salvation, whether it is by living faith or by anticipatory belief in a future revelation (Heb. 11:1-8). Those who cooperate with sufficient grace are further provided with the means for grace to become effective.[1]

This has been a key feature of the classical Christian teaching of grace. An anonymous exegete of the fifth century stated the distinction beautifully: "It so pleased God to give His efficacious grace to many, and to withhold His sufficient grace from none, in order that it might appear from both that what is conferred upon a portion is not denied to the entire race."[2]

---

1. Tho. Aq., ST 2-1.Q111, 3:1135-39.
2. De vocatione omnium gentium 2.25, MPL 17:1073ff.; cf. DT (Pohle) 7:170.

In this way sufficient grace is provided to all categories of recipients: the just, the unjust, and those who have never had the opportunity to hear of God's justice and mercy. It is given not only to those justified by grace through faith, but also to unresponsive and obdurate sinners, those lacking opportunity to hear clear testimony of the divine mercy, those who earnestly seek God, and unbaptized infants. *The sufficiency is offered with the gift; the deficiency follows only from its inadequate acceptance.* As one moves in a progression from those justified by grace through faith to incorrigible sinners, the boundaries of sufficient grace are tested. The first of these is easy to establish; the argument for sufficiency becomes progressively harder as one proceeds along the spectrum.

Sufficient Grace for Those Justified by Grace Through Faith

To the just (*dikaios*, those saved and made upright by faith, Rom. 1:17; 3:26), it is evident that God operates within their specific situations to offer grace sufficient to follow the divine requirement. The sufficient grace promised will be situationally supplied: "God is faithful; he will not let you be tempted beyond what you can bear. But when you are tempted, he will also provide a way out so that you can stand up under it" (1 Cor. 10:13). The promise is that "my yoke is easy and my burden is light" (Matt. 11:30), so that God's "commands are not burdensome" to those "born of God" (1 John 5:3, 4).

Sufficient Grace for Those Without Opportunity: The Unevangelized

Those who have had no reasonable opportunity to hear and respond to justifying grace are distinguished from those who, having heard, reject justifying grace. Those *"heathen"* who have not yet received the Good News of Jesus Christ are contrasted with *apostates*, who having believed have fallen away, and *heretics*, who having heard the apostolic testimony, now pretend to "improve" it.[3]

The Savior of all humanity is equally the Savior of those who have received the law and those who have not received the law. "The Lord in all generations gave opportunity for penance to all who wished to be converted," wrote Clement of Rome.[4] The view that "pagans, Jews, and

---

3. John Cassian, *Conferences* 2.13, NPNF 2:11, 424.
4. Clement of Rome, *First Epistle to the Corinthians* 1.7, DT (Pohle) 7:181.

heretics" lack sufficient grace was generally rejected by the time of the Jansenist controversies.[5] The Apostle promised "glory, honor and peace for everyone who does good: first for the Jew, then for the Gentile. For God does not show favoritism" (Rom. 2:10-11).

God in his mercy does not deny "the help necessary for salvation to those who, without blame on their part, have not yet arrived at an explicit knowledge of God, but who strive to live a good life, thanks to His grace. Whatever goodness or truth is found among them is looked upon by the Church as a preparation for the Gospel."[6]

Sufficient Grace for Those Who Earnestly Seek God

An important implication for the Christian understanding of the religions of the world is embedded in the text of Hebrews 11:6-7: "And without faith it is impossible to please God, because anyone who comes to him must believe that *he exists* and that *he rewards those who earnestly seek him*. By faith Noah, when warned about things not yet seen, in holy fear built an ark to save his family," and thereby before the covenant with Abraham, before the law of Moses, and before the messianic promise to David, Noah "became heir of the righteousness that comes by faith" (ital. ad.).

On this ground the ancient Christian consensus held that sufficient grace is provided for all "those who earnestly seek him" before Christ's coming, and unknowing of Christ's coming. By an implicit faith (*fides implicita*) they embodied a general readiness to trust in what God was anticipatively revealing or is yet to reveal.

Sufficient grace to receive and affirm this implicit faith is given to everyone. It requires no explicit knowledge of or faith in the incarnation or the Triune God, but only a belief in the two phrases mentioned in Hebrews 11:6—the existence of God and the expected ultimate justice of God, even when that justice is not fully understood.[7] The intuition of the existence and justice of God is accessible to natural reason and conscience and consistent with the innate tendencies of human nature. Hence the inference holds that God antecedently wills the sal-

---

5. Alexander 8, "Errors of the Jansenists," SCD §1295, p. 339; cf. Clement 11, "Errors of Paschasius Quesnel," SCD §1379, pp. 347ff.
6. Vatican II, *Dogmatic Constitution on the Church* 2.16, CC 468.
7. Tho. Aq., ST 2-2.Q10.4, 2:1215-16; cf. ST 1.Q14.11, 1:80-81.

vation of all, and that no one is rejected by God except through the exercise of his or her own freedom.[8]

This is why the proclaiming community is free to approach with openness all forms and traditions of the history of religious consciousness.[9] Christianity itself as a religion is not exempt from the judgment of God's holiness upon sin: "The reconciling word of the gospel is God's judgment upon all forms of religion, including the Christian."[10] "Those also can attain to everlasting salvation who through no fault of their own do not know the gospel of Christ or His Church, yet sincerely seek God and, moved by grace, strive by their deeds to do His will as it is known to them through the dictates of conscience."[11]

Sufficient Grace for Unbaptized Infants

The notion that God antecedently wills to save all is especially tested in the issue of the salvation of unbaptized infants, upon which many opinions have been held within the range of orthodoxy. One centrist tradition of interpretation is that expressed by Thomas Aquinas, who said that unbaptized infants enjoy a natural beatitude, and that God mercifully preserves them in a state of innocence. The eternal Lover of souls loves the souls of innocents, and exercises his almighty wisdom by conferring grace on those who without fault of their own are deprived of baptism, which is the ordinary means of receiving regenerating grace.[12]

The following provision was stated by the Westminster Confession concerning elect infants and adults who have neither received baptism nor heard the Word proclaimed: "Elect infants, dying in infancy, are regenerated and saved by Christ through *the Spirit, who worketh when, and where, and how he pleaseth.* So also are all other elect persons who are incapable of being outwardly called by the ministry of the Word."[13]

Each of these cases, however difficult, establishes the single point that God's offer of saving grace is always sufficient. The deficiency lies

---

8. Cassian, *Conferences* 1.3, NPNF 2:11, 325ff., 423-26.
9. Lactantius, *DI* 4.28, ANF 7:131.
10. United Presbyterian Confession of 1967, CC 701.
11. Vatican II, *Dogmatic Constitution on the Church* 2.16, CC 467.
12. Tho. Aq., ST 3.Q66.7.8, 2:2386-88; cf. Q68, 2:2398-2408; DT (Pohle) 7:164-67.
13. Westminster Conf. 10, CC 206, ital. ad.

solely within the fallen will and its distorted receptivity, not in the inadequacy of the gift or Giver.

Sufficient Grace for Sinners Lacking Justifying Faith

God supplies sufficient grace for sinners to be saved, even when they ignore or reject this grace. This applies both to ordinary sinners, who are given sufficient grace to resist temptation and repent, and to obdurate sinners, from whom God never entirely withdraws sufficient grace.

God does not withhold from sinners sufficient grace to resist temptation and repent when they sin. The defect lies not in the grace of God but in the sinner who refuses or neglects the means of grace. No sinner is without the grace of prayer, the exercise of which enables further strengthening by grace. Dame Juliana of Norwich inferred that "it is most impossible that we should ask for mercy and lack it."[14] No divine requirement is given without grace also being given to follow it.

If repentance and faith are duties that require grace, then it is absurd to imagine that God would require a duty for which God refused to supply the grace to fulfill. "The Lord is not slow in keeping his promise, as some understand slowness" (2 Pet. 3:9). "God therefore does not command impossibilities; but in His command He counsels you both to do what you can for yourself, and to ask His aid in what you cannot do."[15]

The gospel is offered to every individual, however deeply racked by sin, as Paul himself powerfully testified: "Christ Jesus came into the world to save sinners—of whom I am the worst. But for that very reason I was shown mercy so that in me, the worst of sinners, Christ Jesus might display his unlimited patience as an example for those who would believe on him and receive eternal life" (1 Tim. 1:15-16). Jesus died even for those who do not want to believe and who will never believe. God's gift is offered whether accepted or not.

Sufficient Grace for Incorrigible Sinners

The obdurate are those who deliberately and repeatedly resist grace, or maliciously reject God's goodwill. Is God's will to save finally frus-

---

14. *RDL* 145.
15. Augustine, *On Nature and Grace* 50, NPNF 1:5:138; cf. DT (Pohle) 7:174.

trated by such obduracy, so that God at long last withdraws sufficient grace from these recalcitrants? No, even the most embittered sinners are given efficacious occasions to repent. Augustine wrote, "The greater and stronger graces which He grants to ordinary sinners, He withholds from the obdurate in punishment of their malice. This is, however, by no means tantamount to a withdrawal of sufficient grace."[16]

Over no depth of sin is it proper to despair.[17] Sinners are lost not because of a defect of God's mercy, but a defect in their reception of it. No living person is wholly beyond being restored by sincere repentance.[18]

This is why early attempts to declare as absolutely unforgivable three of the most noxious capital sins (apostasy, murder, and adultery) were steadily rejected as contrary to the consensual teaching of the church. This is why even the act of despairing of God's grace is itself a sin that can be corrected by the grace of prayer. "Nothing prevents the salvation of the greatest sinner except his own voluntary refusal to accept Jesus Christ."[19]

An amusing distinction was drawn by Thomas Aquinas between *perfect obstinacy*, which exists only in hell, and an *imperfect obstinacy*, which exists on this side of hell among those who have become so obdurate against grace that they have hardly the slightest impulse to repent and turn to do good. Yet even in these cases, sufficient grace remains for prayer, which would enable further graces in time to grow.[20]

THE ANTECEDENT AND CONSEQUENT WILL OF GOD

The eternal divine will to save (*voluntas Dei salvifica*) may be viewed as either antecedent or consequent to the exercise of human freedom in history.

16. DT (Pohle) 7:177.
17. Augustine, *Retractions* 1.12, FC 60:51-58.
18. Fourth Lateran Council, SCD §430, p. 169.
19. "Statement of Baptist Faith and Message," CC 347.
20. Tho. Aq., *Truth* Q24.11, trans. R. W. Schmidt (Chicago: Henry Regnry, 1954), 3:185-88.

Consensual exegesis has distinguished two aspects of God's benevolent will: God's primordial (or antecedent) benevolence, and God's special (or consequent) benevolence. A distinction is posited between God's *antecedent* will to save (*voluntas antecedens,* antecedent to the exercise of human freedom), and God's consequent will (*voluntas consequens*) to reward the just and punish the unjust *consequent* to the exercise of their freedom.

The Benevolence of the Divine Will, Antecedently and Consequently Viewed

On this basis, the universal sufficiency of grace is usually treated in three phases:

1. God's will antecedently is to save all;
2. God's will is to offer grace sufficient to make actual God's universal will to save;
3. Consequent upon the exercise of freedom, God's will is to destine those who freely accept grace to be near to God in eternal blessedness and to destine those who reject grace to be far from God in eternal separation.[21]

The antecedent will of God is that all shall be recipients of redemption, yet not by coercion. The consequent will of God, ensuing upon the free, self-determining responses of persons to believe or not believe, is to redeem those who have faith.[22] A just judge may antecedently will all citizens to live, yet consequent to the fact that some decide to be murderers, he wills that criminals be justly punished. Similarly, God wills antecedently that all should be brought to eternal blessedness, yet consequent to the operation of human freedom to reject grace, God wills that those who so reject grace face the consequences of that rejection as separation from God. From the perspective of the consequences of human freedom, one may apply the following formula: "Whatever God simply wills takes place; although what He wills antecedently may not take place,"[23] if voluntarily refused.

---

21. Hugh of St. Victor, SCF 61-75.
22. Clement of Alexandria, *Stromata* 7.1ff., 8.9, ANF 2:523ff., 565-66.
23. Thomas Aquinas, ST 1.Q19.6.1, 1:108.

In this way it is easy to see the close connection between the doctrines of grace and eschatology. On this basis Prosper of Aquitaine stated the classical formula that "those who are saved, are saved because He wills them to be saved, while those who perish, perish because they deserve to perish."[24] The ancient ecumenical consensus on this universal divine will to save (*voluntas salvifica*) is substantial, unbroken, and oft-repeated.[25] The council fathers at Quiersy taught that "God wishes *all men* without exception *to be saved*, although *not all will* be saved."[26]

God's Antecedent Redemptive Will to Save Is Universal, Impartial, Efficacious, and Ordinate

Since the benevolence of God is primordially offered to all, it is wholly antecedent (Lat.: *antecedanea*, Gk.: *proegoumene*) to its reception or rejection. It is universal, given to all humanity, since, as Scripture attests, Christ died for all (John 3:16; Acts 17:30-31; 1 Tim. 2:4; Titus 2:11). In fact, the grace that saves is offered to all despite the fact that all lack any merit that might cause them to deserve it or ability that might enable them to gain it. Augustine made this very point when, as an African, he taught that God's atoning action was intended not only for Africa (as certain Donatists claimed), but for all the world.[27]

It is offered to all without regard to merit or any condition of earning it. God thereby wills that all should be saved and come to the knowledge of the truth, and offers the necessary means to make fitting response.

Objectively all are reconciled on the cross, even if subjectively only those are finally redeemed who respond in faith and obedience. "He is

---

24. Prosper of Aquitaine, *Pro Aug. responsiones ad capitula calumniantium Gallorum* 8, DT (Pohle) 7:153.
25. Cf. Passaglia, *De partitione voluntatis divinae*, part 3 of *Commentariorum theologicorum* (Rome: Bonarum Artium, 1851), who cites more than two hundred patristic sources on this point; John Chrysostom, *Hom. on John* 27, FC 33:259-67; see also patristic commentaries on John 3:16; Acts 17:30, 31; 1 Tim. 2:4; and Titus 2:11. John of Damascus provided the classical formulation of the consensual distinction between the antecedent and consequent will of God; cf. OF 4.19-21, NPNF 2:9:92-94.
26. Council of Quiersy, A.D. 853, SCD §319, p. 127, ital. ad.
27. *On the Gospel of John* 13.14, NPNF 1:7:92; cf. Rom. 8:32.

the atoning sacrifice for our sins, and not only for ours but also for the sins of *the whole world*" (1 John 2:2). "He is patient with you, not wanting anyone to perish, but *everyone* to come to repentance" (2 Pet. 3:9). "'In the last days, God says, / I will pour out my Spirit on *all* people'" (Acts 2:17, quoting Joel 2:28)—both daughters and sons, young and old, married and unmarried.

If misery is everywhere to be found in the path of sin, so grace is everywhere to be found antecedent and consequent to sin. If in time sin has become universal, grace is universal before time and toward all time.

The universality of God's antecedent will is most explicitly stated in the first letter to Timothy: "This is good, and pleases God our Savior, who wants all men to be saved and to come to a knowledge of the truth. For there is one God and one mediator between God and men, the man Christ Jesus, who gave himself as a ransom for all men—the testimony given in its proper time" (1 Tim. 2:3-6).[28]

The antecedent will of God universally to save is further described by the orthodox teaching of the church as impartial, efficacious, and ordinate. First, God's will to save is *fair and impartial*. The general benevolence of God is called antecedent because it precedes any consideration of human responsiveness to it, disposing itself equally and impartially toward all.[29] Accordingly, no human being of any period of history is left wholly without sufficient prevening grace or neglected by this divine will to save. The Son is sent to redeem the whole world. All human beings are intended recipients of this Word, even those who have not heard it, or upon hearing, have not believed it.[30]

Second, God's will to save all is *sincere and efficacious*. It is said of this antecedent will of God that it is guileless, serious, and active; hence, neither feigned, superficial, nor merely passive. It is not as if God perfunctorily willed that all be saved but hiddenly determined in advance that some would not be saved, in a way that would appear to make God the author of evil.

28. Augustine, *Conf.* 12.17ff., NPNF 1:1:182; *On the Spirit and the Letter* 33.58, NPNF 1:5:109.
29. John Gerhard, *Loci theologici* (Tübingen, Ger.: n.p., 1762–87), 4:169; cf. *DT* (Schmid) 278.
30. L. Hutter, *Compend. locorum theologicorum* (Wittenburgae: Meyerum, 1609), 792; cf. *DT* (Schmid) 279.

The benevolence of God is not an empty vow, a fruitless wish, an indifferent complacency, by which one does not long to effect or obtain the thing which pleases him and which in itself he loves, and, therefore, is not willing to employ the means leading to that end; but it is an efficacious desire, by which God seriously intends, through sufficient and efficacious means, to effect and obtain the salvation of men, in which He is most ardently delighted.[31]

Finally, the antecedent will of God to save is said to be *ordinate* because it deliberately orders and provides those sufficient means through prayer, conscience, reason, and especially the ministry of Word and Sacrament to confer these proffered blessings upon sinners. These means of grace are addressed not to some but to all, to call everyone to repentance, to convert, justify, and regenerate all. These means are provided not grudgingly or barely to justify, but intend to bring all recipients to the full knowledge of the truth.

It Is the World That God So Loved

The New Testament regarded the earthly ministry of Jesus as a testimony in time of the eternal decision of God to redeem whatever might become lost or distorted in creation, even before creation was called forth. All descendants of Adam and Eve thus have Jesus Christ for their mediator.[32]

This mercy is extended to all.[33] "For God so loved *the world* that he gave his one and only Son, that *whoever* believes in him shall not perish but have eternal life" (John 3:16, ital. ad.). God hates nothing that God has made (Wis. 11:24-25). The mercy of God is offered to the whole inanimate and biological creation, but especially toward human beings capable of reflecting the goodness of God like a mirror, even though broken. This applies to every human soul of every time, every race, every culture, every religion. God longs to save all.

The gracious will of the Father toward human fallenness in time results in the sending of the Son whose atoning death accomplishes redemption, and the sending of the Spirit who works to apply that redemption through the ministries of Word, sacrament, and pastoral

---

31. Hollaz, *ETA* 599; cf. *DT* (Schmid) 280.
32. Prosper of Aquitaine, *Grace and Free Will* 2, FC 7:345-50.
33. Trent 6:17, p. 44.

care. This divine intent was anticipated in the biblical narrative as early as Genesis 3:15 (the protoevangelium). Only God could have foreseen from eternity that humanity would fall, and provided a sufficient way to redeem. God loved the world and gave his Son (John 3:16), bore the sins of the world (John 1:29), gave his flesh for the life of the world (John 6:51), and his blood is the propitiation for the sins of the whole world (1 John 1:7; 2:2).

GOD'S CONSEQUENT REDEMPTIVE WILL TO SAVE THOSE WHO ARE RESPONSIVE

Whether God Always Wills Without Reference to Human Willing

If considered abstractly apart from human responsiveness, the general will of God is that all be saved. Yet if that is construed to mean that God saves regardless of human responsiveness, then salvation would be coerced, a premise alien to apostolic testimony. Hence Christ "obtained for all a salvation which, nevertheless, is not applied to all."[34] The accomplishment of God's will is proximately conditioned by the response of human beings to this freely given grace.

The divine resolve consequent to human choice wills that *those should be saved who receive* the salvation offered by grace through faith active in love. This is respectfully called the consequent redemptive will because it follows as a consequence of God's decision to honor, and not coerce, human freedom. The eternal foreknowledge of God knew that if God did not coerce human freedom, some would believe and others would not.[35]

In this way God respects, and does not intrude upon, the human freedom to reject grace. This is clear from Jesus' poignant exclamation concerning the people of Jerusalem: "How often I have longed to gather your children together, as a hen gathers her chicks under her wings, *but you were not willing*" (Matt. 23:37, ital. ad.). Does the unwillingness of the recipient of grace absolutely prevent the stubborn fulfillment and completion of God's desire to save? Such unwillingness may

---

34. Helvetic Consensus Formula 16, CC 316.
35. Augustine, *On the Spirit and the Letter* 58, NPNF 1:5:109.

proximately resist this fulfillment; but it cannot ultimately prevent it, for God has plenty of time.

Suppose a parent wanted to give a son or a daughter a gift that required a strong affirmative response in order that it be meaningfully received. Suppose the gift were an offer of partnership in the family firm. The gift is not an inanimate object but the offering of a relationship of mutuality and promised blessing based on mutual accountability. The gift is costly for the parent and valuable for the youth, but not yet fully recognized by the youth as valuable. The parent wills generally and antecedently that the youth accept the offer. Yet the crucial premise is that this gift requires the free, conscious, studied reception by and commitment of the youth in order to be fully given and received. The will of the parent, which is first antecedent, then consequent to the youth's response, is to honor the youth's freedom to say yes or no, while making it possible to say yes.

Whether There Are Two Competing Divine Wills

Antecedence and consequence in the will of God do not imply two competing divine wills. Rather there is one will of God viewed in two different ways by human recipients of grace in time—as prior to and after human responsiveness. The antecedent will focuses on God's eternal intent to give, the consequent on God's will in answer to historical human responsiveness. The former is universally and equally given, the latter particularly and variably received according to human choice.

After Pentecost the Lord was more ready to give the Spirit than the disciples were to receive: "I am ready to give it even now, but the vessel cannot yet hold it," wrote Cyril of Jerusalem, paraphrasing Jesus; "for a while therefore receive ye as much grace as ye can bear; and look forward to yet more."[36] Grace is in this way justly "distributed in proportion to the vessels, and the capacity of the recipients."[37]

Through the incomparable mercy of divine love, God is inclined to save all; through the incomparable wisdom of divine justice, God brings to nothing those wills that freely reject and obstinately ignore God's mercy and grace. The will of God is one in God, though it may appear differently to creatures in time. "By His antecedent will, God wills that all men be

---

36. Cyril of Jerusalem, *Catech. Lect.* 17.12, NPNF 2:7:127; Luke 24:44-49; 2 Cor. 4:7.
37. Ibid., 16.25, NPNF 2:7:122.

saved if they believe to the end. But those using aright the ordinary means of salvation are those who finally believe. Therefore the antecedent will of God is not overthrown, abolished, or removed by the consequent, but rather passes into the same when the condition is fulfilled."[38]

God does not will saving faith coercively, or without regard for the fulfillment of appropriate conditions leading to the reception of grace. God antecedently wills through reliable and ordinate means to confer saving faith upon all. The consequent will of God to save offers the same divine grace as the antecedent. There is only one difference—God's redemptive will is *consequent to, or follows upon,* human responsiveness. "God compels not (for compulsion is repugnant to God), but supplies to those who seek, and bestows on those who ask, and opens to those who knock."[39]

Finally such matters remain impenetrable, and there is no theological duty to attempt to define conceptually that which transcends human knowing.[40] After attempting to discern the purpose of God amid Israel's folly, Paul exclaimed: "Oh, the depth of the riches of the wisdom and knowledge of God! / How unsearchable his judgments, / and his paths beyond tracing out! / Who has known the mind of the Lord?" (Rom. 11:33-34; cf. Job 5:9, 15:8; Ps. 139:6; Isa. 40:13, 28).

Based precisely on these constraints, the consensual ecumenical tradition has affirmed a profound sense of divine election. The primary awareness is that the freedom to trust God has been utterly and completely elicited by grace. God foreknew this salvation from eternity, yet without coercing freedom. God the Spirit has nurtured, wooed, and coaxed human freedom toward faithful responsiveness.[41]

---

38. Hollaz, *ETA* 588; cf. *DT* (Schmid) 283.
39. Clement of Alexandria, *Who Is the Rich Man That Shall Be Saved?* 10, ANF 2:593.
40. Formula of Concord, "Solid Declaration" 11.54, 55; quoted in *DT* (Schmid) 276.
41. Suppose there had been no sin whatever in history (a fantastic hypothesis, but nonetheless conceivable); would there have been no need for a savior? Scotist and Thomistic traditions of biblical interpretation differ on this question: Duns Scotus held that the incarnation would have taken place even if there had been no sin, that the incarnation's object was not merely the remedy of sin, but to fulfill the eternal purpose of God quite apart from what sin had done to distort the world (Eph. 1:4; 3:11; Stone, *OCD* 286-87). Thomas Aquinas held that the coming of the Savior was provided specifically as a remedy for sin, yet was eternally purposed in the sense that sin was foreknown by God; hence, if there had been no sin foreknown, there would have been no need for a saving remedy for it. "Christ Jesus came into the world to save sinners" (1 Tim. 1:15). There is much room within Christian orthodoxy for such differences, although the latter comes closer to consensual reception.

Why Are So Many, Having Received Sufficient Grace, Unenlightened by It?

How has it happened that so many have remained lost and separated from God, if God has willed that all, simply by believing, should be saved? If God remains eternally the "true light that gives light to every man" (John 1:9), why then do so many remain willfully unenlightened? John Chrysostom answered: "He enlightens all so far as in Him lies. But if some, willfully closing the eyes of their mind, would not receive the rays of that Light, their darkness arises not from the nature of the Light, but from their own wickedness, who wilfully deprive themselves of the gift."[42]

Meanwhile God compassionately reaches out even for those who continually and willfully reject grace (Matt. 23:37), making every possible approach to render grace plausible and believable. Dame Juliana of Norwich wrote: "By his permission we fall, in his blissful love with his might and his wisdom we are preserved, and by mercy and grace we are raised to many more joys."[43]

It was not God's design that men and women be saved contrary to their own wills.[44] Human freedom to reject God's offer remains intact under the divine pardon and permission. God desires that freedom respond in faith but will not intrusively force the gospel on free persons or justice on social processes. Arnobius argued that Christ "invites all alike," and does not "thrust back or repel any one. . . . To all, He says, the fountain of life is open, and no one is hindered or kept back from drinking."[45] This is how the sufficiency of grace has been argued in the face of the history of human rebelliousness.

Did God Cause Humanity to Fall?

God has permitted, but not caused, humanity to fall into sin through the exercise of free self-determination. People have become alienated from God, not because God directly willed it, but because humanity collectively and individually has historically willed it and continues to do so. All descendants of Eve and Adam are trapped in the syndromes

---

42. John Chrysostom, *Hom. on St. John* 8.1, NPNF 1:14:29.
43. Juliana of Norwich, *RDL* 136.
44. Council of Ephesus, SCD §§126ff., pp. 52-53.
45. *Ag. the Nations* 2.64, ANF 6:458-59.

of sin, guilt, anxiety, and death, and all would have perished apart from saving grace.[46]

Though some scripture texts appear to imply that God unilaterally acts to harden the hearts of sinners (Exod. 7:3; 9:12), it would be a misreading of those texts to assume that there would be no cooperation whatever between grace and freedom, for in the same passages it is clear that the same Pharaoh had voluntarily "hardened his [own] heart" (Exod. 8:15) by resisting God's calling and enabling grace.

God prepared vessels of mercy for the divine glory, yet by persuading rather than coercing human freedom (Rom. 9:23). Those not responding in faith (vessels to be bypassed, Rom. 9:22) are viewed as permitted by God temporarily or tolerated with patience by the kindness of God.[47] It is not that God antecedently rejected them apart from any personal responsiveness. Those who say "no" to grace become hardened not by God's direct will but indirectly by God's permission of recalcitrance in the human will.[48] Grace is given sufficiently and does not become insufficient merely by being unreceived.

---

46. Augustine, *Letters* FC 30:193ff.
47. Calvin, *Comm.* 19:367-69.
48. Quenstedt, TDP 3:12; cf. *DT* (Schmid) 280.

PART THREE

HOW GRACE BECOMES FREEDOM

CHAPTER 5

HOW GRACE WORKS IN THE WILL: GRACE-ENABLED FREEDOM

Grace is more than a doctrinal footnote. It is the motivating power of the Christian life. If grace is necessary to know truth, avoid sin, act well, pray fittingly, desire salvation, begin to have faith, and persevere in faith, as the ancient ecumenical writers agree,[1] then it becomes a pivotal concern of Christian teaching and caregiving to understand how grace works in human willing.

WHETHER GRACE SHAPES THE WILL FROM WITHOUT OR RECONSTITUTES AND REEMPOWERS THE WILL FROM WITHIN

The "zap" theory of conversion ignores the most crucial issue: the transformation of the will itself. Grace works to enable the will to will the good. The persistent obstacle to grace is the fact that human willing itself has become corrupted by the history of sin, thus digging its own spiritual grave. This social history becomes further entangled each time an individual wills lesser goods than those offered and situationally available.

God's redemptive will seeks to refashion human willing and loving so as to enable the person once again to will and love the good. Yet this transformation does not occur simply by fiat, because it is the will itself that must be transformed. Such a transformation can only occur meaningfully by the persuasive cooperation of the human will itself.

1. Second Council of Orange, SCD §§174-92, pp. 75ff.

The Consequences of the Fall for the Will

The forbidden fruit never lacks volunteer tasters. They soon become compulsive eaters. Once sin has rebelled against the divine will and raised persistent obstacles to attentive situational listening, the original righteousness of the will prior to the fall does not avail. An uprighted disposition or habituation of the will then becomes impossible to re-acquire, once having rebelled and fallen.[2]

Every moment freedom faces new contingencies. Any one may tend to upset the delicate equilibrium that was once possible under the undiverted attentiveness of original righteousness. Hence the will is inevitably, but not necessarily, prone to fall, under conditions of temptation and contingency.[3] "No one uses his free will well, except through Christ,"[4] for "no one can rise from the depth of that ruin [the defacing of the image of God] through free will, unless the grace of a merciful God raise him up."[5]

Grace does not remake the will by coercion, but only by a history of persuasion, drawing the will back toward the divine requirement. On the cross the prodigal will is offered a wholly pardoned, new beginning point.[6]

The Salvation Which Is by Grace Alone Is Not Without Human Willing

Paul enjoined the Philippians to "work out your salvation with fear and trembling, for it is God who works in you to will and to act according to his good purpose" (Phil. 2:12-13). God works. You work.

"No one can come to me unless the Father who sent me draws him" (John 6:44). Augustine commented that the Evangelist

> does not say, "except He lead him," so that we can thus in any way understand that [the human being's] will precedes. For who is "drawn," if he was already willing? And yet no man comes unless he is willing.

---

2. John Chrysostom, *Hom. on the Statues*, NPNF 1:9:388.
3. John of Damascus, OF 2.25-28, NPNF 2:9:39-42; cf. Niebuhr, NDM 1.
4. Council of Ephesus, SCD §133, p. 54.
5. Ibid., SCD §130, p. 53; cf. Tillett, PS 113-24; Summers, *Syst. Theol.* 2:62-90; Miley, *Syst. Theol.* 2:242-52; Miner Raymond, *Syst. Theol.* 2:308-19.
6. R. Watson, *TI* 2, chap. 27; cf. Pope, *Compend.* 2:55-86, 358-71; Daniel Denison Whedon, *Essays, Reviews, and Discourses* 78-102; A. A. Hodge, OOT 338-47.

Therefore he is *drawn* in wondrous ways to *will* by Him who knows how to work within the very hearts of men. Not that men who are unwilling should believe, which cannot be, but that they should be made willing from being unwilling.[7]

Paul evidenced the affinity of grace and freedom in this passage: "But by the grace of God I am what I am, and his grace to me was not without effect. No, *I worked harder than all of them—yet not I, but the grace of God* that was with me" (1 Cor. 15:10, ital. ad.). Grace is working so as to elicit my energetic responsiveness, while my hard work is being enabled by grace. Grace does not nullify "what I am." Grace is not without behavioral effect. Commenting on Romans 9:16—"It does not, therefore, depend on man's desire or effort, but on God's mercy"—Augustine argued that "if any man is of the age to use his reason, he cannot believe, hope, love, unless he will to do so, nor obtain the prize of the high calling of God unless he voluntarily run for it."[8]

God first prepares the will to be assisted, then "assists it when it is prepared"; hence, grace "goes before the unwilling to make him willing; it follows the willing to make his will effectual."[9]

The Exquisite Cooperation of Grace with Freedom

The salvation prepared for humanity becomes personally received when it is freely accepted within the conditions under which God has freely offered it. "All depends indeed on God, but not so that our free-will is hindered," wrote Chrysostom. God "does not anticipate our choice, lest our free-will should be outraged. But when we have chosen, then great is the assistance He brings to us."[10]

Freedom is the premise of all obedience.[11] Freedom is the incomparable gift of God to humanity,[12] necessary to human nature.[13] Freedom

---

7. Augustine, *Against Two Letters of the Pelagians* 1.19, NPNF 1:5:389, ital. ad.
8. Augustine, *On Grace and Free Will* 5.12, NPNF 1:5:449; cf. Second Council of Orange, CC 39.
9. Augustine, *Enchiridion* 32, NPNF 1:3:248.
10. John Chrysostom, *Hom. on Hebrews* 12.3, NPNF 1:14:425; cf. Methodius, *Concerning Free-Will*, ANF 6:362-64.
11. Tertullian, *Exhortation to Chastity*, ANF 4:51.
12. Clement of Alexandria, *Stromata* 2.15, ANF 2:362.
13. Arnobius, *Ag. the Heathen* 61-65, ANF 6:457-58; cf. Methodius, *Concerning Free-Will*, ANF 6:356-63.

implies that God coworks with humanity.[14] Benedict of Nursia, John Calvin, John Wesley, and Dietrich Bonhoeffer all correctly grasped the corollary insight that discipline is the way to freedom. Only when human willing is awakened and shaped by the divine willing is one made truly free.[15] Faith itself is an act of human willing enabled and disciplined by grace.[16]

Sin remains our own work; free grace God's. "Free will is sufficient for evil, but is too little for good, unless it is aided by Omnipotent Good."[17] "For the commission of sin we get no help from God."[18] God in no way assists the will to do evil. God constantly and sufficiently assists the will to do good; the deficiency lies in the will, not in grace.

Though not the first, Augustine was the most brilliant exponent of how the action of grace can be both

> from the will of man and from the mercy of God. Thus we accept the dictum, "It is not a matter of human willing or running but of God's showing mercy," as if it meant, "The will of man is not sufficient by itself unless there is also the mercy of God." But by the same token the mercy of God is not sufficient by itself unless there is also the will of man.[19]

Ecumenical Teaching of the Affinity of Grace and Freedom

That the synergy of grace and freedom became the consensual teaching of the believing church is clear from the Third Ecumenical Council, held at Ephesus in A.D. 431: "Assuredly free choice is not taken away by this aid and gift of God, but it is set at liberty. . . . For He acts in us that we may both will and do what He wishes, nor does He allow those gifts to be idle in us which He has given to be used and not to be neglected, that we also may be cooperators with the grace of God."[20]

---

14. Origen, *OFP* 3.1, ANF 4:303-24.
15. Augustine, *On Grace and Free Will*, NPNF 1:5:443ff.; cf. *Conf.* 8.5, NPNF 1:1:120-21.
16. Origen, *OFP* 3.1, ANF 4:302-28; Clement of Alexandria, *Stromata*, 2.14-16, ANF 2:361-63.
17. Augustine, *On Rebuke and Grace* 11.31, NPNF 1:5:484.
18. Augustine, *On the Merits and Remission of Sins, and on the Baptism of Infants* 2.5, NPNF 1:5:45.
19. Augustine, *Enchiridion* 9.32, LCC 7:358, commenting on Rom. 9:16.
20. SCD §141, p. 57.

In this same tradition of consent, the Council of Arles (ca. 475) clearly rejected five heresies regarding grace: (1) those opinions which would oversimply argue that the work of human obedience need not be united with divine grace; (2) that after the fall of the first man the free choice of the will was completely destroyed; (3) that Christ our Lord and Savior did not incur death for the salvation of all; (4) that the foreknowledge of God violently impels man to death; and (5) that they who perish, perish by the will of God. The Council then positively reaffirmed the view of Lucidus that "the grace of God is such that I always unite the striving and efforts of man with grace, and I proclaim that the liberty of the human will was not destroyed but enfeebled and weakened, and that he who is saved, was tried; and he who perished, could have been saved."[21]

The ability of the fallen will to cooperate with grace became a vexing issue of early Lutheran scholastic theology. At the Weimar Disputation of 1560, hyperAugustinian advocates argued that the sinner is completely dead to good moral impulses, and that the essential human nature has been so transformed by sin that sin is not simply an attribute but is rather part of the essential substance of human beings.[22] Against this, Victorin Strigel asserted the earlier consensual teaching that sin has not abolished free will but depraved it, and that no inward transformation can be effected without the assent of the will.[23]

Grace does not occur by compulsion. God takes into consideration the condition of humanity as endowed with will.[24] Melanchthon viewed the concurrently cooperative causes of conversion as the Word, the Spirit, and the cooperating human will.[25] Reformed Protestants similarly would confess that the faithful "ought to be diligent in stirring up the grace of God that is in them."[26] Ecumenical teaching insisted that "as often as we do good, God is at work in us and with us."[27]

---

21. Lucidus, Letter of Submission, SCD §160a, p. 65.
22. Weimar Disputation, BOCJ 55; cf. Flacius, *Clavis scripturae sacrae* 2.651ff., SHD 2:369.
23. Weimar Disputation, SHD 2:368.
24. Ibid. This position is in accord with Melanchthon's third revision of the *Loci* of 1543, CR 21:652-58.
25. *Loci* of 1535, CR 21.376-78; cf. LCC 19:22-30, 86-88.
26. Second Helvetic Conf., CC 211.
27. Second Council of Orange, CC 40.

PERPLEXITIES EMBEDDED IN THE CHRISTIAN WITNESS TO THE NECESSITY OF GRACE

Christian reflection on the apostolic teaching of grace remains vexed by persistent dilemmas and seeming inconsistencies. Careful circumspection is required of anyone who wishes to think deeply about grace in spiritual formation. These issues must not be sidestepped by a pious appeal to blind faith, but approached with exegetical honesty. Insofar as perplexities impede the walk of grace, they need to be resolved wherever possible, for if the dynamic of grace can be challenged at its heart, then each step of the walk is made more vulnerable.[28]

What follows is a brief survey of crucial perennial perplexities: whether the fallen will has only the power to sin; whether natural morality is undermined by grace; whether apart from grace anyone can long persevere in good deeds; and whether the intellect may know God apart from revelation.

Whether the Fallen Will Has Only the Power to Sin

When Paul quoted Psalm 14:3 that "there is no one who does good" (Rom. 3:12), the implication was not that all discrete acts of the unjust are equally unjust, as if civic virtue and murder might be absurdly viewed on precisely the same level of culpability. Even amid the history of sin, humanity is not utterly deprived of all capacity for doing any good work whatsoever.[29]

Jesus taught that even the pagans (those without the law) and tax collectors (gross abusers of the law) are found at times loving those who love them and performing certain duties of charity—hence doing natural good deeds (Matt. 5:46-47). It follows, then, that *an act is not in every aspect and consequence sinful merely because it is done by a sinner.*

Jerome commented on Galatians: "Many who are without the faith and have not the Gospel of Christ, yet perform prudent and holy actions, e.g., by obeying their parents, succoring the needy, not oppressing their neighbors."[30] Augustine earnestly admired the best civic virtues of Rome,[31] the temperance of Polemo, and the moral

---

28. Tho. Aq., *ST* 2-1.Q109, 3:1123-31.
29. Ibid., 2-2.Q10.4, 2:1215-16.
30. *Comm. on Gal.* 1.15, DT (Pohle) 7:59.
31. *Letters* 138.3, NPNF 1:1:138, 316.

purity of Alypius.[32] "You are permitted with human love to love your spouse, your children, your friends and fellow-citizens. But, as you see, the ungodly, too, have this love, e.g., pagans, Jews, heretics. Who among them does not love his wife, his children, his brethren, his neighbors, his relations and friends?"[33] Augustine's more difficult task became that of defending against the more subtle Pelagian error that supernaturally good works are possible without the aid of grace, while not perpetuating the Manichaean exaggeration that all natural acts are evil.

This is why it has been considered an ill-advised overstatement to teach without qualification that "all works of unbelievers are sins, and the virtues of the philosophers are vices."[34] "Human nature, created by God, even after its prevarication, retains its substance, form, life, senses, and reason, and the other goods of body and soul, which are not lacking even to those who are bad and vicious."[35]

However deeply trapped in syndromes of sin, one is never intrinsically unable to pray for grace. Surely it cannot be a sin to pray for divine help.[36] Further, while one "cannot merit eternal life without grace, he is, however, able to perform acts productive of some good connatural to man, such as tilling the soil, drinking, eating, acts of friendship."[37]

Whether Natural Morality Is Undermined by Grace

Scripture exhorts sinners to repent, pray for pardon, give alms, and do good: "Repent! Turn away from all your offenses" (Ezek. 18:30).

---

32. Letters 144.2, NPNF 1:1:494; cf. *Conf.* 6.10, NPNF 1:1:97-98; *The Spirit and the Letter* 3.5, 28, NPNF 1:5:494.
33. Augustine, Sermons 349.1, DT (Pohle) 7:81.
34. "Propositions of Baius Rejected" 26, 27, SCD §1027; cf. Alexander 7, "Errors of the Jansenists," SCD §1298.
35. Prosper of Aquitaine, *Contra Collatorem* 36, MPL 51:259; cf. *Defense of St. Augustine*, ACW 32. The view that all works of a sinner are uniformly and necessarily sinful was generally rejected by post-Tridentine teaching; cf. Pius 6, "Auctorem fidei," SCD §§15-23; Clement 11, "Errors of Paschasius Quesnel," SCD §§1351ff., pp. 347-53.
36. Augustine, *On the Spirit and the Letter* 27.48, NPNF 1:5:103-4; cf. *Retractions* 1.15, FC 60:71-73; John 9:31.
37. Tho. Aq., ST 1-2.Q109.5, 1:1127; cf. Luther, Serm. on Isa. 60:1-6, WA 10:1.1:530-31; WLS 3:1158.

"Renounce your sins by doing what is right, and your wickedness by being kind to the oppressed" (Dan. 4:27). Such injunctions could only be addressed to sinners. *If such repentance and prayer and almsgiving were itself a new sin, then scripture would absurdly be commanding the sinner to commit new sins.* Hence, it is not without costly consequences to conclude that all works of mercy done before justification are wholly evil or completely lacking in virtue or grace-enabled goodness.

This is why it has been deemed an exaggeration to expand the doctrine of prevenient grace so far as to imagine that no act can express any action of good without a special act of saving grace. Such an expansion inadvertently tends to undercut any concept of natural law or civic virtue or any thought of morality grounded in human nature.[38]

Whether Apart from Grace Anyone Can Long Persevere in Good Deeds

No one is able, without God's help, to keep even one of the Ten Commandments for any extended period of time.[39] Even one who delights in the law of God may nonetheless have "another law at work in the members of my body, waging war against the law of my mind and making me a prisoner of the law of sin at work within my members" (Rom. 7:23). *Though it might be possible to resist particular temptations for a time by dint of natural wit and courage, it is not possible to resist all temptations perpetually without the help of grace.* This is why those who live by faith and walk in the way of holiness are nonetheless every day called upon to pray, as Jesus taught his disciples to pray, "Lead us not into temptation" (Matt. 6:13).[40]

Though the will is never fated by external necessity to fall, nonetheless, because of its constant attraction to lesser loves, skewed passions, and compulsive concupiscence, when constantly exercised the will is inevitably found vulnerable to falling into sin. Although all nations at some primal level "knew God," they in practice "neither glorified him as God nor gave thanks to him, but their thinking became futile and their foolish hearts were darkened" (Rom. 1:21).[41]

---

38. Juan Martinez de Ripalda, *De Ente Supernaturali* Disp. 20.2 (París: L. Vives, 1871–73), 3:114.
39. Trent 6:13; SCD §806, p. 255.
40. Augustine, *On Nature and Grace* 62, NPNF 1:5:142.
41. Origen, *Ag. Celsus* 3.47, ANF 4:483.

Whether the Intellect May Know God Apart from Revelation

It is difficult realistically to assess the capacity of independent human nature apart from grace, not only with respect to the intellect's ability to know, but also with respect to the will's ability to act.

Natural reason is encumbered by recalcitrant limitations: the brevity of life, the egocentricity of all perception, the inaccessibility of much objective knowledge that would be knowable if one had adequate resources in any particular period of history (e.g., galaxies too distant to observe, the hidden dynamics of atomic structures, the mystery of the origin of the universe). Hence universal, comprehensive, encyclopedic, and ubiquitous knowledge is beyond the reach of any finite, historical mind.[42]

Nonetheless, *though greatly weakened by sin, the ability of natural intellect to reason prudently about causality is not entirely eliminated.* While densely ignorant of the mercy of God, Adam's children are not left without conscience or natural reasoning. While the eyes are profoundly dimmed to God's mercy, they are not wholly blind to God's existence. Hence, the "Gentiles, who do not have the law, do by nature things required by the law . . . their consciences also bearing witness" (Rom. 2:14, 15; cf. Wis. 13:1ff.).

Although saving knowledge of God is impossible without faith's response to revelation, some preliminary natural knowledge of God is accessible to natural reason—for example, that God exists, and that God is just (Heb. 11:6), though not that God is triune or incarnate. That a just God exists is not strictly speaking an article of faith, but an assumption made by reason and experience that may be posited apart from deliberate reflection on God's special revelation. "For since the creation of the world God's invisible qualities—his eternal power and divine nature—have been clearly seen, being understood from what has been made" (Rom. 1:20). Some theological truths (that God is and that God is just) "are not of themselves beyond human reason," and "can, even in the present state of mankind, be known by every one with facility and firm assurance."[43] Thus "faith presupposes natural knowledge, even as grace presupposes nature, and perfection something that can be perfected."[44]

---

42. Tho. Aq., *ST* 1-2.Q109.1, 1:1123; cf. DT (Pohle) 4:258ff.
43. Vat. 1, 3.2, DT (Pohle) 7:54.
44. Tho. Aq., *ST* 1.Q2.2.1, 1:12; cf. DT (Pohle) 7:52.

It was an overzealous Paulinism that departed from Paul by denying all natural capacity of intellect for knowing God by natural means.[45] The consensual ecumenical tradition has often been called on to defend the capacity of reason against both the skeptical challenges of naturalistic reductionism and the anti-intellectual bent of fideistic pietism.

GRACE AS UNMERITED GIFT: THE SHEER GRATUITY OF GRACE

The confession that grace is not merited but freely bestowed had to be defended morally and exegetically by classical interpreters. These perplexities must be regularly inventoried by those who preach grace and care for souls.

Whether One May Acquire a Disposition to Receive Grace

If one does not have a disposition to receive grace, it hardly makes sense to pray for grace. Hence one must first pray for a disposition to receive grace. Those most thirsty are most disposed to hope for and welcome a cup of cold water. So with grace. One prays, first, for a distinct aptness to receive.[46]

The disposition to receive grace requires a complementary grace-enabled effort: the determination to remove obstacles to its reception.[47] Whatever might impede the reception of grace must be pruned away. To pray rightly for grace is to modify one's behavior so that one is readied to receive it, and to remove obstacles to its reception.[48]

If grace could be merited by activity or discipline or preparation, then grace would no longer be a free gift. One cannot actively seize grace, but one may actively work to remove obstacles to the reception of grace. By reinforced habit, disposition, and temperament, the recipient can either cooperate or fail to cooperate with that grace

---

45. Pius 4, "Errors of Paschasius Quesnel" 41, SCD §1391, p. 351; cf. Augustine, *Retractions* 1.9, FC 60:41-50; *On the Predestination of the Saints* 7, NPNF 1:5:500-501.
46. Prosper of Aquitaine, *Grace and Free Will* 11ff., FC 7:375ff.
47. Kierkegaard, *PF* 16-27; cf. DT (Pohle) 7:134.
48. Augustine, *Letters*, FC 30:95-98.

which is contextually given.[49] By cooperating with prevenient grace, further graces are given. God promises to offer subsequent grace to one who puts no impediments in the way to the reception of previous grace.[50]

Whether Prayer Merits Grace

If we pray for grace, does that not imply that prayer merits grace? *Even prayer does not, strictly speaking, merit grace, though we are called to pray for grace.* Prayer is not finally a natural human manipulation of God, but a petition for divine grace. There can be no effective prayer without prevenient grace.

To the semi-Pelagians, who argued that natural prayer merits supernatural grace, the ecumenical tradition was required to respond that "if any one says that the grace of God can be obtained by human prayer, and that it is not grace itself which causes us to invoke God, he contradicts the prophet Isaias and the Apostle who say: 'I was found by them that did not seek me.'"[51] Apart from grace, we do not even "know what we ought to pray for, but the Spirit himself intercedes for us" (Rom. 8:26).

Faith cannot even learn to make the most elementary affirmation, "'Jesus is Lord,' except by the Holy Spirit" (1 Cor. 12:3). "They are mistaken who think that our seeking, asking, knocking is of ourselves, and is not given to us."[52] "Not that we are competent in ourselves to claim anything for ourselves, but our competence comes from God."[53]

The Gracing of Nature

Grace is not resident in nature, but a gift to nature. When grace elevates human nature, it does not denaturalize the human or dehumanize nature. Rather it assists fallen human nature in ways inaccessible to that nature itself.[54] To believe is a work of grace, not of nature. Its steady reception enables one to grow from grace to grace.[55]

---

49. Tho. Aq., ST 2-1.Q111, 3:1135-39; cf. DT (Pohle) 7:149-51.
50. DT (Pohle) 7:148, 149; cf. Tho. Aq., *Truth*, Q14.11.
51. Second Council of Orange, canon 3, SCD §176, p. 76.
52. Augustine, *On the Gift of Perseverance* 23.63, DT (Pohle) 7:144.
53. 2 Cor. 3:5; cf. Council of Mileum, SCD §§103ff., pp. 45, 46.
54. John Chrysostom, *Hom. on the Statues*, NPNF 1:9:401-8.
55. Augustine, Letters 217, FC 32:75ff.; cf. 2 Pet. 3:18; DT (Hall) 5:139-41, 8:250.

Prayer for receiving the bounty of nature is grounded in the conviction that all creaturely goods are the unmerited gift of the Creator, who is not under external obligation to create anything but gives creaturely goods out of unbounded divine grace and mercy. Hence common prayers for health or daily bread or political tranquillity or fair weather are all petitions for natural goods, each one being enabled in time by the free grace of the Creator of all natural goods.[56]

Divine grace, which is eternal, precedes creation, which is in time. A friendly admonition is fitting at just this point. The grace given in creation is not bestowed upon some already naturally existing being, but is a grace that in fact first creates its recipient in order further to bless the recipient. Creation itself is therefore a wholly free gift, the unearned favor of the Creator.[57]

Pelagianism used this truth, however, to promote an error, misleading the Council of Lydda.[58] The error was to assume that created goods, as splendid as they are, could stand as natural graces or talents autonomously and wholly apart from the Giver of all goods (an error opposed by the Council of Mileum).[59] Consequently the ecumenical tradition was forced to resort to an otherwise odd phrase, "supernatural grace," to mark this boundary more clearly, so as to speak of the gift of God that is offered not only through nature but also transcending nature. For if "the faith by which we believe in God is natural," then the distinction between believer and unbeliever is blurred, and everyone automatically becomes a believer, thus diminishing the significance of willed responsiveness.[60]

Whether Human Nature as Such Merits Grace

If grace comes, as we have argued, as sheer gift without merit, previous disposition, or precondition,[61] then what becomes of merit, a concept found frequently in scripture?

---

56. Origen, *On Prayer*, CWS 81ff.; cf. Nemesius, *On the Nature of Man* 42-43, LCC 4:426ff.
57. LG 227ff.
58. A.D. 415, later corrected by the Second Council of Orange, CC 39.
59. FC 30:91-94; cf. Innocent 1, ibid., 121-36.
60. Second Council of Orange, CC 39.
61. Council of Ephesus, SCD §§135ff., pp. 53ff.

Merit is that which one earns which rightly entitles one to reward. One is rewarded for merit, and merit deserves a just reward. Merit is based on justice, not mercy.[62] The language of merit is awkward and uncomfortable in the presence of grace. Grace is not, like a wage, given in return for goods or services, but a gift freely given out of divine love.[63]

Grace does not find merits, but elicits them.[64] After Pelagius had retracted his claim that grace is given according to merit (following the Council of Diospolis, A.D. 415), he continued disingenuously to employ the term "grace of God" as a synonym for the grace given in and with creation. Hence the Second Council of Orange had to define more precisely that grace from beginning to end is given purely as a gift, gratuitously, and thus is not in the slightest way merited.

Do our natural human competencies amount to a kind of grace given in and with creation itself? If so, why is it not proper to say that nature merits grace?

Natural human competencies cannot merit grace, either preparatory or cooperative. Were nature competent to do what grace does, it would take away from grace any necessity for salvation, contrary to apostolic teaching. "For it is by grace you have been saved, through faith—and this not from yourselves, it is the gift of God—not by works, so that no one can boast" (Eph. 2:8-9). "And if by grace, then it is no longer by works; if it were, grace would no longer be grace" (Rom. 11:6). God "saved us, not because of righteous things we had done, but because of his mercy" (Titus 3:5).

Saving grace is the cause, not the effect, of our merit (Matt. 15:14-30; 1 Cor. 4:7).[65] Naturally good works, no matter what the quantity, are unable to acquire qualitatively a legitimate claim to saving grace. God works in us in ways both beyond our working and precisely through our working.[66]

---

62. Tho. Aq., *ST* 1-2, Q114.1.
63. Council of Ephesus, SCD §138, p. 56; cf. Calvin, *Inst.* 2.17.1; 3.13.5.
64. Augustine, *Comm. on John* 86.2, NPNF 1:7:353.
65. Augustine, *On the Predestination of the Saints*, NPNF 1:5:498ff.; cf. *On Original Sin* 24.28, NPNF 1:5:246-47; Tho. Aq., *ST* 1-2.Q114.5, 1:1157.
66. Augustine, *Ag. Two Letters of the Pelagians* 2.21, NPNF 1:5:401; cf. Second Council of Orange, canon 20, SCD §193, p. 79.

CHAPTER 6

THE PERENNIAL BATTLE
WITH PELAGIANISM

The purpose of this chapter is to review a decisive struggle that occurred in the fifth century, but which returns again and again to haunt Christian apologetics in succeeding centuries. Pelagianism bears striking resemblance to the moral self-confidence and anthropological optimism of the nineteenth and twentieth centuries. Hence it is fitting that it be accurately and explicitly described.

The outcome of the Pelagian conflict was decisive for all subsequent Christian theological reflection. Its ecumenical resolution was received in the Protestant tradition, as well as Roman Catholic and Orthodox. Though what follows may appear to be an archaic exercise, upon closer inspection it remains a perennial battle that continues to be contested on various cultural turfs. Even though it was decisively decided ecumenically in the fifth century, it persistently recurs and must be answered anew.

In the early fifth century, Pelagius, a British monk, came to Rome to oppose the doctrines of original sin and prevening grace. He argued that the worst that Adam's sin did for his descendants was to set a bad example, that the descendants of Adam did not inherit corruption, and that it is possible to live without sinning.[1]

---

1. See Pelagius's exposition of Romans 8:29, 9–11 in Alexander Souter, ed., *Pelagius's Expositions of Thirteen Epistles of St. Paul* (Cambridge: Cambridge University Press, 1922); cf. Letter to Demetrias, 8, 16, 17, in R. Evans, ed., *Four Letters of Pelagius* (New York: Seabury Press, 1968).

THE DECISIVE DEBATE ON THE NECESSITY OF GRACE

The Novelty of Pelagian Self-assurance

Rejecting the necessity of preparatory grace, the Pelagians asserted that free will is capable of meriting grace by its own native powers. Accordingly, the power to do good resides naturally in the free will itself, apart from any gift of God to human nature, so that by following the example of Christ, the way of virtue is made clear, and persons of their own will may abstain from sin. Hence there is a need not for any direct prevenient operation of the Spirit upon the human will in order for it to do good, but merely for the Spirit to operate indirectly through conscience and reason.[2]

The Pelagians further taught that the human will is able by its natural capacities to obey God's commands, resist temptation, and retain a continuous state of sinlessness. They went so far as to regard the petition "Forgive us our trespasses" (Matt. 6:12) merely as a subjective expression of humility, lacking any objective referent.[3] In this respect the Pelagians bear a striking resemblance to modern naturalistic advocates of psychological optimism.[4] The more we review this conflict historically, the more it becomes evident that it persists today in modern attire. In resisting Manichaeism, Pelagius (and others such as Celestius and Julian of Eclanum) had exaggerated the native, inborn capacities of human nature in such a way as to underestimate both the power of sin and the need for grace. John Chrysostom, Jerome, and Augustine all had opposed such views. The novel and immoderate views of Pelagius had alarming consequences that caused Augustine to define some issues of original sin, predestination, and perseverance a bit defensively. This became the occasion for further consensual refining of the ecumenical teaching of grace.

---

2. Augustine, *On the Forgiveness of Sins and Baptism* 1.18-23, NPNF 1:5:21-24; cf. Second Council of Orange, canons 5-6, CC 39; Leo, Letters 1, NPNF 2:12:2.
3. Augustine, *On Man's Perfection in Righteousness*, NPNF 1:5:163-67.
4. Abraham Maslow, *Toward a Psychology of Being*, 2nd ed. (New York: Van Nostrand Reinhold, 1982); Carl R. Rogers, *On Becoming a Person* (Boston: Houghton Mifflin, 1961); Sidney Jourard, *The Transparent Self* (New York: Wiley-Interscience, 1971); Donald Meyer, *The Positive Thinkers* (Garden City, N.Y.: Doubleday, 1965).

Wherever it may seem that Cyril of Jerusalem (*Catech. Lect.* 1.17), Athanasius (*Contra gentium,* 30), Basil (Letters, 294), Gregory of Nazianzus (Orat. 31), and Chrysostom (*Hom. on Romans 2*) stress the cooperation of grace and freedom so as to tend argumentatively in a semi-Pelagian direction, it must be remembered that they were battling an older pre-Pelagian heresy, namely, the Gnostic and Manichaean denial of free will, so their task was to encourage the cooperation of freedom with grace. The Eastern tradition's resistance to incipient Pelagianism was already clear in John Chrysostom (*Hom. on Ephesians 4; Hom. on 1 Corinthians 12*).

Between A.D. 411 and 431, no fewer than twenty-four councils faced the question of Pelagianism. It was the burning issue of Augustine's mature life. Though some early actions (such as the Council of Lydda, 415, and the early pronouncements of Zosimus) sided with Pelagius, the ecumenical consensus gradually formed after the Council of Carthage in 418 to reject Pelagianism.[5]

The consensual response was further refined at the councils of Ephesus (431) and Orange (529), which held grace to be necessary for all acts pertinent to salvation. "No branch can bear fruit by itself; it must remain in the vine. Neither can you bear fruit unless you remain in me" (John 15:4; cf. 1 Cor. 12:3). If human nature was unable without the grace of God to "guard the health which it received [in its original righteousness], how without the grace of God will it be able to *recover* what it has lost?"[6]

Augustine did not invent out of whole cloth the teaching of the necessity and sufficiency of grace. A prevailing consensus established long before his efforts, in the midst of controversy, gave it its decisive expression. If the church fathers before Augustine had condoned a Pelagian type of teaching, the councils of both East and West would not have interpreted Pelagianism as a recent innovation. Augustine constantly stressed the exceeding novelty of Pelagianism,[7] appealing to John, Paul, Cyprian, Ambrose, and Gregory of

---

5. Zosimus, Council of Mileum 2, A.D. 416, approved by the Council of Carthage 16, A.D. 418, SCD §105, p. 46.
6. Second Council of Orange, Canon 19, SCD §192, p. 79; cf. CC 42; Augustine, *Enchiridion* 106, NPNF 1:5:271.
7. *On Grace and Free Will,* NPNF 1:5:443ff.

Nazianzus as exponents of the view that "there is nothing of which we may boast as if of our own which God has not given us."[8]

The community of faith had often prayed that schismatics be given grace to be reborn to charity, sinners to repentance, and catechumens to regeneration—all implying grace preceding choice. Who could reasonably pray for grace if grace could be achieved entirely without prayer?[9] Pelagianism was thus viewed from the outset as a mistaken innovation, since the rule of believing was always assumed to follow the established way of prayer (that *lex orandi* precedes *lex credendi*).

The Contested Tradition of Ecumenical Consent on the Nexus of Grace and Freedom

The medieval scholastics combined the ecumenical-Augustinian view of grace with a penitential doctrine of merit that tended to view grace as a quality of the soul enabling one to acquire merit. This tendency motivated the Reformers to return to the Augustinian view. Calvin's view of common grace distinguished universal common grace, general common grace, and covenant common grace.[10] Older Anglican and Arminian teachings of grace stressed that one could obey or resist grace, the human will either concurring or not with grace.[11] The moderate Augustinian ecumenical consensus on the necessity of grace was preserved even in Arminianism: "I ascribe to divine grace the commencement, the continuance, and the consummation of all good. And to such an extent do I carry its influence, that a man, though already regenerate, can neither conceive, will, nor do any good at all, nor resist any evil temptation without this prevening and exciting, this following and cooperating, grace."[12]

Some aspects of Calvin's view of the bondage of the will[13] appealed to patristic reference primarily in that portion of Augustine which, embroiled in the controversy with Pelagius, focused defensively on the radical necessity of grace, not its relation to free will, which Augustine

---

8. *On the Gift of Perseverance* 50, NPNF 1:5:546.

9. Celestine 1, Decretals, MPL 45:1759; Council of Ephesus, SCD §126, p. 52.

10. Abraham Kuyper, *Calvinism* (Princeton: Fleming H. Revell, 1899), 179ff.

11. Howard Watkin-Jones, *The Holy Spirit from Arminius to Wesley* (London: Epworth, 1929).

12. J. Arminius, quoted in Tillett, PS 114; cf. Arminius, *Works* 2:177-235.

13. *Inst.* 2.3.10.

affirmed as a great mystery. Even Augustine's more extravagant statements on the hegemony of grace[14] are amenable to orthodox, consensual interpretation. For even there it is clear that his deeper concern is to show that the will is strengthened, not negated by grace. Elsewhere Augustine made it clear that "to yield consent, indeed to God's summons, or to withhold it, is the function of our own will."[15]

As the five points of Dort were rejected by the emergent moderate Calvinist-Arminian-Anglican consensus in Protestantism, so the points of Jansenius of 1653 (total depravity, irresistible grace, and limited atonement) were rejected by the Roman magisterium.[16] Insofar as the Dort and Jansenist traditions were consistently pursued, it became increasingly difficult to teach that the cross assures all humanity sufficient grace for salvation. An absolute double predestinarianism tends to limit grace to efficacious grace, in such a way as to neglect prevenient, sufficient, and cooperating grace.[17] Grace is not the simple, direct, omnicausal will of God that nothing can resist, but rather a gift in which God condescends to cooperate with human freedom, and where responsive freedom is enabled to cooperate freely with grace.[18]

Here as everywhere we seek to follow the scriptural teaching as consensually remembered by the sacred tradition of the Ecumenical Councils and the most widely received of the ancient Christian writers. The local synods that supplied the definitions for later ecumenical consent on these questions met over a long period of time, refining a broadly received consensus of exegetical interpretation. The basic claim of orthodox Christian teaching is that these consensual definitions (Ephesus, Orange, Quiersy, and Arles) are perennially reliable, and having been ecumenically defined under challenge in the first five centuries, have not been substantively amended, but only extended and refined in accord with the Vincentian canon. All local synods and subsequent

---

14. *On Admonition and Grace* 12.38, NPNF 1:5:487.
15. *On the Spirit and the Letter* 60, NPNF 1:5:110; cf. Augustine, Sermon 163.11.13, DT (Pohle) 7:229.
16. Innocent 10, *Cum occasione*, SCD §1092, p. 316.
17. Bernhard John Otten, MHD 2:234ff., 507ff.; cf. Calvin, *Inst.* 3.21; Cornelius Jansenius, *De gratia Christi* 3.3, in Tetrateuchus, *Sive commentarius in sancta Jesus Christi evangelica* (Louvanii: Guiliemi Stryckwont, 1699).
18. Melanchthon, *Loci*, LCC 19:22-30; cf. Trent 4, SCD §§793ff., pp. 248ff.; Clement 11, SCD §§1359ff., pp. 348ff.

confessions must be tested by correspondence with the Ecumenical Councils, which constitute the textual criterion of ecumenicity.[19] The ecumenical consensus has held closely together the freedom of the will and the efficacy of grace. These are not contradictory, but complementary. But the explanation of their relation differs considerably among different exegetical traditions.

Reflection on the riddle of grace has focused on whether grace is necessary for every aspect and shade of developing human action that would tend toward salvation. Two opposite errors must be avoided: either exaggerating the capability of natural will to accomplish salutary acts without grace (Pelagianism); or the utter incapacity and impotence of the natural will to do anything whatever pleasing to God (an irrational, pseudo-Augustinian antinomianism that tends to undermine natural morality and civic virtue). In sum, Pelagianism errs by assuming that the appropriation of God's action can proceed without God's grace. Antinomianism errs by assuming that justification needs no continuing work of the Spirit to guide persons to its full reception.

THE EFFECTIVENESS OF GRACE

Efficacious Grace

By efficacious grace we mean grace that is not merely offered but is also being effectively received. It is a grace which comes to fruition in the will by enabling active human consent, as distinguished from the prevenient and sufficient grace which works prior to consent.

Grace is not forever ineffective. From time to time grace bears fruit amid the conditions of human freedom, becoming effectively appropriated. The worshiping community is privileged to behold and celebrate these fruits. If God offered only that grace that could be forever frustrated by human rejection, God would not be as wise or omnipotent as the true God who offers grace abundantly and enables it to become effective without crushing human freedom.[20]

---

19. Confession of Dositheus, CC 486-89.
20. John of Damascus, OF 2.25-28, NPNF 2:9:39-41.

Efficacious grace is a further refinement of the idea of cooperating grace. Cooperating grace is never intrinsically insufficient and never able to be made perpetually ineffective, although it may be willfully resisted.[21] The distinction between cooperating and efficacious grace is this: Cooperating grace may be received or not received. Efficacious grace by definition is that grace which is received.

Even where the will is most recalcitrant, grace is still said to be "sufficient," for grace would have sufficed to guide the will had the will not resisted. It is not inconsistent to say that sufficiency from God's side may be met with resistance from the human side. "God anticipates us, calls, moves, aids; but we must see to it that we do not resist."[22]

Grace Even When Effective Still Presupposes the Freedom to Resist

In scripture the work of grace does not characteristically appear as coercive or neglectful of human freedom, but rather enables and completes it.[23] This premise of mutuality is prophetically typified in Zechariah: "'Return to me,' declares the Lord Almighty, 'and I will return to you'" (1:3; cf. Jer. 30:21). In saying "You always resist the Holy Spirit!" just before dying, Stephen assumed that his persecutors were capable of resisting God, who had not compelled the will irresistibly (Acts 7:51).

If grace compels free will, all appeals and exhortations to the will would be absurd.[24] Isaiah poignantly wondered: "What more could have been done for my vineyard / than I have done for it? / When I looked for good grapes, / why did it yield only bad?" (Isa. 5:4).[25] "Take away free will," remarked Bernard of Clairvaux, "and there will be nothing left to save; take away grace and there will be no means left of salvation."[26] "It is only as response is made by faith to divine grace that true freedom is achieved."[27]

---

21. Paul 5, SCD §1090, p. 314; Alexander 8, SCD §§1295-96, p. 340.
22. Melanchthon, *Loci* (1543 ed.), CR 21:658; cf. DT (Pohle) 7:43.
23. Augustine, Letters, 157.2.10, MPL 33:677.
24. For a catena of patristic writers on this subject, see Robert Bellarmine, *De gratia et libero arbitrio* in *Opera oratio postuma,* 9 vols. (Rome: Gregorian University, 1942–50); cf. Otten, MHD 2:507ff.
25. Wesley, "On God's Vineyard," WJWB 3:107; cf. WJW 7:202-13.
26. *Of Grace and Free Will* 1.2, in *The Works of Bernard of Clairvaux* (Spencer, Mass.: Cistercian, 1970–), vol. 7.
27. Edinburgh Conference on Faith and Order, CC 572.

In honoring the human liberty God created, God "does not employ force," wrote Irenaeus. Thus, those who act upon God's good counsel will receive honor "because they have done good, *though they were free not to do it*; but those who do not do good will experience the just judgment of God, because they have not done good, *though they were able to do it.*"[28] Similarly, Augustine maintained that "no one is guilty because he has not received," but only because he "does not do what he ought to do."[29]

Post-Tridentine Thomistic and Augustinian Definitions

The issue may be examined from the viewpoint of *either* the grace that acts upon the will (which was the preference of the Thomistic and Dominican traditions), *or* the will that is acted upon by grace, stressing either active or receptive agency (the latter being the preference of the Jesuit traditions that devised Molinism and Congruism).

By Thomistic we mean in this case the Spanish scholastic followers of Thomas Aquinas, notably the tradition of Domingo Soto, Domingo Bañez, Melchior Cano, and Teresa of Avila,[30] though not Thomas himself.[31] They argued that *sufficient grace* confers the power to act, but not the act itself; hence, to sufficient grace must be added *efficacious grace,* which does not become effective merely as a result of the consent of the will, but rather is efficacious of itself intrinsically, yet works through the free consent of the will.[32]

Meanwhile post-Tridentine Augustinians proposed a different psychology of grace: If the heavenly delectation (pleasure, delight, choice) is weaker than concupiscence (*delectio carnalis*), the will fails to act in the way particularly invited by grace. The will is not overpowered, but left free to choose between good and evil. Sufficient grace gives the will the possibility of salutary action, but not the desire or wish to act. Efficacious grace leads the will to the desiring

---

28. *Ag. Her.* 4.37.1, ital. ad., ANF 1:518.
29. *On Free Choice of the Will* 3.16, DT (Pohle) 7:47; cf. Joyce, *CDG* 119ff.; E. J. Wirth, *Divine Grace* (New York: Benzinger Brothers, 1903).
30. See, e.g., St. John of the Cross, *Selected Writings* in CWS; Gonet, *Clypeus theologiae Thomisticae* (Parisiis: Sumpibus Antonii et Guillemi de la Cort, 1669), 1659ff.
31. *ST* 1-2.Q110.111.
32. DT (Pohle) 7:235.

performance of salutary acts, which are not within the power of free will as such.[33]

This position will be recognizable to Protestants as much nearer to Calvin, though not going so far as that of later Calvinists or Jansenists in questioning the moral efficacy of free will. However, it is doubtful that this view can appeal sufficiently to Augustine, even though it is sometimes called by his name. Augustine did not view pleasure as the well-spring of all supernaturally good deeds, or concupiscence as the distinguishing mark of sin.[34]

Ambiguities in the Thomistic definition of efficacy and in the Jesuit-Augustinian definition of agency led to the development of Molinism and Congruism, both of which are validly arguable within the realm of orthodox teaching.

The Molinist Scientia Media

The Jesuit Luis de Molina (in his work *Concordia liberi arbitrii cum gratiae donis*, 1588) attempted to reconcile the divisive issues between Augustinianism and semi-Pelagianism. As Calvinist orthodoxy was focused chiefly on the defense of the sovereignty of God's grace, so were the post-Tridentine Thomistic and Augustinian formulae. As Arminius and moderate Anglicanism and Wesley were focused primarily on the defense of free will, so was the Molinist formula. In this way the Dominican versus Jesuit debate in Catholicism corresponds to many aspects of the Calvinist versus Arminian debate in Protestantism. Although some may find these arguments somewhat tedious, they remain important contributions of a highly nuanced study of grace, and deserve careful attention.

In Molina's view, only by the consent of the will does sufficient grace become efficacious grace. By resisting, the will can make grace ineffective. In consenting, the will is not adding to the power of grace, but grace is aiding the will in its free responsive activity.[35] Grace and will

---

33. Norisius, *Vindiciae Augustinianae*, MPL 47; L. de Thomassin, *Memoires sur las Grace*, 2nd ed. (Paris: 1668); and Lawrence Berti, *De theologicis disciplinis* (Bassini: Remondini, 1739).

34. *Comm. on Ps.* 79.13, NPNF 1:8:384; cf. DT (Pohle) 7:248-55.

35. Molina, CLA, Q14.23.

work together in simultaneous concurrence *(concursu simultaneo)* like two workers tugging a vessel with one rope.

God foreknows not only the free actions of each and every rational creature, but also their hypothetically free actions, their multiple possible futures, and their varied potentialities, by means of God's *scientia media* (dialectical or middle knowledge of means), whereby God knows all possible means by which each creature's freedom acts in each future contingent situation. God foresees what free creatures under any given circumstances will do or not do. The omniscience of God grasps and encompasses eternally what each act of freedom would assume in each case of facing specific contingencies. Only in this way is the power of efficacious grace consistent with the radical contingencies of free will.[36] *Scientia media*, a knowledge of contingent futures, is the crucial premise of Molinism, retaining a place for human freedom without falling into semi-Pelagianism. Molina argued that God foresaw those who would cooperate with grace, yet this foreseen free activity of the will was regarded only as a means, not a cause, of predestination.

Dominican critics of Molinism (much like Calvinist critics of Arminianism) wondered if grace might have thereby become undervalued in exchange for an overvaluing of freedom. It seemed to some deplorable that grace should depend for its effectiveness upon human freedom. Scripture does not say "God acts, but only if I agree," but rather "God acts whether or not I agree." This is what caused Bellarmine to press further toward the development of Congruism.

Congruism and the Principle of Parsimony

Jesuits such as Roberto Bellarmine, Francisco de Suarez, Leonhard Lessius, and Claudius Aquaviva devised a more finely tuned form of the grace-freedom dialectic called the grace of congruity. The thesis of Congruism is that God confers grace for the performance of good works in accordance with such human circumstances as God foresees will be most favorable to its use. Grace is offered economically under conditions most fitting to and congruous with its contextual operation.[37]

Only that grace which is contextually needed is given, in order to make sufficient grace efficacious. Example: The parent knows that one

---

36. Ibid., Q19, Art. 6.2.
37. Augustine, *To Simplician* 1.2.13, LCC 6:395.

child needs a slight nod of the head for correction, while another may need explicit persuasion. Similarly, grace is constantly being adapted to variable circumstances, forming its influence in ways congruous with specific changing contingencies according to the principle of parsimony—economically, sufficiently, yet sparingly within the context.

Only God the Spirit knows how to administer grace in these variable, proportional, contextual ways.[38] Grace is offered prudently with specific regard to different times, places, inclinations, passions, and dispositions.[39]

Congruism beholds human willing concretely and contextually as functioning within social and personal situations, richly interwoven with historical contingencies. Grace works congruently with changing circumstances to persuade and woo the will, but parsimoniously and only to that degree required in the situation.[40] In this way, "Grace does not depend on but controls and fashions the circumstances of the recipient."[41]

The relation of grace and freedom is understood not woodenly or mechanistically but personally and analogically. Grace depends not on free will for its efficacy or power, but on dialogical relations. God's foreknowledge of contingencies (*scientia media*, knowing of means) is complete and utterly effective and in no way is subject to any supposed divine self-deception.[42]

Congruism comes closer to the intent of the earlier ecumenical consensus of the councils of Ephesus, Arles, Orange, and Quiersy than its scholastic alternatives. God's incomparable power is the power to adapt graciously to highly specific circumstances, not merely the power to stand over against them. This theory intends to confirm divine omnipotence without denying human self-determination.

These arguments on congruence were brilliantly anticipated by Thomas:

---

38. Augustine, *On Grace and Free Will* 1-12, NPNF 1:5:443-49; cf. Gregory the Great, *Pastoral Care* 3.1, NPNF 2:12:24.
39. Franciscus Suarez, *Opera omnia*, 29 vols. (Paris: Apud Ludovicum Vives, 1856–78), vol. 25: *De auxilio efficaci.*
40. Otten, MHD 2:493ff.; cf. B. Jungmann, *De gratia* (Ratisbone: Fridericus Pustet, 1882).
41. DT (Pohle) 7:266; cf. C. Pesch, *Praelectiones dogmaticae*, vol. 5, *De gratia* (Friburgi Brisgoviae: Herder, 1894–1909).
42. Augustine, CG 5.9.4, NPNF 1:2:90-92.

God can know many things simultaneously . . . not only all that is, but all that can be. Therefore, as our intellect potentially and virtually knows those infinite objects for which it has a principle of cognition, so God actually contemplates all infinities. . . . For He knows them according to His manner of being, which is eternal and without succession. Consequently, as He knows material things in an immaterial way, and many things in unity, so in a single glance He beholds objects that do not exist at the same time.[43]

Molinist teaching that God knows contingent futures remains a useful contribution to the defense of free will. The Congruist teaching of the contextuality and economy of grace remains a useful clarification of how grace relates to variable circumstances.

COUNTERING THE SEMI-PELAGIAN ERROR

John Cassian and Faustus of Riez sought to build a bridge between Augustine and Pelagius by asserting that faith begins with the will, but ends in requiring grace in Christ; that freedom on its own initiative can secure the gift of perseverance without grace; that baptismal grace for infants depends on divine foreknowledge of their future merits; and that God allows to increase what he has seen to arise from our own effort.[44]

These views are usually called semi-Pelagian, but more accurately might be described as semi-Augustinian since they were so strongly conditioned by the premises of Augustine's views of grace and freedom. These writers, sympathetic to the Antiochene, Alexandrian, early Latin, and early monastic traditions, feared the annihilation of human freedom, the introduction of fatalism and Manichaeism, and the subtle tendency toward antinomianism.

These views were meticulously answered by the elderly Augustine (in his works *On the Predestination of the Saints* and *On the Gift of Perseverance*), and subsequently by Prosper, Fulgentius, and Celestine. Much of this thinking was consensually received by the Second Council of

---

43. Tho. Aq., *Compend.* 133, p. 142.
44. Cassian, *Conferences* 2.13, NPNF 2:11:422-35; cf. Faustus of Riez, Epist. 1, "To Lucidus," MPL 58:835-37.

Orange (A.D. 529) and other councils, which asserted the necessity of grace for each and every step on the way to saving faith.[45] In answering semi-Pelagianism, Rome (as represented by Celestine, Hormisdas, and Boniface II) largely took the Augustinian position, but carefully avoided commitment to extreme aspects of Augustine, such as absolute double predestinarianism.

Five arguments were required in the orthodox ecumenical rejoinder to semi-Pelagianism:

1. Prevenient grace is necessary for the very inception of faith.
2. Both prevenient and cooperating grace are radically required for each and every salutary act that leads to and follows from justification.
3. Even one in a state of sanctifying grace is still impotent to perform salutary acts without the aid of efficacious grace.
4. No one even in a state of sanctifying grace is able to avoid venial sin or infirmities of knowledge and will for an extended period of time.
5. No one can persevere in the way of holiness without the grace of God.

Prevenient Grace Necessary Precisely for the Commencement of Faith

If God had not initially called, no one would be answering.[46] "No one can come to me unless the Father who sent me draws him" (John 6:44), declared Jesus. "This is why I told you that no one can come to me unless the Father has enabled him" (John 6:65). Such drawing and enabling is precisely what is meant by prevenient grace. These scriptural statements would be false if the natural human will were capable of performing salutary acts without grace, which is the specific tendency of semi-Pelagian arguments. *So prevenient grace is necessary for the very inception of faith.*[47] Even the earliest judgments one forms as to the plausibility of revelation are already shaped by prevenient grace at work in the intellect.[48] "What do you have that you did not receive?" (1 Cor. 4:7; cf. Eph. 2:8).

---

45. CC 38.
46. 2 Thess. 2:14; cf. 1 Cor. 1:24-26; Rom. 8:30; Chrysostom, *Hom. on 1 Cor.* 29, NPNF 1:12:168-75.
47. Second Council of Orange, Canon 5, SCD §178, p. 76.
48. Augustine, *On the Predestination of the Saints*, NPNF 1:5:498ff.

Grace Leads Toward and Follows Every Salutary Act

Both prevenient and cooperating grace are radically required for each and every salutary act that leads to and follows from justification. As Augustine pointed out, in John 15:5 Jesus did not say "'Without me you can *perfect* nothing,' but '*do* nothing.' For if He had said *perfect*, they might say that God's aid is necessary, not for beginning good, which is of ourselves, but [merely] for perfecting it."[49] Adoption into a family is a metaphor that can occur only through the action of another, not finally on one's own initiative.

Augustine sympathetically understood that the preceding Eastern church fathers had been very busy combating the Manichaeans in their time. They had to reject decisively the view that human freedom is a slave to fate. Hence it was useful for them to argue for the integrity of free will. Yet they would have rejected semi-Pelagianism had they been faced with it, as is evident from the prayer of Ephraem Syrus: "If I possess anything, Thou hast given it to me. . . . I ask only for grace."[50]

Acts are said to be spiritually *salutary*—from *salus*, health, salvation—when they have a healthful, salvific, life-saving effect. A salutary act[51] is one that nurtures, enables, and deepens life in the spirit, either by preparing for the reception of justifying grace, or, following justification, by deepening the union of the believer with Christ.[52]

Effective Grace Required for All Salutary Acts

Against the semi-Pelagians, who held that one is able to avoid sin altogether and retain a state of grace unremittingly without supernatural assistance, the consensual tradition argued that *even one in a state of sanctifying grace is still impotent to perform salutary acts without the aid of efficacious grace.* "We can of ourselves do nothing to effect good works of piety without God either working that we may will, or co-operating when we will."[53] Those who say that God inertly or passively awaits our willing run the risk of misapplying the scripture

---

49. Augustine, Ag. *Two Letters of the Pelagians* 2.8, NPNF 1:5:399; cf. Phil. 2:12.
50. *In Margaritam*, MPG 86:2107-9; cf. *DT* (Hall) 7:110.
51. Denoted *actus salutares* or *agere ad iustificationem* or *agere ad salutem* in scholastic theology.
52. *DT* (Pohle) 7:82.
53. Augustine, *On Grace and Free Will* 17, NPNF 1:5:450-51; cf. John 15:5; Thirty-nine Articles of Religion 17, CC 272; Otten, MHD 1:306ff., 374-79.

that "it is God who works in you to will and to act according to his good purpose" (Phil. 2:13).[54]

Infirmities Unavoidable

No one even in a state of sanctifying grace is able to avoid venial sin or infirmities of knowledge and will for an extended period of time. It is virtually impossible for those who are justified to avoid committing sins of haste or surprise over an extended period of time except by a special work of grace.[55] The Council of Carthage (A.D. 418) declared that no child of Adam has ever avoided unconscious faults and errors.[56] A venial sin does not wholly deprive the soul of sanctifying grace, though it disposes the soul in the direction of spiritual death. Venial sins came to be viewed in penitential practice as allowable, excusable faults committed without awareness of their seriousness or without full or deliberate knowledge or consent. This did not imply an irreversible fall from sanctifying grace or a destruction of the state of grace. Venial was distinguished from mortal sin, which ultimately causes the spiritual death of the soul and a fall from grace.[57]

When James wrote "We all stumble in many ways" (James 3:2*a*), he may have been referring to such unconscious faults, for his next sentence is: "If anyone is never at fault in what he says, he is a perfect man, able to keep his whole body in check" (James 3:2*b*), which suggests that a mature, fully developed life of faith active in love was in his view possible, yet not without stumbling.

It may be of venial or unpremeditated "sins of surprise" that John speaks when he says, "If we claim to be without sin, we deceive ourselves and the truth is not in us" (1 John 1:8). Yet the same writer seems to be speaking of spiritually calamitous (not venial) sin when he said later, "No one who lives in him keeps on sinning" (1 John 3:6). What might appear to be a contradiction in the passage is resolved by some ancient writers by discriminating between "a sin that leads to death," a recalcitrant ungodliness which prevents communion with God, and sin that "does not lead to death," particular sinful acts which

---

54. Council of Orange 4, CC 38.
55. Trent 6:23; cf. Wesley, "On Perfection," WJW 6:1-23.
56. SCD §§101-9, pp. 44-48.
57. Augustine, *On Marriage and Concupiscence* 1.17-32, NPNF 1:5:270-76.

leave room for a future restoration through repentance (1 John 5:16, 17). This is why John can say on the one hand that the regenerate do not sin (1 John 3:9; 1:6; 2:6), yet assume that some sin remains among the regenerate, as well as the need for the regular confession of sin (1 John 1:7; 2:1, 2).

In this way it is said that "though a righteous man falls seven times, he rises again" (Prov. 24:16). "There is not a righteous man on earth / who does what is right and never sins" (Eccl. 7:20) in the sense of constant impeccability or freedom from unconscious error or faulty perception. Erotic desire *(concupiscentia)* remains in the regenerate; it requires volition to become culpable.[58]

If those in scripture who are known to have walked in the way of holiness (Abel, Enoch, Melchizedek, Abraham, Samuel, Nathan, Elijah, Micaiah, Simeon, Anna, Judith, Esther, Elizabeth) could be assembled and asked whether they had lived without sin, Augustine concluded that they would all exclaim with one voice: "If we claim to be without sin, we deceive ourselves."[59]

The Perseverance of the Saints

The final argument, *no one can persevere in the way of holiness without the grace of God,* responds to the semi-Pelagian view that one is able to persevere in righteousness by one's own power. The Second Council of Orange defined that "even those who are reborn and holy must implore the help of God, in order that they may be enabled to attain the good end, or to persevere in the good work."[60]

Scholastic writers set forth an ingenious distinction between perfect and imperfect perseverance. In an hypothesized "perfect perseverance," baptismal innocence would be preserved in a state of grace until death. In a more realistic "imperfect perseverance," faith perseveres despite imperfections and infirmities to the end without ceasing to be saving faith.[61] This saved the doctrine of election from the pretense of having to present perfected saints in order to validate God's electing love.

---

58. Ibid., 1.25-40, NPNF 1:5:274-80; cf. Tho. Aq., *ST* 1-2.Q82, 1:956-58.
59. 1 John 1:8; Augustine, *On Nature and Grace* 42, NPNF 1:5:135.
60. Canon 10, CC 40; cf. Benjamin B. Warfield, *Two Studies in the History of Doctrine* (New York: Christian Literature Co., 1897).
61. Trent 6:11, SCD §804, p. 253.

The actual process of perseverance requires a series of efficacious graces, including regular hearing of the Word and communion with the risen Lord at his Table. The Christian life is precisely that life that is filled with such enabling graces.[62]

Cyprian interpreted the seven petitions of the Lord's Prayer as seven prayers for perseverance, whereby the church "prays that the unbeliever may believe" and "that believers may persevere."[63] Would not the Lord's Prayer be a mocking prayer, reasoned Augustine, if the gift of perseverance were merely a fantasy, and not a distinct gift, and that all the time the possibility and power of perseverance were in human hands?[64]

Jesus charged his disciples to "watch and pray so that you will not fall into temptation" (Matt. 26:41). The faithful do not cease to pray for perseverance in faith, grounded in the Son's promise: "I tell you the truth, my Father will give you whatever you ask in my name."[65] Epaphrus was commended by Paul as one "always wrestling in prayer for you, that you may stand firm in all the will of God, mature and fully assured" (Col. 4:12).

Perseverance is a gift for which the faithful pray, not a work that is merited.[66] "This gift of God may be obtained suppliantly, but when it has been given, it cannot be lost contumaciously."[67] Insofar as justifying faith is true and lively, "the sanctifying spirit of God is not extinguished nor vanished away in the regenerate, either finally or totally."[68]

---

62. Joyce, CDG 142ff.
63. Cyprian, *Treatise* 4, "On the Lord's Prayer," ANF 5:449-51.
64. *On the Gift of Perseverance* 1-6, NPNF 1:5:526-28.
65. John 16:23; cf. Domenico Palmieri, *De Gratia Divina Actuali* (Paris: M. Alberts, 1836), Thesis 36.
66. Calvin, *Inst.* 3.20.
67. Augustine, *On the Gift of Perseverance* 10, DT (Pohle) 7:127; cf. NPNF 1:5:529.
68. Irish Articles 38, COC 3:534.

PART FOUR

ON PREDESTINATION AND THE PERMISSION OF RECALCITRANCE

CHAPTER 7

THE MYSTERY OF FOREKNOWING AND ELECTING GRACE

The reader may remain puzzled as to how human freedom and divine foreknowledge can be held so closely together by classical Christian reasoning and not regarded as contradictories. This chapter seeks to clarify the logic of the intersection of foreknowledge and freedom.

The foregoing discussion of the contextuality of grace (Congruism's stress on the situational application of grace to the specific condition of human freedom) and of God's sufficient knowledge of all mediating contingencies *(scientia media)* clears the way for the discussion of two of the most difficult questions relating to grace: the problems of predestination and the divine will to permit recalcitrant sin.

First, the question of divine foreknowledge. Free human willing in response to grace occurs in time. It is consensually held that all time is presciently known by God through incomparable eternal wisdom. "I make known the end from the beginning" Isaiah says of Yahweh (46:10). No conceivable future is unknowable to the eternal God. This is hard for human consciousness to grasp or remember since consciousness is from the outset conceived, informed, steeped, and bound in time. So how is it possible that foreknowing is not contrary to human freedom?

ON FOREKNOWING GRACE

The Premise of Eternal Foreknowing

Only God adequately sees the end from the beginning. "Before a word is on my tongue / you know it completely, O Lord" (Ps. 139:4).

Eternal foreknowledge belongs to God's character as omniscient. Since God is eternally present to all moments—past, present, and future—God foreknows how free agents will choose, but that foreknowing does not determine their choice.[1]

"God's foreknowledge is nothing else than that God knows all things before they happen,"[2] for God has a relation to time entirely different from the one we have. Only an eternal and incomparably wise One could have this foreknowledge. God's vision differs entirely from all human and historical vision by being able to envision not only discrete events but all the contingencies of each, their unfolding vicissitudes, and the final end of history in eternal simultaneity without diminishing history's significance or robbing freedom of its own effects.[3]

All this is said to be easy for God, for whom nothing "is too hard" (Gen. 18:14; Jer. 32:27), for God is eternal. "God knows, in His eternity, all that takes place throughout the whole course of time," argued Thomas, using this analogy: "God knows the flight of time in His eternity, in the way that a person standing on the top of a watchtower embraces in a single glance a whole caravan of passing travelers."[4]

Whether Divine Foreknowing Implies the Robbery of Human Freedom

"The events are known by God because they exist, and do not exist because He knows them."[5] God's foreknowing (*prognōsis*; Lat.: *prescientia*) as such does not necessitate or foreordain explicit events of freedom, but eternally foresees them and all contingencies surrounding them. God's foreknowing of future events does not eliminate or diminish natural causality or human reason or will.[6]

Augustine hammered out this succinct analogy: "Just as you do not, by your *memory* of them, *compel past events* to have happened, neither does God, by His *foreknowledge, compel future events* to take place." So

---

1. John of Damascus, *Dialogue Ag. the Manicheans* 79, FEF 3:346, §2382.
2. Formula of Concord 11.1, BOC 494.
3. John of Damascus, OF 2.30 NPNF 2:9:42-43; cf. Calvin, *Inst.* 3.21; Barth, *CD* 2.1.553ff.; 4.4.24ff.
4. Tho. Aq., *Compend.* 133, p. 142.
5. Chrestos Androutsos, *Sumbolike* (Athens: I. A. Leurottoulou, Sids, 1930), p. 66; cf. Gavin, *Aspects* 222.
6. John of Damascus, OF 2.30, NPNF 2:9:43.

"God foreknows all the things of which He is the Author, but He is not Himself the Author of all that He foreknows."[7]

Origen had sharpened the same distinction early on: Divine foreknowledge means *not that anything will happen because God knows that it will, but that, because it will happen, God already knows it.*[8] Hence God's foreknowing does not "impose any necessity upon things foreseen."[9] Pastors and caregivers will save themselves considerable trouble by grasping this distinction. Those who doubt that these questions arise in daily pastoral care have not yet exposed themselves fully to the risk of the pastoral office.

What at first seems paradoxical upon closer inspection becomes a crucial point in defense of human freedom: The specific content of God's foreknowledge in a sense hinges on how the will decides. For *it is precisely how the will freely decides that God eternally foreknows.* Divine foreknowledge does not abolish human freedom but knows its contingencies and choices from the heart, since God inwardly knows the experiencing, deciding subject in all of his or her contingencies. So it is ironically less precise to say that human willing depends on divine foreknowledge, than that the particular events understood by divine foreknowledge hinge on the specific decisions and concretions of human willing in time.

The fact that God (who sees all from the beginning in eternal simultaneity) *foreknew* what the believer's response would be does not imply that God is *coercing* the act of belief, or irresistibly determining a particular response, but rather that God is empathically foreknowing both the options that a particular person's freedom will experience and how one will freely choose.[10] The Spirit's call intends to be efficacious, but not absolutely irresistible.[11] The inward call seeks to render the hearer capable of obedience, which itself is an act of freedom. Those who not only hear the invitation, but respond to it in repentance, faith, and obedience, are characteristically denoted in scripture as the "chosen" (*eklektos*, 1 Tim. 5:21; 2 Tim. 2:10; Titus

---

7. Augustine, "For God foreknows but does not author evil," *Free Choice*, FEF 3:39, §1547, ital. ad.
8. *Ag. Celsus* 2.20, ANF 4:440; cf. *DT* (Schmid) 275.
9. Quenstedt, TDP 1:539.
10. Nemesius, *On the Nature of Man*, LCC 4:410.
11. Bonaventure, *Life of St. Francis*, CWS 291-93.

1:1). By choosing to respond to the divine call, one is not diminishing, but enhancing one's freedom.

God's Foreknowing of Evil Steeped in Mystery

God's foreknowing does not make God the author of events contrary to God's will. Whatever evil God foreknowingly sees that will emerge as a result of alienated freedom, God is able to overrule so as to bring good out of evil proportionally as the situation requires. God's foreknowing does not limit either divine or human power.[12] "God foresees everything," concluded John of Damascus, "yet does not foreordain everything," if evil is found in history.[13] The consensual tradition tersely rejected the demoralizing idea that some may be "foreordained to evil by the power of God."[14]

That God foreknows that disaster will finally catch up with idolatry-prone human willing does not imply that God causes evil or compels any to do wrong.[15] Without grossly coercing freedom, God may curb or hedge freedom's lust for folly, or impose "a limit on its duration," so that in spite of its absurdity, even folly may minister indirectly to draw humanity toward divine mercy.[16]

Apostolic teaching stood in awe of the previously hidden, pretemporal purpose of God, which became known in time only incrementally through an extended series of dispensations or periods of the history of covenant, through which the Son was recognized as the incarnate mediator.[17] Insofar as humanity lacks revelation, faith, and hope, this unfolding remains a mystery and offense to human understanding.

ON PREDESTINING GRACE

It was Augustine (not Arminius, as some imagine) who first explained that *"predestination is nothing else than the foreknowledge and*

---

12. Clementina, *Hom.* 3.43, ANF 8:246.
13. John of Damascus, OF 4.21, NPNF 2:9:94, cf. pp. 42-44.
14. Second Council of Orange, CC 44.
15. Origen, *Ag. Celsus* 2.20, ANF 4:440.
16. Formula of Concord 11.3, BOC 405.
17. Irenaeus, *Ag. Her.* 4.21, ANF 1:492-93; cf. Augustine, CG 16-18, NPNF 1:2:309-97; Barth, CD 4.2.823ff.

the preparation of those gifts of God whereby they who are delivered are most certainly delivered."[18]

Thomas astutely noted that the locus of the doctrine of predestination "is in the One who predestines, and not the one predestined," just as the teaching of providence has less to do with "the things provided for" than "the mind of the provider."[19]

Romans 8:28-30—The Textual Nucleus of the Doctrine of Predestination

Most elements of classical predestination teaching are textually embedded in a single passage, Romans 8:28-30, which speaks of:

> God's foreknowing of the outcomes of human freedom in all its contingencies;
> God's working for the good of those who love him;
> God's working for those who are effectually called according to his purpose;
> the eternal decree of God's primordial will to save;
> the work of the Spirit to conform the faithful to the likeness of the Son, by which the elect are brought to the hearing of an effectual calling, to justifying faith, and finally to eternal blessedness:

"And we know that in all things God works for the good of those who love him, who have been called according to his purpose"—a promise made antecedently in principle to all, but in fact received only by those who in deed and truth love God. "For those God foreknew [*proegnō*] he also predestined [*proōrisen*] to be conformed to the likeness of his Son, that he might be the firstborn among many brothers." The destiny of the elect is to be at long last conformed to Christ in eternal blessedness. "And those he predestined, he also called [*ekalesen*]; those he called, he also justified [*edikaiōsen*]; those he justified, he also glorified [*edoxasen*]" (Rom. 8:28-30). "Glorified" suggests that the future glorification of the faithful is so definite as to be regarded as if already accomplished. Here time is being telescoped as if seen by God eternally. Since this is clearly an apostolic teaching,

---

18. Augustine, *Of the Gift of Perseverance* 14.35, NPNF 1:5:539, ital. ad.
19. Hence "predestination is a kind of type of the ordering of some persons toward eternal salvation existing in the divine mind," Tho. Aq., ST 1.Q23.2, 1:126, trans. altered; cf. DT (Pohle) 8:190; Nemesius, *On the Nature of Man*, LCC 4:397-428.

"It would be as impious to deny predestination as to oppose grace itself."[20]

The predestination of which Paul spoke in Romans 8:29-30 is directly premised by the foreknowing of God, which assumes the rational use by human beings of their natural light and free will (1 Tim. 2:4-6; 2 Cor. 5:15).[21] God knows in advance those who will respond in faith to saving grace, who by the right use of their will and knowledge of revealed truth will lay hold of that truth, trust in it, and who thereby will be justified. But this does not imply that God decides for them or substitutes direct divine causality for all human causes.[22]

Conversion has scant meaning if grace operates by a necessity that entirely overrides all human willing (Prov. 1:24-25; Isa. 5:4; Matt. 11:21; Acts 2:38; 2 Cor. 6:17). Salvation is offered by grace and accepted by free will, itself enabled by grace. The Westminster Confession rightly spoke of God the Spirit "effectually drawing them to Jesus Christ; yet so as they come most freely, being made willing by his grace."[23] To avert the premature impression that what follows is shaped more by Arminian than ancient ecumenical teaching, I will be making constant reference to the consensual teaching of the first five centuries, and to Reformed and Lutheran sources that steadily confirmed it. The ancient consensual argument is a far more subtle and dynamic form of predestinarian thinking than much of the polemics of the followers of Dort would allow.

Predestination Is to Salvation

The strict and proper usage of the term "predestination" is classically reserved for the election of the blessed, for God does not unilaterally or antecedently destine some to eternal separation, but only as a consequence of their own free choice.[24] Predestination is essentially eternal blessedness for those in a state of grace, and only therefore negatively

---

20. Prosper, Epistles, To Rufinus, DT (Pohle) 7:192.
21. 1 John 2:2; cf. Acts of the Synod of Jassy, Moldavia, 1641-43, COC 2:305-10; Confession of Dositheus 3, CC 487-88.
22. Council of Valens 3, SCD §§320-25, pp. 127-31; cf. Acts of the Synod of Constantinople, 1638, 1672.
23. Art. 10, CC 206.
24. John of Damascus, OF 2.30, NPNF 2:9:41-43.

and secondarily eternal separation for those who willfully remain in a state of sin.[25]

By predestination we refer to whatever God has willed and decreed *antecedent* to human freedom, a point already established. However much God antecedently wills that all might be saved, and provides grace sufficient for salvation, it is evident from scripture that through their own choice some do not actually receive this grace (Matt. 25:41). God's will to save all, viewed *consequently* to the self-determination of human freedom, ends in the salvation only of some, because some do not receive it.[26]

In the first four centuries various texts on calling, election, and predestination were received without much controversy and with a high degree of ecumenical consent. After the beginning of the fifth century, these ideas were further tested through a more rigorous interpretative process that would extend over many generations before they obtained, at least proximately, ecumenical reception as the mind of the believing church. Among alternative positions that were developed, sought general lay consent, and had to be adjudicated, were (a) the late Augustinian teaching of absolute predestination (qualified by Thomas Aquinas and extended by Calvin), (b) the moderated predestinarian exegesis, of the pre-Augustinian eastern tradition, sustained in the West by the Second Council of Orange. These views are due a postcritical reevaluation.

The Dilemma of Absolute Predestination

Did God first decree a certain number elect and only subsequently provide them with effective grace to persevere to that end? Advocates of absolute predestination answered yes, but usually after making a momentous distinction: In relation to God's primordial will, *in order of intent* the predestination to election is before the provision of means of grace; but *in order of time*, grace is concretely provided through an unfolding history, and only then is eternal blessedness received as a reward of Christ's merit acquired by the aid of grace. The aging Augustine of the anti-Pelagian controversies, Thomas Aquinas, and Calvin

---

25. Augustine, Letters, FC 30:276ff.; cf. John Cassian, *Conferences*, NPNF 2:11:190-91, 325ff.
26. Prosper of Aquitaine, *Grace and Free Will* 2-8, FC 7:345-66.

set forth this pattern of reasoning, which lays claim to being an important tradition of interpretation.

Though Romans 9 is often thought to support absolute predestinarian exegesis, it is subject to so many divergent interpretations that it is difficult to place it in a determinative doctrinal role in relation to other passages that speak more clearly. The theme of the passage is: "Does not the potter have the right to make out of the same lump of clay some pottery for noble purposes and some for common use?" (Rom. 9:21). The metaphor is employed to show that freedom may yield itself fully to be molded like clay, not to show that God absolutely predestines some to heaven and others to hell. When Paul wrote: "Jacob I loved, but Esau I hated" (Rom. 9:13; cf. Mal. 1:2-3; see also Rom. 9:16-18), the theme was the radical nature of grace, not absolute predestination to damnation.

Insofar as Augustine at some points of his public debate seemed to be arguing for absolute double predestination (e.g., in *The Gift of Perseverance* and *The Predestination of the Saints*), he tended to strain the received consensual teaching of the church fathers who preceded him (Irenaeus, Athanasius, virtually all eastern fathers, Hilary, and even Ambrose). Later, Prosper, Fulgentius, Calvin, and Bellarmine would follow Augustine's lead with variations.[27] The pre-Augustinian eastern tradition was seldom attracted to the theory of absolute double predestination.

The language of foreordination becomes problematic at the point at which it yields the impression of unilateral divine omnicausality—implying that all secondary causes are negated, or that free human agency is obliterated by the divine decree, which amounts to an assault on the Christian teaching of creation. Etymologically, "preordain" (from *ordo*, order—to establish by decree or appointment) and "predestine" (from *destinare*, to decree beforehand by mandate, design, or appointment) are close cognates. Both differ substantially from preknowing, omniscience, prescience, and precognition, all of which imply the awareness and permission but not the direct appointment or establishment in advance of an event or action. A still different nuance emerges in the idea of predetermination (*pre* + *de* + *terminare* = to

---

27. Paulus Orosius, *Liber apologeticus contra Pelagium*, MPL 31:1175-1216; cf. Petavius, *Theological Dogmatics* (Barri-Ducis: L. Guerin, 1864–70) 10:9; Felix Oswald, *Die Lehre von der Heiligung* (Münster: Aschendorff, 1870), 242.

limit in advance), a fixing of limits, that which sets boundaries before-hand.[28]

The Predestinarian Exegesis of Pre-Augustinian Orthodoxy

The alternative to absolute predestination is the view that God's will to save all is based on an antecedent (sometimes called a hypothetic) decree contingent on a future condition. God mercifully wills to save all antecedent to their choice, yet according to his justice God wills the separation of sinners from his holiness consequent to their choice. If so, the pretemporal divine decree is not simple and absolute but con-ditional upon grace being freely received.[29] Accordingly, only those are predestined to blessedness who freely receive grace by faith. It is only when conceived from the viewpoint of God's foreknowledge that one can speak of this hypothetic decree becoming a fixed decree. "God first prepared the gifts of grace, and then elected to eternal life those whose good use of the gifts He foresaw."[30]

By faith the believer cooperates with grace so as to make effective the antecedent, pretemporal decree of predestination to life. In so doing, the decree becomes no longer hypothetical, but is now a fulfilled election into an actual or absolute decree, with the result that by faith one's name becomes written indelibly into the book of life (Luke 10:20; cf. 2 Pet. 1:10).

If God absolutely and pretemporally decrees that particular persons shall be saved and others damned, apart from any cooperation of human freedom, then God cannot in any sense intend that all shall be saved, as 1 Timothy 4:10 declares. The promise of glory is conditional on grace being received by faith active in love. This seems clear from Paul's exclamation: "I have fought the good fight, I have finished the race, I have kept the faith. Now there is in store for me the crown of righteousness, which the Lord, the righteous Judge, will award to me on that day—and not only to me, but also to all who have longed for his appearing" (2 Tim. 4:7-8).

---

28. Augustine, *On Admonition and Grace* 23ff., NPNF 1:5:481ff.; cf. Nemesius, *On the Nature of Man*, LCC 4:397-420; Barth, CD 2.2.
29. John of Damascus, OF 4.19-21; NPNF 2:9:92-94; cf. Alexander of Hales, Albertus Magnus, and Leonhard Lessius for medieval and scholastic expositions of this view; Francis de Sales, *Treatise of the Love of God* (New York: P. O'Shea, 1868), 3:5.
30. Bucanus, *ITLC* 1.7; cf. DT (Pohle) 7:206.

The premise of the parable of the last judgment is that those separated might have been placed on the right hand had they chosen differently (Matt. 25:34-35). Chrysostom astutely grasped this dialectic: "Because I knew beforehand that *you would become what you are*" through your freedom, you are brought near to or far from the divine holiness.[31]

Likewise, in the West prior to Augustine the already prevailing consensus had been clearly expressed by Ambrose: "For He did not predestine before He foreknew, but He predestined a reward to those whose merits He foresaw."[32] Similarly, predestination was aptly defined in Lutheran orthodoxy as "the eternal decree of God to bestow eternal salvation upon all of whom God foresaw that they would finally believe in Christ."[33]

A thousand years before Protestantism, the Second Council of Orange defined several positions as ecumenical teaching. The council repudiated an extreme absolute double predestinarian position that God pretemporally decreed a specific number of elect for glory and reprobate for damnation. It pointedly omitted the later Augustinian doctrine of irresistible grace, yet accepted most other aspects of Augustine's teaching on grace and free will. It rejected both the notion that persons are predestined to do evil, and the Pelagian view of unmarred natural free agency.[34]

Those who held that the freedom of the soul remains unimpaired after Adam, having fallen into the error of Pelagius, were admonished by the Apostle that "sin entered the world through one man, and death through sin, and in this way death came to all men, because all sinned" (Rom. 5:12).[35] Those who imagined they could make right choices without grace were referred to John's Gospel: "Apart from me you can do nothing" (John 15:5); and to Paul: "Such confidence as this is ours through Christ before God. Not that we are competent in ourselves to claim anything for ourselves, but our competence comes from God"

---

31. Chrysostom, *Comm. on Matthew*, Hom. 79.2, NPNF 1:10:476, ital. ad.; *Hom. on John* 27, FC 33:259-67.
32. *On Faith* 5.6.82, NPNF 2:10:294; Augustine refines this view in *On the Gift of Perseverance* 41, NPNF 1:5:542.
33. Hollaz, *ETA* 604.
34. CC 38.
35. Second Council of Orange 1, 2, CC 38.

(2 Cor. 3:4-5). "God loves us for what we shall be by his gift, and not by our own deserving."[36]

The Permission of Recalcitrance

It would be contrary to the wisdom and justice of God to insist that the condemnation of sinners is either without cause or directly caused by God. God created no one deliberately for the purpose of condemnation.[37] God "foreknew the one would make a right use of their free-will, and the other a wrong."[38] On the basis of this foreknowing, it may be said that God predestined some to glory, yet permitted the fair judgment of recalcitrant sinners, who freely choose to resist divine grace.

The Third Council of Valence (A.D. 855), brought together in good balance the otherwise conflicting themes that God foreknows "eternally both the good deeds which good men will do, and the evil which evil men will do," for "in Him future things have already taken place. . . Certainly neither [do we believe] that the foreknowledge of God has placed a necessity on any wicked man, so that he cannot be different." The Council concluded against the view that "the wicked thus perish because they were not able to be good"; rather "because they were unwilling to be good, they have remained by their own vice in the mass of damnation." God foreknew their malice but did not predestine it.[39]

God from eternity knew with certainty all future things and ordered them to reside within layers of causality, yet not in such a way that all things occur by a direct divine causality that eradicates all other causes.[40] Humanity remains free to do good with grace or to choose evil having rejected grace.[41] These conciliar actions express the main lines of classical Christian exegesis on predestination.[42]

---

36. Ibid., 12, CC 41.
37. Saxon Visitation Articles (1592) 2, COC 3:185.
38. Confession of Dositheus 3, CC 487.
39. SCD §§321-22, pp. 128-29.
40. Council of Quiersy, SCD §316, p. 126; cf. Council of Valence 3, SCD §§321-22, pp. 127ff.
41. Council of Ephesus, SCD §134, pp. 54ff.; Lateran Council 3, SCD §400, p. 155.
42. Leo 9's Symbol of Faith of 1053 similarly distinguished that "God predestined only the good things, but that He foreknew the good and the evil"; SCD §349, p. 142.

Whether God Predestines Freedom to Fall

The essential logic of classical predestination teaching is that every-one who will perseveringly believe in Christ to the end will certainly be saved.[43] Some have used the word "predestination" in a less restrained sense to refer equally to the saving of the faithful and the damnation of the unfaithful. In ecumenical teaching, predestination principally means the divine decree concerning the salvation of fallen humanity, not the damnation of those who neglect this salvation. "God's predestination is the cause of the standing firm of many, but for no one is it the cause of their falling."[44]

The failure of absolute double predestination to gain ecumenical consent hinged on the fact that it tended to locate the decree of elec-tion simplistically in the antecedent will of God, ignoring any divine willing consequent to human responsiveness. Orthodoxy places elec-tion not exclusively in the antecedent will of God, but also in God's consequent willing.

43. Hollaz, *ETA* 630; *DT* (Schmid) 287.
44. Prosper of Aquitaine, *Responses to Objections of Vincent*, FEF 3, 2033, p. 191.

CHAPTER 8

ELECTION MADE SURE THROUGH FAITH

To be called or invited does not imply that one necessarily will accept the invitation. One's calling and election must be *"made sure,"* which requires effort and responsiveness: "Make every effort to add to your faith goodness; and to goodness, knowledge; and to knowledge, self-control," and thereby "be all the more eager to make your calling and election sure" (2 Pet. 1:5, 10). Salvation is not extorted but elicited through moral means by God's own persuasive self-giving love, which empowers the moral freedom of the hearer.

ELECTING GRACE

The Elect

The elect (*eklektos*, chosen, selected—Matt. 24:22-31; Mark 13:20-27; Rom. 8:33) are those called into the *ekklēsia*, through whom God's outreaching love has become revealed by its behavioral fruits: "For we know, brothers loved by God, that he has chosen you, because our gospel came to you not simply with words, but also with power, with the Holy Spirit and with deep conviction" (1 Thess. 1:4-5).

One may be called without being chosen (Matt. 22:14). *The call issues in accomplished election only when freely accepted.* If one is called and does not respond to the call, the call has been aborted. Election is not wholly dissociated from repentance, faith, and obedience. Election occurs through the work of the Spirit in justifying, regenerating, adopting, and sanctifying the hearer, who becomes thereby set apart from and for the world, consecrated to God.

That "few are chosen" (Matt. 22:14) "does not mean that God does not desire to save everyone," for some may not hear the Word at all, or hear and despise it, or "bar the ordinary way for the Holy Spirit, so that he cannot work in them; or, if they do hear the Word, they cast it to the wind."[1]

When Luke wrote that "all who were appointed for eternal life believed" (Acts 13:48), it is not implied that all self-determination was eradicated in the act of believing. It is a wooden reading of this text to assume that God foreordained eternal life for particular individuals before time and, without any willing cooperation from them, they believed. In the same passage, Luke had just written that Paul and Barnabas had freely proclaimed the gospel to the Jews in Galatia, that they had debated and rejected it, and hence the apostles had turned to preach to the Gentiles (Acts 13:16-47). The same text appeals to all to be accountable, warning against indecisiveness, and assuring that "everyone who believes is justified" (Acts 13:39).

Faith Receives but Does Not Merit Election

Faith is not a meritorious cause of election, but it is constantly attested as the sole condition of salvation. Faith merely receives the merit of atoning grace, instead of asserting its own merit. God places the life-death option before each person, requiring each to choose. The *eklektos* are those who by grace freely believe. God does not compel or necessitate their choosing. Even after the initial choice of faith is made, they may grieve and quench the Spirit.[2]

Faith is the condition under which God primordially wills the reception of salvation by all. "He chooses us, not because we believe, but that we may believe; lest we should say that we first chose Him."[3] Faith receives the electing love of God not as if it had already become efficacious without faith, but aware that God's prescience foreknows faith like all else.

In accord with ancient ecumenical consent, predestination was carefully defined in centrist Protestant orthodoxy as

the eternal, divine decree, by which God, from His immense mercy, determined to give His Son as Mediator, and, through universal preach-

---

1. Formula of Concord 20.11, *BOC* 496.
2. 1 Thess. 5:19; cf. Miner Raymond, *Syst. Theol.* 2.423.
3. Augustine, quoted in Bancroft, *CT* 239; cf. John 15:16.

ing, to offer Him for reception to all men who from eternity He foresaw would fall into sin; also through the Word and Sacraments to confer faith upon all who would not resist; to justify all believers, and besides to renew those using the means of grace; to preserve faith in them until the end of life, and in a word, to save those believing to the end.[4]

Election Is to Sanctification: Ephesians 1

The central theme of the Letter to the Ephesians is Christ's eternal purpose in establishing, fashioning, and completing his body, the called-out people. It is not that humanity has chosen God but that God has chosen to give himself to humanity unreservedly. Every aspect of the plan of salvation has its source in God's grace, which awakens and enables but does not eliminate human responsiveness.[5]

This electing love is intended for sanctification. The visible fruits of holiness validate and manifest the premise of election: "For he chose us in him before the creation of the world to be holy and blameless in his sight. In love he predestined us to be adopted as his sons through Jesus Christ" (Eph. 1:4-5).

God has set in motion a complex plan in which those who believe in Christ will be adopted into the family of God and be given sufficient grace to become accountably conformed to his Son. All this is "in accordance with his pleasure and will—to the praise of his glorious grace, which he has freely given us in the One he loves" (Eph. 1:5-6; cf. Rom. 8:12-17, 29). "In him we were also chosen, having been predestined according to the plan of him who works out everything in conformity with the purpose of his will" (Eph. 1:11).[6] This does not relieve human recipients of responsibility to answer accountably in faith active in love. The priority of grace to freedom is everywhere evident in Ephesians without negating either divine or human freedom.

Paul appealed to his hearers that they "not grieve the Holy Spirit of God, with whom you were sealed for the day of redemption" (Eph. 4:30). This assumed some capacity on the part of believers for resisting the Spirit. "For we are God's workmanship, created in Christ Jesus to

---

4. Hollaz, *ETA* 609; cf. *DT* (Schmid) 285; Melanchthon, *Loci*, LCC 19:24-30.
5. Athanasius, *Life of Antony* 10-24, NPNF 2:4:199-202.
6. Calvin, *Inst.* 1.16-17; cf. 2.11-14.

do good works, which God prepared in advance for us to do" (Eph. 2:10). It is by God's choice that the gospel has been given, and by faithful freedom that the gospel is received (Eph. 1:6).[7]

Conditionality in Responsible Election

The passage most crucial to the responsiveness of the elect is Romans 9–11, from which, by a disputed interpretation, the ideas of double predestination and compulsively irresistible grace have derived principal support. The grief of Paul is a primary factor in the context of personal disquietude in which this passage was tortuously written, for Paul stated clearly at the outset: "I have great sorrow and unceasing anguish in my heart" (Rom. 9:2). Paul was not sorrowful because God had from eternity by an inflexible decree of reprobation damned some to death. Rather, he was sorrowful because *so many of God's own called people were willfully rejecting God's own coming.* Nor was Paul anguished because God had failed to keep promises to the descendants of Abraham, but because they were failing to respond freely to God's promise-keeping. Yet they remained the people of promise, recipients of covenant, of election, Torah, and temple. "It is not as though God's word had failed. For not all who are descended from Israel are Israel" (Rom. 9:6).

Who, then, constitutes the true Israel? Those to whom, like Abraham, faith is accounted righteousness. God's promise to Israel, rightly understood, is continually being fulfilled in Christ. The promises to Israel were never meant to imply that they were given without conditions or simply on the basis of blood kinship or without faith. "On the contrary, 'It is through Isaac that your offspring will be reckoned.' In other words, it is not the natural children who are God's children, but it is the children of the promise who are regarded as Abraham's offspring" (Rom. 9:7-8, referring to Gen. 21:12).

Paul felt heavy of heart not because God had pretemporally rejected the Jews (the dismal premise of much later anti-Semitism), but because some had freely chosen to neglect the Good News of God's coming. The subject of the discourse in Romans 9–11 was not the eternal election or reprobation of particular individual persons to eternal life or death, as individualistic exegesis has sometimes argued, but rather the

---

7. Barth, *CD* 2.2.60-76, 102-15; cf. Miley, *Syst. Theol.* 2.263.

election of the Gentiles to be recipients of the promise equally with the descendants of Abraham, based on faith's free response to grace.[8] As Yahweh had said through Hosea, "I will call them 'my people' who are not my people" (Rom. 9:25, referring to Hos. 1:9-10); so Christ was calling the Gentiles, who are not fleshly or physical heirs of Abraham but were being prepared to become heirs of the promise through faith. The promise to Abraham was realized through a remnant—not through the whole mass of Israel, but through the spiritual Israel of faith (Rom. 9:27).

In distributing his blessing to all humanity instead of only to some, God remains sovereign by the same sovereignty that elected Jacob and not Esau. Does this make God unjust? Not at all! (Rom. 9:14).[9] This is the same One Who Is who said to Moses: "I will have mercy on whom I will have mercy" (Exod. 33:19), whose purpose in election stands "not by works but by him who calls," as Rebekah knew (Rom. 9:10-12). The admission of the Gentiles to equal privilege was not an occasion on which the elect people might make any sort of warranted complaint, for grace "depends not on human will or exertion, but on God who shows mercy. For the scripture says to Pharaoh, 'I have raised you up for the very purpose of showing my power in you, so that my name may be proclaimed in all the earth'" (Rom. 9:16-17 NRSV).[10]

Pharaoh had been spared in the plague of boils because God intended to permit Pharaoh to play a part in the revelation of divine grace through the exodus of Israel from Egypt. When Paul recalled that God "hardens the heart of whomever he chooses" (Rom. 9:18 NRSV), he was dealing with a particular aspect of the relation of God's sovereignty and human freedom—namely, the ability of God to circumvent and judge previous human arrogance, and allow it freely to make its own self-inflicted mistakes. The passage need not refer to divine reprobation to eternal death. Paul throughout assumed that Pharaoh continued to exercise his self-determining freedom amid folly, willfully resisting doing what was right. God temporarily permitted Pharaoh to mock justice and bring ruin on himself that by his own folly he might become an inadvertent means of the divine purpose. "For God thus blinds and

---

8. John Chrysostom, *Hom. on Ephesians* 5, 6, NPNF 1:13:70-79; cf. Calvin, *Inst.* 3.20-24; Barth, *CD* 2.2.118ff., 306ff.

9. Barth, *CD* 2.2.13ff.

10. Miner Raymond, *Syst. Theol.* 2.419.

hardens, simply by letting alone and withdrawing His aid."[11] In such ways God makes even human wrath to praise him (Ps. 76:10).

The enigma of grace is that "the Gentiles, who did not pursue righteousness, have obtained it" (Rom. 9:30), while some of Israel, having once pursued righteousness, have in the meantime missed its palpable incarnation. This is why Paul was anguished. "Because they pursued it not by faith but as if it were by works. They stumbled over the 'stumbling stone'" (Rom. 9:32; cf. 1 Pet. 2:8), not because God predestined them to stumble, but because they rejected the ancient hebraic premise that salvation comes by faith. "Since they did not know the righteousness that comes from God and sought to establish their own, they did not submit to God's righteousness" (Rom. 10:3).

Even amid all this stumbling and obstinacy to Christ, Paul still confessed that his "heart's desire and prayer to God for the Israelites is that they may be saved" (Rom. 10:1). He reminded them of God's encouraging word to Elijah: "I have reserved for myself seven thousand who have not bowed the knee to Baal" (Rom. 11:4; cf. 1 Kings 19:18). "Again I ask: Did they stumble so as to fall beyond recovery? Not at all!" (Rom. 11:11).

This assumes that both Jews and Gentiles are faced with a genuine choice: faith or unfaith. The reception of God's electing love hinges upon their yea or nay decision, foreknown by God from eternity, but without coercively predetermining their human freedom.[12]

Whether Human Freedom Limits Divine Sovereignty

God's incomparable power includes and embraces God's permission to humanity to say no. When Pilate spoke of his power over Jesus, Jesus answered: "You would have no power over me if it were not given to you from above" (John 19:11). Pilate had a power to decide—tragically so. He did decide, and Jesus died. But Pilate's power was derived and not independent. So it is with every human person: God grants us power to say no to the good incarnate.

Though temporarily freedom is able to resist divine grace, God's purpose in history will in the long run be carried out, even if in the short run thwarted by human defiance.[13] It is not a limitation of the divine

---

11. Augustine, *On the Gospel of St. John* 53.6, NPNF 1:8:293.
12. Cyprian, Treatise 12, ANF 5:547.
13. John Chrysostom, *Hom. on John*, Hom. 84, FC 41:417-27.

sovereignty that God grants this temporary and finite freedom to humanity, but an expression of the greatness of God's compassion and parenting care and joy in companionship. This does not limit God's capacity, but stands as a freely given self-constraint of God's actual scope of activity within and for the wretched history of sin.

God primordially wills that all should be saved and come to the knowledge of the truth, but in the limited time between creation and consummation, human beings are given freedom to resist, to "grieve the Spirit," to backslide, to play out their freedom in folly. Meanwhile, the Spirit woos, but does not force; persuades but does not coerce; judges, hedges, and draws, but does not obliterate the precious gift of vulnerable human freedom.[14]

The Spirit of God draws or leads the sinner from one phase to another, gradually, in proportion as one is found having a disposition to responsive hearing. Grace flows ordinarily from prevenient grace through the grace of baptism through the grace of justification toward sanctifying grace leading toward consummation in glory. The power by which one cooperates with grace is grace itself. In this way God draws all to himself, eliciting a hunger for righteousness and a desire for truth.[15]

God does not compel but elicits and draws persuasively; God nudges the human will not as a mechanical force, but according to moral suasion shaped by divine love and justice. Scripture does not teach the absolute passivity of will as it is influenced by effective grace. Grace elicits faith, not simply as one billiard ball bumping another, but always in such a way that faith is one's own personal act. One is never so free as when obedient and responsive to grace.

The Damascene articulated the consensual view in the East: "Had God kept from being made those who through His goodness were to have existence, but who by their own choice were to become evil, then evil would have prevailed over the goodness of God. Thus, all things which God makes He makes good, but each one becomes good or evil by his own choice."[16]

Augustine spoke similarly for the West: "Neither did any future event escape God's foreknowledge nor did His foreknowledge compel

---

14. Clement of Alexandria, *Stromata* 6.9, ANF 2:496-98.
15. Journet, *CWI* 1.31-35.
16. John of Damascus, OF 4.21, FC 37:387, 388.

any one to sin." It was within God's power to prevent men and women from sinning, "But God preferred to leave this in their power, and thus to show both what evil could be wrought by their pride, and what good by His grace."[17]

Whether It Is Absurd That Yahweh Covenanted with Israel Rather Than Another

If God is to become known within the frame of mundane history, then that knowledge must begin at some distinct point in real time. If the plan of salvation is to be worked out through events, not ideas alone, then its inbreaking into history must be inaugurated at some particular juncture in time, not generally or everywhere.

Only a too-tidy rationalism pretends that truth appears in every time and place identically, as if following some predisposing axiom of absolute rational equality. That is not the way the One Who Is became self-disclosed, nor is it the way truth is revealed in ordinary human circumstances such as those that prevail between lovers or between parent and child, where the *truth* of the relation is revealed through personal *events*.

Yahweh chose Israel to be the means by which all others might in time behold the divine glory. Israel was called to service, not to boast in its own chosenness as if election were an end in itself. Yahweh loved Israel first and others through Israel. Yahweh chose Abraham first and others through Abraham. Why? The answer lies wholly in grace—the mercy and good pleasure of the divine will. "The Lord did not set his affection on you and choose you because you were more numerous than other peoples, for you were the fewest of all peoples. But it was *because the Lord loved you* and kept the oath he swore to your forefathers that he brought you out with a mighty hand and redeemed you from the land of slavery" (Deut. 7:7-8, ital. ad.).

The specific reasons in the divine mind why God chose Jacob and not Esau are not for us to know. It is enough to know that they hiddenly embrace a divine plan that is becoming fully revealed in the Son through the Spirit. Meanwhile Yahweh continues eternally to love, and hence to choose, Israel, even when Israel is temporarily unfaithful (Jer. 31:2-4).

---

17. Augustine, CG 14.27, NPNF 1:2:282.

THE REFINEMENT OF PREDESTINARIAN TEACHING THROUGH CONTROVERSY

Augustinian Reasoning on the Specific Number of the Elect

Since God foreknows the choices of self-determining persons, God grasps already those who will share in eternal blessedness. They are countable, but only to God. It is of this collection—those foreknown by God to exercise their freedom either for or against saving grace—that vexing questions concerning the number of elect have been raised. Since only One foreknows, only One knows that number and can already name them by name, not because this is already decreed by unilateral foreordination, but because God's knowing is contemporary with every moment in time, including future moments with all their contingencies.[18]

What follows is a recapitulation of Augustine's argument on the number of the elect, which later would be consensually refined. Augustine argued that God had decreed before time that only a certain number were elected for salvation, leaving the remainder to perdition, and that the elect were drawn to faith by an irresistible grace. It was for these elect, and not for the whole of humanity, that Christ died, in this view. The glory of God was the predestined end of creation, the purpose for which the whole plan of providence and redemption was initiated. Adam's fall brought misery on all humanity. The freedom to do good and abstain from evil was lost.

The consequence is not that free will has been destroyed altogether, but that whenever we use freedom, we distort and cannot choose or do the good. Humans remain free to choose, but they cannot avoid sinning since they are trapped in the anxieties and guilts endemic to the precariousness of human freedom. All humanity shares Adam's sin. The freedom not to sin (which Adam originally was given) has been lost not only to Adam but to human progeny. It is not that the image of God has been completely destroyed, but that it has become grossly distorted and defaced. From among the mass of the fallen, God elected a number (in Augustine's view, exactly the number of the fallen angels) to eternal life, leaving the remainder for the just recompense

---

18. Augustine, *On Admonition and Grace* 13.39, NPNF 1:5:446-47; cf. Tho. Aq., *ST* 1.Q23.7.3.

of their sins. The work of the Son and Spirit is effective for the elect. An efficacious grace brings them into the life of faith and enables them to persevere. They will be brought to the knowledge of the truth and persevere in holy living to the end. God chooses as God pleases, yet there is no injustice in these choices, for it is only by compassion that any are chosen. The elect receive infinitely more than their due, while the reprobate receive just what their sins deserve. So argued Augustine.[19]

Countering Exaggerations

One cannot deny that much of the argument here outlined gained fairly wide consent in much of western Christianity, though in detail it never gained prevailing consent in the East. Some important aspects, however, became highly contested and failed ultimately to gain general consent in the West, especially:

a. that Adam transmitted sin through physical, sexual generation;
b. that the grace by which the elect are brought to salvation is irresistible; and
c. that God predestined from the mass of reprobates a specific number for eternal life, while the remainder were pretemporally consigned to damnation.

When later followers of the tradition of Augustine exaggerated his views or presented them defensively, this predictably elicited another reactionary wave of defensive semi-Pelagianism that asserted a natural competence in all persons to move toward grace, an ability not fundamentally injured by sin. Some Augustinian apologists came to view grace as locked into a deterministic world view of unilateral divine omnicausality. Some opponents of Augustine came to view grace too simplistically as finally dependent on free human agency. Against both these extremes, the consensual tradition east and west found it wiser to argue the priority of grace to freedom in a way that preserves human

---

19. Augustine, CG 22.24, NPNF 1:3:502-4; 12.3, 14, pp. 246, 251; cf. *On the Grace of Christ* 1.1-9, NPNF 1:5:217-20; *On the Gift of Perseverance* 35, 47-48, NPNF 1:5:507-8; *On the Predestination of the Saints* 19, NPNF 1:5:378-79; Ag. *Two Letters of the Pelagians* 1.5; 3.254; Hodge, *Syst. Theol.* 332.

accountability by viewing predestination as the divine foreknowing of human acts of freedom.

Medieval scholasticism continued to be divided over these issues. Thomas Aquinas argued that "God wills all men to be saved by His antecedent will . . . and not by His consequent will."[20] Thomas Bradwardine, twelfth-century archbishop of Canterbury, anticipated the predestinarian views later to be developed by Wyclif and Calvin. The consensus, however, was for a more moderate view that asserted the universal scope of redemptive grace and preserved free human agency, a position that had long been consistently held by chief orthodox teachers in the East.

Lutheran and Calvinist Definitions

Although Luther, as a former Augustinian monk, held largely to Augustinian premises on predestination, the maturing Melanchthon taught that human will is graciously enabled to cooperate with divine grace in conversion. The consensual Lutheran Formula of Concord shied away from extreme forms of both synergism and absolute double predestination. It denied that the natural human being could cooperate with regenerating grace, arguing that regeneration is entirely the work of God,[21] that God loves fallen humanity, wills the salvation of all,[22] and sent his Son for all; and that God elects some and not others because he foresaw that some would believe and persevere and others would not. The elect are those who God foresees will have faith. God predestines only the elect, not the damned.

The controversy was influentially renewed by Zwingli and Calvin, who pressed the hyper-Augustinian position to its logical conclusion, strongly emphasizing absolute double predestination. "We call predestination God's eternal decree, by which he [compacted] with himself what he willed to become of each man. For all are not created in equal condition; rather, eternal life is foreordained for some, eternal damnation for others."[23]

Calvinists soon became divided over competing interpretations of

---

20. *ST* 1-1.Q23.4, 1:128.
21. Formula of Concord 11, *BOC* 494-98.
22. Hollaz, *ETA* 599.
23. Calvin, *Inst.* 3.21.5.

the logical order of decrees: According to the *supralapsarian* view (holding that the election of individuals preceded the fall), the first decree was predestination—the election of some persons and angels to eternal life and the reprobation of others to eternal death. The decree to create followed the decree to predestine. Only then did God permit the fall. The next decree provided a plan of redemption by which salvation was provided for the elect. Finally the efficacious calling of the elect was decreed. Hence some of those fallen were pretemporally elected to grace, while others were predestined to glorify the divine justice through their reprobation. Creation is given in order to allow a predestined redemption and damnation. In supralapsarian teaching the decree is first to save some and condemn others, then to create both elect and reprobate, then permit the fall of both, then provide salvation for the elect only (cf. Theodore Beza, Peter Martyr, Franciscus Gomarus, and William Twisse).

The order of decrees is changed in the *infralapsarian* view (sometimes called sub- or postlapsarianism), which held that the election of individuals occurred after the fall. God first determined to create the world, then permitted the fall, then elected some of the fallen, sending his Son for their redemption, leaving the remainder to suffer the just punishment of their sins, and providing for the effectual calling of the elect. In both cases, salvation is provided only for the elect.[24]

Moderating Calvinism in the English Tradition

The Anglican Thirty-nine Articles of 1563 contained an article on predestination that represents a moderated Reformed teaching. It returned to the earlier ecumenical tradition by affirming a "predestination to life," not eternal death: "Predestination to life is the everlasting purpose of God, whereby (before the foundations of the world were laid) he hath constantly decreed by his counsel secret to us, to deliver from curse and damnation those whom he hath chosen in Christ out of mankind, and to bring them by Christ to everlasting salvation, as vessels made to honour." Those who have received this excellent benefit

---

24. Ibid., 3.21-24; cf. Witsius, *OFD* 2; Strong, *Syst. Theol.* 778-79; Erickson, *CT* 3.918.

are effectively "called according to God's purpose by his Spirit working in due season; they through Grace obey the calling; they be justified freely; they be made sons of God by adoption; they be made like the image of his only-begotten Son Jesus Christ; they walk religiously in good works, and at length, by God's mercy, they attain to everlasting felicity."[25] The order of salvation proceeds from the grace of calling, through justification, adoption, and regeneration, to glorification, a doctrine "full of sweet, pleasant, and unspeakable comfort" to the godly. Nothing is said of double predestination, irresistible grace, or limited atonement.

The most influential statement of predestination in the English-speaking tradition is Article 3 of the Westminster Confession: "God from all eternity did, by the most wise and holy counsel of his own will, freely and unchangeably ordain whatsoever comes to pass; yet so as thereby neither is God the author of sin, nor is violence offered to the will of the creatures, nor is the liberty or contingency of second causes taken away, but rather established." It is argued that "although God knows whatsoever may or can come to pass upon all supposed conditions, yet hath he not decreed any thing because he foresaw it as future." "By the decree of God, for the manifestation of his glory, some men and angels are predestinated unto everlasting life, and others foreordained to everlasting death." "Their number is so certain and definite that it can not be either increased or diminished." These have been elected

without any foresight of faith or good works, or perseverance in either of them, or any other thing in the creature, as conditions, or causes moving him thereunto; and all to the praise of his glorious grace. As God hath appointed the elect unto glory, so hath he, by the eternal and most free purpose of his will, foreordained all the means thereunto. . . . The rest of mankind God was pleased, according to the unsearchable counsel of his own will, whereby he extendeth or withholdeth mercy as he pleaseth, for the glory of his sovereign power over his creatures, to pass by, and to ordain them to dishonor and wrath for their sin, to the praise of his glorious justice.[26]

25. Art. 17, CC 272.
26. CC 198, 199.

The Gradual Protestant Retrieval of the Ancient Ecumenical Consensus on Grace and Freedom

Only after a century of Protestant experience did the decisive confrontation occur through which the older ecumenical tradition of grace and freedom again became clarified.[27] When Jacobus Arminius (professor of theology at Leiden, d. 1609) rejected the extreme form of absolute double predestination, he was attacked by Franciscus Gomarus (1563–1641). Arminius was defended by James Uytenbogaart and Simon Episcopius in the Five Points of Remonstrance (1610), which were debated by Dutch Protestantism in the years leading to the Synod of Dort (1618–1619). The Remonstrance represented a substantial reappropriation of pre-Augustinian eastern patristic consensus:

1. Against unconditional double predestination to election and damnation, the argument was again advanced that election is received by faith. If unreceived the election has been negated or simply unreceived. God's eternal purpose is to save by grace those that believe and persevere in obedience. Election is not just given by arbitrary fiat without human responsiveness, but its reception is conditional upon faith. The elect are precisely those who God by eternal foreknowing is able to foresee will accept the offer of salvation (Rom. 8:29; 1 Pet. 1:2). God's decree was not to damnation but to election. God elected that all who repent and believe should be saved. Whether a particular moral agent believes or disbelieves is not pretemporally determined by God.[28]

2. The universality of atonement was reasserted, against the view that Christ died only for the elect. Against limited atonement, God primordially desires all persons to be saved (1 Tim. 2:3-4). The scope of

---

27. A further moderated Calvinism was proposed by Moses Amyraldus (Amyraut) of Saumur, in France (d. 1664), who held (as had the ancient Catholic tradition) that Christ made the salvation of all humanity possible *if* they believe in Christ (the *decretum universale hypotheticum*). By this hypothetical universalism of grace there was posited a dim revelation of grace in nature and history apart from the gospel, which would make the rejection of the reprobate more plausibly just and intelligible, since all are guilty of rejecting either the general or special offer of grace (*Traité de la predestination et de ses principes* [Saumur: I. Lesneir & I. Desbourdes, 1634]). The moderate Calvinist Second Helvetic Confession of 1675, composed by Heidegger, noted that even though "mention is made of the small number of the elect, yet we must hope well of all, and not rashly judge any man to be a reprobate" (CC 138).

28. COC 3:545ff.

atoning grace is human history. God finds no pleasure in the death of sinners (Ezek. 33:11; 2 Pet. 3:9). The juridical verdict manifested on the cross was in favor of humanity as a whole.[29]

3. Moral freedom was reasserted against a moral necessity unilaterally determined by total depravity. Against absolute natural inability, the regeneration of the will is enabled through prevenient grace. By grace all are invited to pray for the grace of repentance and faith. The summons to repentance would make no sense if there could be no possible response to it. That response is enabled not by natural ability, but by prevenient grace. Persons are responsible only for those acts in which their volition enters. Lacking free moral agency, humanity would be in a state of absolute necessity. Neither the choice of good nor that of evil would be within human power, even supposing the help of grace. Liberty is essential to human nature and cannot be lost without the loss of humanity. Yet this ability is insufficient for salvation, for it needs the prevenient and cooperating grace of God in order to respond to grace in conversion and holy living. All humanity remains naturally inclined to evil by an inveterately corrupted nature. "Apart from me you can do nothing" (John 15:5). Grace is offered to all, some of whom cooperate with grace toward redemption. These are predestined to life in the sense that God's elect "have been *chosen according to the foreknowledge [kata prognōsin]* of God the Father, through the sanctifying work of the Spirit, for obedience" (1 Pet. 1:2). Those chosen are those who God foresees will freely accept salvation.

4. The resistibility of grace was reasserted against irresistible grace and the absolute efficacy of effectual calling. All good works are attributed to God's grace alone, yet this grace does not coerce the will to act against one's inclination, but may be resisted and rendered ineffectual by the perversity of one's will. If the Holy Spirit were irresistible, Stephen could not have meaningfully said to his persecutors that they were prone repeatedly to resist the Holy Spirit (Acts 7:51). What moral meaning could preaching or repentance have if salvation had been pretemporally decided? Is not preaching insincere if there is by God's predetermination no possibility of response? It is contrary to divine sincerity to make an offer that cannot under any circumstances be accepted. The calling of God is not irresistible but efficacious, work-

29. Cf. Saxon Visitation Articles, COC 3:189.

ing not by outward constraint but effectively and proportionally in accord with the distinctive makeup of human psychological processes (Phil. 2:12-13).

5. Against the decree of the absolute final perseverance of the believer was reasserted the possibility of backsliding, falling from grace, and apostasy.[30]

These are the five points of Arminian teaching, whose patristic referents largely remain lodged in the pre-Augustinian East and the post-Augustinian conciliar actions.[31]

Over against these points stand the five points of Dort, which represent a reappropriation of a rigorous application of the Augustinian view, which tended to dominate in certain periods in the West:

1. Total depravity: Fallen humanity is incapable of any good, except by the Spirit.
2. Unconditional election by double predestination: God elects a definite number to salvation, justly leaving the others to perdition.
3. Limited atonement: The sacrifice of Christ effects only the salvation of the elect.
4. Irresistible grace: The call certainly, infallibly, and efficaciously elicits regeneration.
5. Perseverance of the saints: The elect may fall into grave sins, but the electing God so preserves them that they never fall entirely out of grace (from these points comes the "TULIP" acronym).[32]

Karl Barth's reevaluation of the doctrine of election amounted to a critique of scholastic Calvinism, and a return to the pre-Augustinian patristic teaching, stressing that God is for us in Jesus Christ, not against us, that God's will is to elect, not reject humanity, which as a whole is chosen in Jesus Christ. Christ is the electing God and the elected human, freely obeying the Father by sharing in the human con-

---

30. Articles of Remonstrance, COC 3:545-49.
31. Much of the Anglican and Methodist traditions followed in this older Greek and pre-Augustinian tradition; cf. Saxon Visitation Articles, COC 3:189; Wesley, "The Scripture Way of Salvation," WJW 6:42; Fletcher, *Works* 1:37ff.
32. Synod of Dort, COC 3:581-97; cf. Westminster Confession, CC 212.

dition, choosing reprobation, perdition, death, and burial, only to be raised from the dead. Universal election does not imply universal salvation. Though all are elect, only some elect their election. Even when humanity rejects God, God does not reject humanity. Hence all human rejections are to be viewed in a penultimate sense.[33]

THE LOST

Those Eternally Separated from God's Holiness

Reprobation refers to the decree of God to be eternally separated from those who are self-determined to refuse the means of grace and remain in sin. Just as in the case of predestination, God's decree is connected primarily with God's eternal foreknowledge of subsequent acts of freedom. Thus, in the case of reprobation, God's decree of separation is an eternally resolved decree toward those who God foreknows will separate themselves from the goodness of God. Reprobation is "God's foreknowledge of the wickedness of some creatures" and the preparation of their separation.[34]

God has neither predestined anyone to evil, nor saved anyone unwillingly.[35] The canons of Arles renounced the view that the free choice of the will was completely destroyed after the fall; that they who perish, perish by the will of God; and that Christ did not incur death for the salvation of all.[36] The awkward idea that God unilaterally predestines specific persons to evil flows against the stream of massive biblical testimony that celebrates the divine attributes of justice and mercy, the primordial will of God to save all humanity, and the sufficiency of grace.

There is in classical ecumenical teaching no absolute pretemporal decree or positive predisposition of God to damn individual persons. There is rather a negative reprobation contingent on and consequent to the exercise of self-determining human freedom, by which God bars

---

33. Barth, *CD* 2.2.145-75.
34. Lombard, *Sent.* 1.40; cf. Calvin, *Inst.* 3.21.5.
35. Council of Quiersy, SCD §§316-21, pp. 126-27.
36. Letter of Renunciation of Lucidus, Council of Arles, SCD §160*a*, p. 65.

recalcitrant sinners from eternal blessedness, excluding them from effective election.[37]

Prosper provided the classical distinction between positive predestination and negative reprobation: "Of their own will they went out; of their own will they fell; and because their fall was foreknown, they were not predestined [to eternal blessedness]. They would, however, be predestined if they were to return and persevere in holiness; hence God's *predestination is for many the cause of perseverance, for none the cause of falling away.*"[38] Augustine summarized: "He who falls, falls by his own will; and he who stands, stands by God's will."[39]

As God foreknew those who would respond in faith, he also foreknew those who would not. Concerning unfaithfulness *(apistia)* these sayings of Jesus were remembered: "Whoever does not believe will be condemned" (Mark 16:16). "Whoever rejects the Son will not see life" (John 3:36). How are the impenitent punished? Simply by being excluded from the inheritance of eternal salvation—"Depart from me" (Matt. 25:41). The final divine rejection of sin is an act of the consequent divine will by which God allows impenitent sinners to be justly brought to nothing.

The Self-condemnation of the Reprobate

The Council of Quiersy spoke of "only one predestination of God, which pertains either to the gift of grace or to the retribution of justice."[40] "Omnipotent God wishes *all men* without exception *to be saved* (1 Tim. 2:4) although not all will be saved. However, that certain ones are saved, is the gift of the one who saves; that certain ones perish, however, is the deserved punishment of those who perish."[41]

God allowed but did not directly cause or preordain the resistance to grace of disbelieving humanity.[42] Since sinners, "through their own

---

37. Gonet, *Clypeus Thomist., De Praedest.,* 2.5.5.2.23, DT (Pohle) 7:216; cf. J. B. Franzelin, *De Deo Uno* (Rome: Soc. de Prop. fide, 1870), 583.
38. Prosper of Aquitaine, *Responses to Objections of Vincent,* MPL 51:155ff., ital. ad.; cf. Fulgentius, *Ad monimum* 1.1, MPL 65:151; Petavius, *Theological Dogmatics* (Barri-Ducis: L. Guerin, 1864–70), 10.7ff.
39. Augustine, *The Gift of Perseverance* 8.19, NPNF 1:5:532.
40. SCD §316, p. 126.
41. Council of Quiersy, SCD §317, p. 126.
42. Council of Valence 3, SCD §321, p. 128.

wicked choice, and their impenitent heart, have become vessels of dishonour, there is, as is just, decreed condemnation, we do confess. But of eternal punishment, of cruelty, of pitilessness, and of inhumanity, we never, never say God is the author, who telleth us that there is joy in heaven over one sinner that repenteth."[43]

The general benevolence of the divine will provides salvation for all, but respects human freedom and its vulnerabilities, and knows that only some will respond in faith. This is not a diminution of human dignity or freedom, but an honoring and sustaining of it. The intent of God to save all does not imply that God absolutely wills to save all whether they want to be saved or not, but that God wills that all may be saved by means appropriate to the nature of human freedom and moral integrity.[44] "When we elect a president, we do not need to hold a second election to determine that the remaining millions shall be non-presidents," remarked Emery Bancroft. "As water naturally runs downhill, so sinners if let alone will go down to ruin. The decree of reprobation is simply a decree to do nothing—a decree to leave the sinner to himself."[45]

Whether Faith Can Be Lost: The Possibility of Final Apostasy

Grace keeps us from falling, but the neglect of the means of grace may result in the loss of good conscience. In Judas we see the prototype of the final apostasy of one who is called but does not follow, willfully resisting grace (John 20:4-6).

Paul, even with assurance of his salvation, grasped the possibility of his own apostasy, and struggled against it, aware that he himself could be "disqualified for the prize" (1 Cor. 9:27). Even the elect who were "firmly established in the truth" (2 Pet. 1:12) were exhorted to "make all the greater efforts to make God's call and choice of you certain" (v. 10, Goodspeed).[46]

Whoever endures or perseveres *(hupomeinas)* "to the end will be saved" (Matt. 10:22). Yet this must not be presumptuously assumed

---

43. Confession of Dositheus 3, CC 488-89.
44. Irenaeus, *Ag. Her.* 4.37.1-3, ANF 1:518-21; *DT* (Schmid), 272.
45. CT 241.
46. Cf. Articles of Remonstrance, COC 3:545-49; Arminius, Letter to Collibus, *Works* 2.689ff.; W. King, A *Discourse on Predestination* (London: J. Murray, 1821); Watson, TI 2:25-27.

as "an absolute certainty, though all ought to place and repose the firmest hope in God's help. For God, unless men themselves fail in his grace, as 'he has begun a good work, so will he perfect it, working to will and to accomplish.'"[47] Those who freely believe and grow in grace will be saved, persevering to the end. God has purposed from eternity to save those he foresaw would persevere in faith active in love.

Those who persevere do not fall from grace. They are those foreknown by God to persevere in faith (1 Pet. 1:1-4; John 10:28). This election is therefore said to be (from the viewpoint of the divine foreknowing) immutable, irrevocable, particular, and eternal (Eph. 1:4; 2 Thess. 2:13; Matt. 20:16; 24:24; Rom. 8:29-30). Although the elect may subjectively experience for a while the loss of indwelling grace (Ps. 51:12; 1 Cor. 10:12), they persevere (Matt. 10:22; Rom. 8:38; Phil. 2:12).

Chrysostom magnificently observed that the treasure of grace "not only is preserved, but also preserves the house where it is stored up." God "placed the treasure [of grace] not in a stone vessel but in an earthen one." The vessel is weak precisely to reveal the power of the treasurer to preserve the vessel. The treasure is "not preserved by the vessel, but itself preserves the vessel."[48]

Against Presumption

The believer ought not to "so far presume as to state with absolute certainty that he is among the number of the predestined, as if it were true that the one justified either cannot sin any more, or if he does sin, that he ought to promise himself an assured repentance. For except by special revelation, it cannot be known whom God has chosen to Himself."[49]

Such matters remain finally impenetrable to empirical analysis. There is no theological duty to attempt to define conceptually what transcends human knowing.[50]

---

47. Trent 6:13, p. 38; cf. Phil. 2:13.
48. John Chrysostom, *Eutropius*, NPNF 1:9:260.
49. Trent 12 (Sixth Session, Justification).
50. Formula of Concord, "Solid Declaration" 11:54, 55, *BOC* 625; cf. *DT* (Schmid) 276; Rom. 11:33-36; Isa. 40:13; 40:28; Job 41:11; 5:9; 15:8; Ps. 92:5; 139:6.

The Westminster Confession cautiously concluded:

> The doctrine of this high mystery of predestination is to be handled with special prudence and care, that men attending the will of God revealed in his Word, and yielding obedience thereunto, may, from the certainty of their effectual vocation, be assured of their eternal election.[51]

> If anybody teaches the doctrine of the gracious election of God to eternal life in such a way that disconsolate Christians can find no comfort in this doctrine but are driven to doubt and despair, or in such a way that the impenitent are strengthened in their self-will, he is not teaching the doctrine according to the Word.[52]

> Let Christ, therefore, be our looking-glass, in whom we may behold our predestination.[53]

---

51. CC 199.
52. Formula of Concord, "Epitome" 11, BOC 497.
53. Second Helvetic Conference, CC 140.

PART FIVE

WHERE THE HISTORY OF GRACE MEETS
THE MYSTERY OF PERSONAL CHOICE

CHAPTER 9

THE COVENANT HISTORY OF GRACE

My personal meeting with the risen Lord and the enlivening Spirit takes place in the context of a far-reaching history, which profoundly illuminates its personal significance. Only as I enter into this extended story of the history of grace am I being formed evangelically.

My individual spiritual formation does not occur apart from this discernible history of grace. To pretend to speak of personal spiritual formation while forgetting the history of the Spirit is to abstract person from context, and thus proceed with an abstract and fleshless understanding of grace.

Grace is known through the history of its disclosure. This is why there is such a close link in Jewish and Christian thinking between grace and history. The coming of grace in time is ordinarily reported in narrative style, not as a deductive sequence of propositions, but as a specific history, a sequence of remembered events.

This is not ordinary history, however, but rather the history of the covenant between God and humanity. This is why the Hebrew Scriptures and New Testament writings play such a crucial role in personal spiritual formation.

The crux of the complex story of saving grace in history can be told in a single paragraph, but only by condensing a long, intricately stitched story:

The descendants of Adam and Eve, having willfully lost the favor of God, live out the brokenness of the divine image, trapped in syndromes of despair, anxiety, pride, and guilt. All would have perished in this condition had not God by grace provided a plan of salvation. Moved by compassion for fallen humanity, God sent his only Son to assume human nature, to do and suffer what was necessary for their salvation. This salvation is promised to all who comply with the terms and conditions of covenant—repentance and a trusting faith that becomes active in love. This call to salvation is addressed to me personally, and through me to all I meet.

This tangled history, viewed at a glance, is a chronicle of the divine-human covenant.

GRACE EXPRESSED AS COVENANT HISTORY

To grasp the narrative as a whole, we do well to inquire directly into its center: the nature of covenant, its representative participants, symbols, rites, ratification, and effects. The notion of covenant (Heb.: *berith*, Gk.: *diathēkē*) is lodged in the heart of the Jewish and Christian teaching of saving grace.

Covenant formed the relational matrix in which the specific events of the history of salvation were played out and understood. The divine-human covenant was thought of not as merely a contractual agreement, but rather more broadly as an *oikonomia*, a divine plan moving through many stages, a "Disposition or Arrangement assumed by the One Supreme purpose of grace."[1]

The Unequal Partners of the Covenant of Grace

The gracious covenant between Yahweh and Israel was between decidedly unequal partners: the transcendent rescuer of those in bondage and the vulnerable needy who before the covenant were no people, the "fewest of all" (Deut. 7:7). The covenant was offered by God to the people, not the reverse. Like creation, Yahweh brought Israel into being out of nothing. The parties of the divine-human covenant are God the Covenant-initiator, and humanity the covenant-respondent.

The whole of humanity is represented by Adam, fallen history by Noah, the elect people by Abraham, the people under divine requirement by Moses, and the forming of the people into a distinct royal tradition and identity in history by David. Each of these leading representative recipients of the covenant has a story, and together their story in time becomes my story, the story of grace taking eventful form.[2]

1. Watson, *TI* 2:94; cf. Eph. 1:10.
2. Calvin, *Inst.* 1.8; 2.1-10; cf. H. R. Niebuhr, *The Meaning of Revelation* (New York: Macmillan, 1960).

The covenant itself is a gift, hence grace. The blessing of the covenant is promised on the simple condition that recipients are willing trustingly and joyfully to receive it. It is for those who hunger and thirst for it. There is no merit in this hunger or willingness. Intended for all, this gift is not finally received until the requisite receptivity is present (Romans 3–4; Hebrews 11).

In ancient Israel a covenant was said to be "cut." Ordinarily sacrificial victims were slain in forming agreements. In a general sense anything agreed on between two parties under such conditions could be called a covenant. Two tribes could covenant for peace. A man and woman could covenant to marry. Business partners could covenant to trade. The victor could covenant with the vanquished to spare them. An affectionate relation between two friends such as David and Jonathan could be manifested by a covenant. Covenant could be made between equals (e.g., Abraham and Abimelech, Gen. 21:32), or unequal parties (God and Israel, Jer. 11:1-17).

Covenant as a Social Transaction, Not Exhausted by Intrapersonal Analysis

Those who enter into the covenant of grace do not enter singly on an individual, detached, or solitary basis, but as communities, families, tribal and national units, where the willing of the community configures the destiny of personal willing.

The covenant was between God and the people as a whole, and through the whole, each member individually. Yahweh met and dealt with individuals, but the covenant promises to Israel were chiefly directed toward the collective community, and through it each individual person.[3] The covenanting people were viewed in scripture as if considered together multigenerationally as a single corporate subject.

This is why in the early history of Israel it could be said that the sins of the fathers could be visited on the children, and that the reward or punishment of the head or member of a family embraced the whole family (Lev. 26:39; Lam. 5:7). The notion of individual free agency and private accountability was a later, postexilic development. Immortality

---

3. Exod. 32:13; cf. H. W. Robinson, *Redemption and Revelation* (New York: Harper and Bros., 1942).

was viewed at first less as individuated or personal, than as God's everlasting promise to Israel as a people (Jeremiah 33; Acts 7).

In speaking of the covenant of marriage between believers and unbelievers, Paul grasped the interwovenness of human destinies in covenant relation: "For the unbelieving husband has been sanctified through his wife, and the unbelieving wife has been sanctified through her believing husband" (1 Cor. 7:14)! Since human beings live in covenant communities, their eternal accountability to God is deeply intermeshed in the choices made by those with whom they exist in covenant.[4] The radically intergenerational and social nature of covenant histories shapes and conditions the history of grace.

The Testament of Grace Is Enacted Through Sacrificial Death

In the dispensation from Adam to Abraham, when human moral knowledge was in its infancy, sacrifices were instituted. Sacrifice was not an arbitrary or meaningless institution. Utilizing available symbols of pastoral life, sacrifice pointed dramatically to the central fact of the divine-human alienation: Guilt in relation to justice requires expiation, which occurs by the shedding of blood (Numbers 7; 1 Sam. 16:1-5; Heb. 9:22). But how could this be an expression of grace?

The classical exegetes argued that animal sacrifice was instituted by the appointment of divine providence, not as a device of human reason or sociological imagination. The connection is remarkable: Adam and Eve were required to make coats of skins to clothe themselves under the harsh conditions that prevailed east of Eden. The animals had to give their very lives in order for humans to be warm, a situation not necessary in Eden. The killing of animals for warmth had a providential purpose, according to the ancient writers: to show human beings the reality of death, and their own mortality as sinners.[5] By their need to keep warm, God was teaching fallen humanity that "man's fate is like that of the animals; the same fate awaits them both: As one dies, so dies the other" (Eccl. 3:19).

In the Hebrew Bible, the forming of covenant was ordinarily accompanied and attested by some sacrifice, where the parts of a sacrificial

---

4. Luther, Comm. on 1 Corinthians, LW 28:34-36.
5. Ambrose, *Isaac*, FC 65:10-12; cf. pp. 416-17; Basil, *Hexaemeron*, NPNF 2:8:95ff.; WL 352ff.

animal were divided, the flames (implying God's own holy, purifying, fiery presence) passed through the sacrificial animal, and the parties to the transaction thereby ratified the covenant. The Paschal lamb served as a continuing annual recollection of the enduring covenant between Yahweh and Israel (Exod. 12:27).

The language of covenant was borrowed from legal, diplomatic, and domestic metaphors, each of which was destined to become basically transformed in the light of the coming incarnate Son. As early as Gideon it was anticipatively revealed that "all the sacrifices of the Gentiles are to be abolished, and only the sacrifice of the Lord's passion is to be offered to God."[6]

The New Testament covenant of grace was in time finally to be ratified on the cross by the sacrifice of "the Lamb that was slain from the creation of the world" (Rev. 13:8). "Christ is the mediator of a new covenant," according to Hebrews, "now that he has died as a ransom to set them free from the sins committed under the first covenant" (Heb. 9:15). He thus became the pledge and surety to humanity of the blessing of God received through his atoning death, and the pledge to God on behalf of humanity in compliance with all the conditions of the covenant. "Because of this oath, Jesus has become the guarantee of a better covenant" (Heb. 7:22).

This covenant is a new testament, bearing the essential marks of legal testamentary disposition.[7] This *berith* (Gk.: *diathēkē*, Lat.: *foedus*, pact, covenant, testament) indicates a binding promise made by God and fulfilled through Christ. Where the execution of a testament or will occurs, there must be a death. The death of the testator precedes the transfer of ownership. To a ratified testament one cannot make incidental additions. Once made it stands as a completed, authenticated will. All requirements of a testament are found in the divine-human covenant: a testator (the eternal Son), the ratification of the testament by the death of the testator (the cross), and the heirs of the testament (the faithful; Heb. 8:6; 9:16-17).[8]

---

6. Ambrose, *The Holy Spirit*, FC 44:37.
7. Heppe, RD 374.
8. Wollebius, CTC 21, RDB 117ff.; cf. Witsius, OFD 2:2:5; Braun, DF 1.3.4, 4, in Heppe, RD 374.

COVENANT TIME

The scripture texts imply a working distinction between the *pretemporal* covenant relationship between the Father and Son, and the covenant of grace *in time* between God and the people.[9]

The Pretemporal Covenant of Grace Between the Father and the Son

In the pretemporal covenant of redemption, the Father sends, the Son is sent. This is the plan that was hidden for ages (Eph. 3:9) but revealed in these last days: Christ came into the world to execute a pardoning, rescuing action foreseen from eternity (Eph. 1:3-14).

The terms of the pretemporal Father-Son covenant are as follows: The Father gave the Son a work to do, sending him into the world to assume human nature so as to perform the work, and promised his incomparable blessing to humanity when the work was complete. All elements of covenant are therefore pretemporally in place: responsible parties, a condition, a promise, an agreement. An obligation was undertaken by the Father (enabling the mission and offering the gift), and by the Son (assuming human nature, suffering and dying for the redemption of humanity, Col. 1:15-20; Philippians 2).

Only the Incarnate One could be a party both to the pretemporal purposing of God (since the Son was "with God and was God"), and to the covenant with all humanity (since he was a man and obedient to law), and a mediator of that same covenant between God and fallen humanity. Christ, being human and a descendant of Adam, Abraham, and David, is a member of the covenanting human community—all humanity, and representatively, Israel—without ceasing to be at the same time the mediator and fulfiller of the covenant.[10]

Jesus understood that the Father had "sent me into the world" (John 17:18). It is this work that Jesus completed in time through his suffering and death, praying: "I have brought you glory on earth by completing the work you gave me to do" (John 17:4). Paul similarly wrote: "But when the time had fully come, God sent his Son, born of a woman, born under law, to redeem those under law, that we might receive the full rights of sons" (Gal. 4:4-5). "This is how God showed his love

---

9. Irenaeus, *Ag. Her.* 4.9.3ff., ANF 1:472-73.
10. John of Damascus, *OF* 3.19, NPNF 2:9:68; cf. *WL* 344ff.

among us: He sent his one and only Son into the world that we might live through him" (1 John 4:9).

The promise of the Father was to secure this filial work by offering the Spirit without measure, that the Son's humanity would be constantly and sufficiently replenished by grace, even so as to deliver him from the power of death and return him to the Father's side among the heavenly hosts, that all things in heaven and earth should ultimately become united in him. The Father would then send the Spirit to whomever the Son willed, those who were "his own" by faith, that all the faithful would be drawn to the Father, that this kingdom of grace would embrace and bless all nations, and be made known to all sapient and spiritual intelligence throughout time and eternity (John 14–17; Romans 5–7).

The Personal Engagement in Time of the Covenanting God

What the Father and Son determined in eternity was manifested in time in the covenant of grace. Christ became the mediator *(mesitēs)* and surety or pledge of the covenant. Through his life, death, and resurrection, God ratified the new covenant with fallen humanity (1 Tim. 2:5; Gal. 3:19-20).

The pretemporal covenant required an actual life lived in time, becoming bone of our bone and flesh of our flesh, being made like us in every way except without sin. He voluntarily fulfilled all righteousness, living under the law without spot or blemish, bore our sins, became a curse for us, and offered himself as a sacrifice for the sins of the world. This is the atoning, reconciling work of Christ.[11]

Although the divine plan to redeem was fully conceived and formulated in the eternal pretemporal counsel of the triune God prior to creation, its recognition and reception within the conditions of human history was gradual in occurring, through a specific history of the covenant relationship, sometimes called dispensations or covenant economies or providences (Calvin, *Inst.* 2.6-11). The history of salvation embraces and recounts a series of dispensations of the covenant of grace *(administratio foederis gratiae)*, variously called the Noachian, Patriarchal (or Abrahamic), Mosaic (or Sinaitic), and Christian dispensations or economies or ways of ordering the divine-human relationship.

---

11. Luther, SML 6:224ff.

Irenaeus spoke of a threefold dispensation of the covenant of grace: the primitive period of divine human covenant from Adam to Moses, in which the law was written on the heart; the Mosaic covenant, in which the law was codified in external commandments, during the time from Moses to Christ; and the new covenant in Christ, in which the law was again written on the heart by the renewing power of God the Spirit. Reformed theologians similarly spoke of three dispensations: prior to law, under law, and fulfilling the law (*ante legem, sub lege, post legem*).[12]

The sequence of time of the covenant before Christ is sometimes conceived in three periods: Adam and Eve through Noah to Abraham and Sarah (for all humanity, based on the protoevangelium of Genesis 3:15), Abraham and Sarah to Moses (for all humanity through the seed of Abraham, based on Genesis 15 and symbolized by circumcision), and Moses to Christ (for the set-apart people of the law, based on Exodus 20, narrowing finally to a remnant). The one divine-human covenant takes these several forms through its long course of unfolding history.[13]

The Unity of Diverse Covenants

There are not multiple, separable divine-human covenants that differ in substance, but essentially only one covenant of grace administered through varying times, places, economies, circumstances, symbol systems, and dispensations. Though the covenant is one, dispensations of the covenant are many, spanning more than forty centuries. Each discrete moment points finally to its fulfillment in the One who is "the same yesterday and today and forever" (Heb. 13:8).

In all forms of divine-human covenant, salvation is promised and faithful obedience required. The essential terms of covenant remain the same under varying historical circumstances before and after the incarnation. In both testaments God promises blessing and remission of sins to those who repent and believe.[14]

Irenaeus applied this analogy: The work of God is like an athletic contest which requires that one meet various contingencies. Though

---

12. Cocceius, *SDF* 10:278ff.; cf. Leonardus Riisen, *Francisci Turretini compendium theologiae* (Amsterdam: n.p., 1695), 10:17; Irenaeus, *Ag. Her.* 4.9-16.
13. Calvin, *Inst.* 4.15, 4.16; cf. Wollebius, *CTC* 21, RDB 117-20; Heppe, RD 395.
14. Zecharius Ursinus, *Commentary on the Heidelberg Catechism* (Cincinnati: T. P. Bucher, 1851), 97-100; cf. Heppe, RD 392.

the wrestler remains a single person, his strategies vary over an extended contest, in God's case an ages-long contest.[15] These varying conditions of many centuries have required varying expressions of the one divine-human covenant.

The Time of Expectation and the Time of Fulfillment

Time, under the conditions of covenant, is divided into the time before and the time after God's own coming. This is why all participants in the covenant may be classified in these categories: those who live in expectation of the coming Christ, and those who live already in union with Christ by faith. These are distinguished from those who do not expect the Christ.[16] Attitudes toward history may thus be grossly differentiated into two views: those who do not expect a salvation event, and those who do.[17] Among those who have lived out of expectation of a messianic event, some view it as yet to come, others as already having come.

This distinction is implied in the division of scripture into the former and later testaments. The premise is that the one divine-human covenant was differently administered before and after Christ. As the covenant of works was formed with Adam, so was the covenant of grace formed with Christ (Rom. 5:12-21; 1 Cor. 15:21-22, 47-49).[18] The notion of an *old diathēkē* (testament, covenant, 2 Cor. 3:14) refers to documents witnessing the entire expectation that preceded Christ (from creation to incarnation). It is called "old" not because it has become outmoded, but because it has been gloriously completed and fulfilled by that which is incomparably "new"—Jesus Christ, the personal fulfillment of God's plan of redemption.[19] Any talk of old and new must avoid the naïve view that the covenant with Israel has been abandoned, which would tend to slope toward anti-Semitism.

The Christ to come was foreshadowed constantly throughout the history of Israel in its laws, ceremonies, sacrifices, prophets, and historical expectations.[20] Both old and new covenant "have had, and

---

15. Irenaeus, *Ag. Her.* 4.16.3, ANF 1:481; 4.36.2, ANF 1:515.
16. Cocceius, *SDF* 10.277.
17. Reinhold Niebuhr, *NDM* 2.1ff.
18. Augustine, *CG* 13.23, FC 14:336ff.
19. Irenaeus, *Ag. Her.* 4.9-10, ANF 1:472-73.
20. Council of Florence, *SCD* §695, p. 220.

still have, one fellowship, one salvation, in one and the same Messiah; in whom, as members of one body, they are all joined together under one head, and by one faith are all partakers of one and the same spiritual meat and drink. Yet here we do acknowledge a diversity of times, and a diversity in the pledges and signs of Christ promised and exhibited."[21]

Only the cross could have made the covenant of law understandable as "old" (Heb. 8:13). Yet the one divine-human covenant has remained substantially the same over all its periods of mutation: God promises grace to sinners, calling for radical responsiveness.[22] Testaments new and old sound the same chords: There is one God (1 Tim. 2:5-6), who offers salvation out of mercy first by law, and then by personally coming to fulfill the law (Jer. 31:31-34; Matt. 5:17; Rom. 13:8-10; Heb. 8:13).

The Levitical law was the requirement of the one God in its own time and dispensation (Rom. 7:12),[23] offering not only fear of God but also grace.[24] After God's own coming, the precepts of the law became the basis for understanding how deeply humanity is enmeshed in sin. Christ himself is the fulfillment of the law, the end of the law understood as condemnation, so that the observance of the renewed law continues to belong to the covenant people.[25]

The Spirit as promised in the old covenant is in the new covenant poured out upon all flesh (Joel 2:28-29; Acts 2:17). What the prophets longed to see has appeared (Luke 10:21-24; 1 Pet. 1:10-11). With the Son through the Spirit, the law becomes written on our hearts as promised (Jer. 31:33-34; Romans 8). Those who were "separate from Christ, excluded from citizenship in Israel and foreigners to the covenants of the promise, without hope and without God in the world" have "now in Christ Jesus" been "brought near through the blood of Christ" (Eph. 2:12-13).

> Come, ye faithful, raise the strain
> Of triumphant gladness;
> God hath brought his Israel

---

21. Second Helvetic Conference, CC 142.
22. Clement of Alexandria, *Stromata* 4.16, ANF 2:428.
23. Council of Toledo, SCD §28, p. 13.
24. Leo 9, SCD §345, p. 141.
25. Trent 6, SCD §§804, 828-37, pp. 253ff.; cf. SCD §§712, 1356-57, 1519-20.

> Into joy from sadness;
> Loosed from Pharaoh's bitter yoke
> Jacob's sons and daughters;
> Led them with unmoistened foot
> Through the Red Sea waters.
> 'Tis the spring of souls to-day;
> Christ hath burst his prison,
> And from three days' sleep in death
> As a sun hath risen;
> All the winter of our sins,
> Long and dark, is flying
> From his light, to whom we give
> Laud and praise undying.[26]

The covenant is not removable by human neglect, caprice, or negation. It is established by divine promise as an eternal covenant (Heb. 13:20; Hos. 11:1-11) whose peace shall not be removed (Jer. 33:20-25). "Just as no one can set aside or add to a human covenant that has been duly established, so it is in this case. The promises were spoken to Abraham and to his seed" (Gal. 3:15-16). It is promised that the seed would continue; hence, it was expected that Abraham, Isaac, Jacob, David (anticipatory types of faithful respondents) would have an enduring inheritance, however unlikely that at times might have seemed.

> The tide of time shall never
> His covenant remove;
> His Name shall stand for ever,
> His changeless Name of Love.[27]

26. John of Damascus, "Come, Ye Faithful," hymn, trans. John Mason Neale, HPEC 157.
27. James Montgomery, "Hail to the Lord's Anointed," 1821, HPEC 90.

CHAPTER 10

THE FULLNESS OF GRACE RECEIVED

We are being formed spiritually as persons by One who has met us personally in history. Those who are formed by the Spirit in the mind of Christ find themselves entering into this extended story as if the history of grace were becoming their own history.

The thesis that completes this study is that the deeper relevance of grace for spiritual formation is understandable only by viewing one's own personal story of grace in light of the cosmic-eschatological history of grace.

THE SEED OF WOMAN: REDEMPTION PREFIGURED

Salvation was to come through human seed. God's way of rescuing humanity would come through one fully human. It was revealed gradually that the promised seed would be the seed of woman, the mother of all living, through the seed of Abraham as prototype of the faithful, and descendant from the royal seed of David (Gen. 13:15-16; Ps. 18:50; 22:23; 48).

The Protoevangelium

The divine purpose to redeem humanity was uniquely declared immediately after the fall, according to the classical exegesis of Genesis. This came in the cryptic form of a promise that one to come from the seed of woman would cause the power of evil to be bound. This passage, often called "protoevangelium" or "earliest gospel," is an anticipatory form of the coming Good News of redemption. The essence of this promise is hidden in the Lord's address to the serpent after the fall: "I will put enmity / between you and the woman, / and between your offspring and hers; / he will crush your head, / and you will strike his heel" (Gen. 3:15).

The serpent stood as a metaphor for the tempter, the superintelligent deceiver, the enemy, upon whom the curse was surely to fall at some later unspecified date. Crushing the serpent's head meant a fatal injury.[1] The offspring of the serpent are the co-conspirators of Satan (John 8:44; Eph. 2:2). The offspring of Eve are all humanity. A redeemer from among the woman's seed would deal a death blow to Satan's head at the cross. Satan would cause the redeemer to suffer (strike his heel).[2]

The one by whom the redeemer would come would be female (from the seed of Eve); the redeemer promised who would crush the demonic power would be male ("he will crush," as a "man born of woman"). In this way the gender complementarity of the salvation event was anticipated from the outset: God through a man born of woman turning toward the sinner in mercy to reverse the human condition from sin to promised salvation by grace (Gal. 4:4).

This gender complementarity is coupled with an image that would play a decisive role throughout the history of salvation: *seed*. The seed of woman is the means of promised salvation. Later the seed of Abraham and the seed of David would serve as metaphors of the promise of the ultimate overthrow of the arch-deceiver (Rom. 1:3; 4:13-18).[3]

The Typological Irony

Ponder this typological irony: The tempter of humanity who had beguiled our first parents would at some time be fully cast down. This overcoming would occur precisely through the offspring of the woman who had just been tempted and had fallen with her creation partner, Adam. This is the first biblical prediction of a coming salvation by One who would guilelessly undo what the tempter of human freedom guilefully had done, One who by pure goodness would bind up the strong man. The seeds of salvation history are thus already sown in the early chapters of Genesis.[4]

---

1. John Chrysostom, *Hom. on Gen.* 17, FC 74:238-46.
2. Calvin, *Comm.* 1:170-71.
3. Luther, Lectures on Genesis 3.15, WLS 3:121; cf. WA 42:146.
4. Calvin, *Comm.* 1:167-71; cf. Pius 10, SCD §2123, pp. 545-46.

"It was while Eve was yet a virgin that the ensnaring word had crept into her ear which was to build the edifice of death. Into a virgin's soul, in like manner, must be introduced that Word of God which was to raise the fabric of life; so that what had been reduced to ruin by this sex, might by the selfsame sex be recovered to salvation."[5] Ambrose reasoned that it was fitting that a woman be appointed as first messenger of the gospel to all humanity, in order "that she who first had brought the message of sin to man should first bring the message of the grace of the Lord."[6]

The protoevangelium promised *that*, not *when*, this overcoming would occur. The binding of the strong man (Mark 3:27) would not occur without a struggle, or without blood or suffering. There would be a lengthy enmity in history between humanity and the tempter. Humanity would be bruised. Yet by this means the head of the enemy would be crushed (Gen. 3:15).

Human Unity in Eve: Mother of All Living

The seed of this woman would be the Savior, and all human history would come from her and be unified in her. Hence she was called Eve (life-giving) "because she would become the mother of all the living" (Gen. 3:20).

A brief interlude is called for in this narrative: There has recently emerged astonishing scientific support for the inchoate biblical intuition that all of the human family is indeed one, and shares a literal lineage from a single mother or very small group of mothers. Geneticists have discovered that there are genetic markers that plot migration routes of millennia past. There is high probability that the gene migration is consistent with what is known of the fossil record, namely, that Africa is the ancestral home of all *homo erectus* genes. This research has hinged on the identification and tracking of a mitochondrial DNA gene that is passed on to women only—it does not exist in the male. Genetic researchers have taken these genes, sliced them in segments, and examined them with auto-radiography. In every case the mother has a gene fragment that the father does not have. Each mitochondrial gene of a succeeding generation has

---

5. Tertullian, *On the Flesh of Christ* 17, ANF 3:536.
6. Ambrose, *Of the Holy Spirit* 3.11.7, NPNF 2:10:145.

more variations than that of the preceding generation. A correlated approach studied placentas of women of different races, looking for those with the greatest number of mutations, hence the oldest threads (those most mutated). Researchers found that the Kung people of the African Kalahari had the greatest number of mutations, and thus, according to this hypothesis, theirs would be the oldest known strand of genes. Further, these genetic researchers have discovered that there are three branches of gene pools that have distinct similarities. But there is also remarkable evidence that these three sets of gene pools were all linked together in a single pool about 200,000 years ago. Hence all mitochondrial genes came from one source.

Researchers have hypothesized on the grounds of this evidence that there was a literal, and not merely mythical or symbolic, Eve of Africa who was the source of the human gene pool, and that all human beings are descended from her. But was there a sole founder of the human race? Some geneticists argue that there were perhaps at most a few thousand women from whom this original human gene pool could have come, rather than a single woman; in any case there would not have been more. Either hypothesis (of a single woman or a small number in a distinct location) has profound implications for our understanding of human history.

Accordingly, all human beings of all times are a part of a single human family with a single female lineage to a single woman or a very small group of women. Each one of us therefore carries a powerful message in our genes from our human past. If this is so, the entire history of humanity, and thus the history of grace, is a single, biologically unified story. This message seems to be consonant with the biblical understanding that God has made of one family all the nations of the world (Acts 17:26), and that one woman is the mother of all living, all of whom were to be embraced by the grace of which scripture seeks to give an account.

God had placed the first parents, whom Hebrew scripture named Adam and Eve, in a completely sufficient environment for their unfettered happiness, warning them that if they disobeyed they would die. Amid this abundance they were clearly warned not to eat of the fruit of the tree of knowledge of good and evil. Tempted to be like gods, they ate the forbidden fruit, died spiritually, and the consequences of their disobedience affected all their posterity (Gen. 3:1-24).[7] They immediately experienced guilt and alienation in relation to God, became vain in their imaginations, ashamed, anxious, and were expelled from the garden paradise, yet with the promise of a future overcoming of the enmity between God and humanity (Gen. 3:14-19).[8]

Subsequent humanity became ever more deeply impaired through the free exercise of fallen freedom. The end of the entire human experiment might have been deemed justifiable. Yahweh, however, permitted the fall of Adam and Eve to become not the end of humanity but the basis of a greater revelation of divine grace that would reveal to humanity God's more excellent mercy and justice. The violation of the original covenant requirement became the occasion for the revelation of the new covenant of grace (Romans 5).[9]

The initial, cryptic promise of salvation to our first parents was repeatedly renewed and amplified, in each phase looking more intently toward God's own coming in the flesh. Numerous anticipations of the coming deliverance were offered by God, to provide human history with a plausible basis for hope in God's own coming.[10]

THE GENERAL PREPARATION OF HUMAN HISTORY FOR THE INCARNATION OF GRACE

Whether God Might Have More Wisely Allowed a Shorter Interval Between Adam and Christ

But why was the coming of grace Incarnate delayed so long? Gregory of Nyssa reasoned that God waited until "wickedness had reached its utmost height, and there was no form of wickedness which men had not dared to do, to the end that the healing remedy might pervade the whole of the diseased system."[11] God let human freedom go its own way until it descended to its own self-chosen nadir to show that God desires

---

7. Wesley, Treatise on Original Sin, WJW 9:191ff.
8. Cf. Kierkegaard, *The Concept of Anxiety* (Princeton: Princeton University Press, 1980).
9. Wesley, "God's Love to Fallen Man," WJWB 2:422-35; cf. WJW 6:231-41.
10. Wollebius, CTC 21, RDB 117-20.
11. *Great Catech.* 29, NPNF 2:5:498.

not to coerce humans into a reconciled relation, but rather to draw them there by their free choice.

The salvation event occurred "many centuries after the original sin was committed" in order that a fitting "time should elapse to make possible the reception of a holy mystery. On the one hand, man should be left for some time without a Saviour, that, under ever increasing hardships, he should realize the greatness of his disease, and himself call in the aid of the Physician. And on the other hand, Israel needed previously to be shaped and educated."[12]

Thomas Aquinas explained the extended interval this way: God first left man in the freedom of his will under the natural law so that he might come to know the strength of his own nature. "Then, when he had failed, he received the law. On the law being given, the disease gathered strength by the fault, not of the law, but of man's nature, so that when his own weakness was thus made known, he might cry out for the Physician, and seek the help of grace."[13]

In order for salvation rightly to unfold in a way suitable to the human condition, it was necessary that God prepare human history for the reception of a saving event consistent with human freedom and moral accountability, as well as divine justice and compassion. A lesser or simpler or non-historical salvation would have been far less costly and time-consuming. But God would not stoop to bullying the very human freedom created at such cost.[14]

Such a salvation would have to be capable of transforming precisely the free human behavior shaped by the history of human social interchange. It would be set in motion gradually through a process of divine disclosure. Hence in history we find the gradual revelation of a plan of redemption that was not fully clarified until the fullness of time (Gal. 4:4), when the promised man born of woman appeared, eternal Son of the eternal Father.

Irenaeus contrasted Adam's temptation and Christ's overcoming— the tree by which disobedience came and the tree of the cross of obedience.[15] This plan is even now still moving toward its comprehensive

---

12. *A Holy Catechism* 31 (London: Patriarchal Press, 1861), p. 26.
13. *ST* 3.Q1.5, 3:2030-31; cf. *Sermons of St. Leo on the Incarnation*, NPNF 2:12:144, 145; Stone, *OCD* 54.
14. Origen, *OFP* 2.9, ANF 4:291-92.
15. Irenaeus, *Proof of the Apostolic Preaching*, ACW 16:69-70.

application in history. Meanwhile humanity was gradually being prepared for this saving event through the complex pedagogy of law, promise, covenant accountability, exile, suffering, sacrifice, priesthood, and ritual. This could only happen through an extended history of covenant dispensations.[16]

The Covenant with Noah and the Promise of Restraining Grace

"The Lord saw how great man's wickedness on the earth had become, and that every inclination of the thoughts of his heart was only evil all the time. The Lord was grieved that he had made man on the earth, and his heart was filled with pain. So the Lord said, 'I will wipe mankind, whom I have created, from the face of the earth'" (Gen. 6:5-7). The flood is not merely a story of destruction, but of salvation and new beginnings, where through a single family of faith the whole of covenant history was given a gracious, fresh start (Genesis 6–9).

After the household of Noah had been saved, he built an altar and sacrificed burnt offerings of cleansed animals (Gen. 8:20). "The Lord smelled the pleasing aroma and said in his heart: 'Never again will I curse the ground because of man, even though every inclination of his heart is evil from childhood. And never again will I destroy all living creatures'" (Gen. 8:21; cf. Eph. 5:2 for a corresponding New Testament metaphor). The promise was that God would never again destroy the earth, but would protect his covenant people until the history of grace would be appropriately accomplished (Gen. 9:13-16). The form of Noah's worship was vicarious sacrifice in which ritually clean animals were offered. This sacrifice had a vicarious character—one life given for another. The classical exegetes could not help seeing in this narrative an anticipatory intimation of the coming sacrifice of God the Son.[17]

In the covenant with Noah, all living things surviving the flood were embraced by this renewed divine-human covenant "established between me and all life on the earth" (Gen. 9:17). The condition of covenant was that Noah and his descendants should abstain from blood and regard human life as sacred. Human government was insti-

---

16. Gregory of Nyssa, *The Life of Moses*, CWS 89ff.
17. Aphrahat, *Select Demonstrations* 6.3, NPNF 2:13:365-66; cf. Augustine, CG 16.24, NPNF 1:2:323-24.

tuted. Sin was to be restrained by legitimated civil power (Rom. 13:1-3; Titus 3:1).

In the gracious rainbow covenant, God promised that the regular succession of seed time and harvest, the natural rhythms of night and day, winter and summer, would reliably continue. The natural order would be sustained so that it could be studied and received as an intelligible order. It is a covenant that displays the grace commonly given to all humanity. Yet no sooner had this covenant been established than the people of Babel were found building an idolatrous tower. Again judgment was visited on humanity, human history became scattered, and language confused.[18]

The Light Coming into the World

The common preparatory grace of God continued to work within the whole of human history. All were being gradually prepared for a single incomparable saving event. "God did this so that men would seek him and perhaps reach out for him and find him, though he is not far from each one of us" (Acts 17:27).[19]

Throughout human history generally, "The true light, which enlightens everyone, was coming into the world" (John 1:9 NRSV). The light referred to is Jesus Christ. This light was faintly shining not in some but in all humanity *(panta anthrōpon)*.[20] Metaphorically, the light was for centuries "coming into the world." It is a light that illumined all humanity in a dim, anticipative way during all the laborious centuries in which the light was slowly dawning.[21] Hence the Second Helvetic Confession could assume "that those who were before the law and under the law, were not altogether destitute of the Gospel."[22]

In this universal history, divine grace remained hiddenly present in conscience, which the Bible viewed as universally present wherever human consciousness exists, for it is consciousness judging itself (Rom. 2:12-16). But at some point this striving must end, because of the finitude of human life and history. "My Spirit will not contend with man forever, for he is mortal" (Gen. 6:3).

18. Theophilus, *Letter to Autolycus* 2.31-32, ANF 2:106-7.
19. Calvin, *Comm.* 19.163-70.
20. Augustine, *Letters*, FC 18:153-56.
21. Augustine, *Hom. on John*, Tr. 2, FC 78:66-74.
22. Second Helvetic Confession, COC 3:259; cf. Formula of Concord 12, BOC 498-501.

Grace Amid the Corruptibility of the History of Religions

While it may be argued that any religion is better than none, since *religio* by definition engenders awe and moral duty, it is even more true that all religion is subject to the corruption of self-assertiveness and sin. The general history of religion remembered in the Bible is largely a history of idolatry, of adoring perceived goods more than the source of the greatest good, of corrupted awareness of the holy, and of legal striving after self-justification (Mic. 1:7; 1 Cor. 8:1-10). Some forms of godliness were never obliterated among the children of Eve, yet no phase of human history remained uncorrupted. Conscience was in principle adequate to point to knowledge of God, but in historical fact it proved to be limited and corruptible.

Meanwhile God was preparing a special people to be "entrusted with the very words of God" (Rom. 3:2), set apart from all others. Through their own special history as a covenant people, they learned of the coming salvation, of their own moral inadequacy, and of God's majesty and mercy. Through the seed of Abraham, all nations were to be blessed (Gen. 22:18).

DISPENSATIONS OF COVENANT GRACE FROM ABRAHAM TO CHRIST

With Abraham the focus of covenant history shifted from the general mass of humanity to a special people. Abraham was called to leave his country and follow the call of Yahweh into a new land. Abraham obeyed, and God covenanted with him, promising him a fruitful land and a blessed posterity.

Two complementary promises characterized the covenant with Abraham: earthly land and spiritual seed (Gen. 12:3, 7; 13:14-17; 15:5-18; 18:18; 22:17, 18). The people of God were to receive the promised land, and through their seed the Messiah would come. Similar promises were given to Isaac (Gen. 26:2-5), Jacob (Gen. 28:3, 4, 14; cf. Gen. 35:1-12), and their progeny.[23]

---

23. Cyril of Alexandria, Letters 55, FC 77:15ff.

Abraham: The Prototype of Faith Expecting Grace

The gracious divine-human covenant, which offered righteousness and eternal life, required faith and obedience. Abraham radically trusted God even when commanded to sacrifice his beloved son and sole heir, Isaac, the very one through whom the promise was to be mediated.[24] Classical Christian exegetes viewed that event as a prototype not only of radical faith, but also of the figurative offering up by God the Father of his only Son (Heb. 11:17).[25] Abraham's reply to Isaac was viewed in the light of the history of Jesus: "God himself will provide the lamb for the burnt offering, my son."[26] Isaac prefigured Christ by carrying "the wood of his sacrifice, just as the Lord bore the wood of the Cross."[27]

Abraham became the prototype of radical trust in God, believing indeed against contrary evidence, even when the fulfillment of the divine promise seemed absurd.[28] Abraham thus has become "the father of all who believe but have not been circumcised, in order that righteousness might be credited to them" (Rom. 4:11).[29] Paul viewed Abraham as the father of all who live by faith. "Those who believe are children of Abraham. The Scripture foresaw that God would justify the Gentiles by faith, and announced *the gospel in advance* to Abraham" (Gal. 3:7-8, ital. ad.).[30]

With Abraham a covenant people was first elected, then gradually, through a laborious history, called to covenant accountability. "You only have I chosen / of all the families of the earth" to be "brought up out of Egypt" (Amos 3:2, 1). "When Israel was a child, I loved him, / and out of Egypt I called my son. / But the more I called Israel, / the further they went from me" (Hos. 11:1-2).

From the protoevangelium to Mount Moriah, it was becoming gradually evident that the disaster of Eden would be reversed. The

---

24. Clement of Rome, *First Epistle to the Corinthians* 10, ANF 1:7; cf. Ambrose, *On Belief in the Resurrection*, NPNF 2:10:190.
25. Irenaeus, *Ag. Her.* 4.25, ANF 1:495-96; cf. John Chrysostom, *Hom. on Hebrews* 25, NPNF 1:14:477-81.
26. Gen. 22:8; cf. Ambrose, *Isaac, or the Soul*, FC 65:10-14; cf. Kierkegaard, *F&T*.
27. Clement of Alexandria, *Christ the Educator* 1.5, FC 23:23.
28. Cf. Kierkegaard, *F&T*.
29. Tho. Aq., *ST* 1-2.Q98.4.1, p. 1028.
30. Irenaeus, *Ag. Her.* 4.5, 6, ANF 1:467-69.

reversal would come through the descendants of Abraham, who would multiply as the stars of heaven and bear fruit for the whole world. Abraham typified all who were "looking forward to the city with foundations, whose architect and builder is God" (Heb. 11:10). The temporal blessing promised was not an end in itself, but a means and a type of a coming spiritual blessing to humanity that would appear in God's own coming.

The sign of entry into the Abrahamitic covenant was circumcision, symbolizing the putting off of the flesh or limitation of the natural life of self-assertiveness in order to enter into a new life in the Spirit. The whole world would be blessed through this chosen seed, which would become purified from its fleshly nature and readied to be heir of the promise. Having been justified by faith, Abraham "received the sign of circumcision, a seal of the righteousness that he had by faith while he was still uncircumcised" (Rom. 4:11). The male foreskin was to be excised eight days after birth as a penitential indication that our human condition had become corrupted through the abuse of freedom, and that this covenant community was being separated from the world. This sign acknowledged that we humans are incorrigibly egocentric, as especially seen in male sexuality, and stand in radical need of new birth by God's own Spirit (Gen. 17:11-23; Deut. 10:16; 30:6; Col. 2:11).[31]

Circumcision was the expression and evidence of that grace by which God elects, marks, and sets aside a people for his own. It was a metaphor for sanctification. Those who have uncircumcised ears do not listen to the divine address (Jer. 6:10), and those who have uncircumcised hearts have not been inwardly changed by grace to radical consecration of all their worldly powers (Lev. 26:41; Ezek. 44:7, 9; Deut. 10:16; 30:6; Rom. 2:28-29).

Reading the Covenant Promise from the Vantage Point of Its Fulfillment

Since grace has a history, historical recollection and interpretation are intrinsic to the community of faith. A hermeneutic interlude is here required. A determinative element of New Testament writings is the pervasive assumption that the Old Testament promises are being

---

31. Amandus Polanus, *Syntagma Theologiae Christianae* (Hanover: C. Marnium and J. Aubri, 1610).

reliably fulfilled in the history of Jesus and the new Israel.[32] Classical Christian writers consistently followed this pattern, viewing the Messiah as being constantly present already in the address of the Word of Yahweh to the patriarchs, Moses, prophets, and psalmists.[33]

Early Christians thought it quite appropriate to search the scriptures and behold in Genesis or Jeremiah the anticipated coming of the triune God active in the history of Israel in a way that pointed beyond the events reported in these texts to a salvation event yet to occur. It is understandable that this assumption may appear objectionable to those who assume that the psalms and Isaiah must be read *exclusively* in relation to their historical surroundings, and not extrapolated to a later time. Yet such an exclusion is prone to misunderstand the New Testament, failing to recognize the anticipations of the fulfillment of God's purposes in history, and how thoroughly Hebraic prophecies were in fact fulfilled in Jesus.[34]

The church understood the New Testament to constitute a completed canon, fulfilling what was promised in the Hebrew Bible. Nothing further was needed in addition to the apostolic testimony to God's own coming.[35] All subsequent disclosures of the divine will and discernments of the Spirit would thereafter be best grasped in the light of the coming of the Son.

Dispensations of Covenant Grace from Moses to Christ

Reviewing the thread of covenant dispensations leading to Moses, we can see that: the command to rest on *shabbath* was given with the creation of time; Noah's rainbow symbolized a covenant with the whole of surviving humanity, intensely aware of the value of human life; Abraham's promise was of a covenant of grace focused on a particular people, to be given a land, and whose seed would bless the world. In the Mosaic dispensation of salvation history, from Moses to Christ, all that had been gained in previous periods was preserved, enhanced, and deepened by means of a legal-sacrificial system that embraced the full range of the political, economic, priestly, and domestic realms. The

---

32. Niceta of Remesiana, Explanation of the Creed, FC 7:48.
33. Augustine, *Trin.* 14, FC 45:411-49.
34. Irenaeus, *Ag. Her.* 4, ANF 1:462ff.
35. Synod of Laodicea, 59, NPNF 2:14:158-59.

Torah set forth a detailed structure for priesthood and sacrifice antici-pative of God's own coming.[36]

The *parties* of the Mosaic form of covenant were Yahweh and the people of Israel. The *promise* was that the people would be blessed and protected to enable their historic mission to be fulfilled. The *condition* of the covenant was obedience to law, epitomized by the decalogue given at Sinai (Deut. 5:2-3; Isa. 59:20-21; Jer. 31:33). A land was pre-pared, an exodus provided, a people freed from bondage, so that they could participate in God's overarching redemptive purpose.[37]

Through the Aaronic priestly and sacrificial system of Mosaic law, Israel grasped anticipatively the central principle of God's redemptive activity, that redemption occurs through sacrifice (Exodus 28–32). The definitive sign of the Mosaic covenant was the passover, by which the sacrificial offering of a lamb signified Israel's exodus from Egyptian slav-ery and birth as a people. The Paschal lamb implied that the redemp-tion of the nation would occur through substitutionary blood sacrifice (Exodus 12; Mark 14).

The synagogue system was devised to enable continuity in the wor-ship of the exiled community. Through exile the people of Israel devel-oped competencies in languages, trade, flexibility, and survival matched by few other human communities—all a part of the rigorous intergenerational pedagogy of grace. Thereafter the Jews were scattered increasingly throughout the world. It was through this lived history of suffering, captivity, exile, yearning for deliverance, and remembrance, that Israel learned to trust providential grace. Through these curious paths and providential hedgings of the way, Israel was being prepared to mediate, and the world to receive, the Good News of God's own coming (Hos. 2:6; Lam. 3:7; Job 1:10).

Law as Schoolmaster to Grace

The law paved the way to Christ by convicting of sin and calling to repentance. The law pointed toward the gospel; it served to increase the consciousness of sin (Rom. 3:20; 4:15; Gal. 3:19; Heb. 12:24).[38]

---

36. Ambrose, Duties, NPNF 2:10:21, 42; On the Mysteries, 9, p. 324; cf. Gregory of Nyssa, The Life of Moses.
37. Gregory of Nyssa, The Life of Moses, CWS, pp. 37ff.
38. Luther, *Comm. on Gal.*, MLS, pp. 99-134.

Murder was forbidden. There would be no bearing of false witness. All property belonged to Yahweh. The nation was Yahweh's. "Israel was holy to the Lord, / the firstfruits of his harvest" (Jer. 2:3). "'As a belt is bound around a man's waist, so I bound the whole house of Israel and the whole house of Judah to me,' declares the Lord, 'to be my people'" (Jer. 13:11).

Though sacrifices symbolized the divine-human reconciliation, the heart of this covenant was grace, which elicits moral obligation. Yahweh said: "I desire mercy, not sacrifice, / and acknowledgment of God rather than burnt offerings" (Hos. 6:6). "For when I brought your forefathers out of Egypt and spoke to them, I did not just give them commands about burnt offerings and sacrifices, but I gave them this command: Obey me, and I will be your God and you will be my people" (Jer. 7:22-23).

"Moses was faithful as a servant in all God's house, testifying to what would be said in the future" (Heb. 3:5). The promised atonement for the sins of the world had not yet occurred in history, though it was certainly formed in the divine will and anticipatively glimpsed by the prophets. Its promise was fully effectual to all who expected God's own coming.

The godly in Israel were justified not by the law itself, but by faith in the promised coming of God to which the law pointed. All who believed in the coming salvation would be viewed by God as already cleansed and reconciled. God's own coming was viewed as "the end of the law" (*finis legis,* Rom. 10:4), which had served as a tutor to a people in their youthful minority, leading to Christ (*paedagogus ad Christum*). "So the law was put in charge," having a custodial or guardian or schoolmaster function, "to lead us to Christ" (Gal. 3:24).

The Mosaic "ceremonies, sacred rites, sacrifices, and sacraments" were "established to signify something in the future, although they were suited to the divine worship at that time," yet "after our Lord's coming had been signified by them, [they] ceased, and the sacraments of the New Testament began."[39] Among Mosaic signs of the promise that would later be understood in the New Testament as fulfilled were: the exodus itself (1 Cor. 10:12), the feast of manna, water flowing from the rock (1 Cor. 10:3-4), shedding of blood (Heb. 9:18-20), and the tabernacle (Heb. 9:11).

---

39. The Council of Florence, 1438–1445, SCD §712, p. 228.

The Seed of David

The Messiah was expected to come from "the tribe of Judah, the Root of David" (Rev. 5:5). "A shoot will come up from the stump of Jesse; / from his roots a Branch will bear fruit. / The Spirit of the Lord will rest on him" (Isa. 11:1-2).

Like the promise to the seed of Abraham, the promise concerning the seed of David had two complementary aspects: The first was the promise of a well-ordered, safe earthly *land* (as secured through the kingly rule of David and Solomon). The coming salvation would appear through the *progeny* of David, a type of the Messiah as coming Ruler of God's own kingdom. "I will raise up your offspring to succeed you, who will come from your own body, and I will establish his kingdom" to "endure forever" (2 Sam. 7:12, 16).

The hermeneutical key to many of the psalms (traditionally understood as Davidic psalms) lies in this messianic hope, according to patristic exegesis. David was remembered as having rightly grasped the theocentric purpose of the governance of Israel. The king in himself was nothing. The relation of the kingdom to God's justice and God's coming was everything. The royal office was to be rightly exercised by Yahweh himself. The very purpose of governance in Israel was messianically understood. Hence the language of the Psalms is at times emphatically messianic. Yahweh himself is the rightful king in the present and the coming king in the future (Ps. 22:28; 24:1-10). The messianic king is exalted above all the earth (Ps. 2:6; 110:2-6), even though he suffers and experiences abandonment (Ps. 22:1-22). The king is to be freed from the corruption of death (Ps. 16:9-10). The kingdom is universal (Ps. 2:10-12; 110:5-6), and everlasting (Ps. 145:13). The king is the Son of Yahweh (Ps. 2:7), a priest forever after the order of Melchizedek (Ps. 110:4). Such messianic references in the Psalms appeared to apostolic and classical exegetes as references to the history of Jesus.[40]

Israel lived out a curious status among nations: *In* but not *of* the nations, it was forbidden to imitate them or depend on standard armaments, horses, and fenced cities for defense (Hos. 1:7; 8:14). The nation was set apart, a kingdom of priests, a holy nation (Exod. 19:6). In his denunciation of Israel, Amos could say: "Hear this word the Lord

---

40. Jerome, *Hom. on Ps. 36*, FC 48:270-79; Basil, *Exegetic Hom.*, 20, FC 46:333-40.

has spoken against you, O people of Israel—against the whole family I brought up out of Egypt: 'You only have I chosen / of all the families of the earth'" (Amos 3:1-2).

Messianic expectation had general reference to a deliverance in the future, but without present possession. Israel possessed sufficient understanding in the present to live in trust, while confidently expecting more light to show forth in the future. The priestly office pointed toward a complete cleansing of the covenant community at some future time. The hope was awakened of an Anointed One who would bring Israel rightly before God, to mediate fully between the people and God (Ps. 2:2; 89; Isaiah 45).

THE SENDING OF THE SON

The Narrowing of Israel's Covenant Remnant to Jesus Christ

In all these ways the Davidic expectation made reference not only to an earthly kingdom, but also to God's own coming, whose flesh would not see corruption, whose kingdom would have no end, who would combine a priestly and kingly office of unique origin, yet who would suffer on behalf of others, and whose suffering would be the source of blessing for all humanity.

These characteristics found in the messianic elements of the Psalms and prophets shaped the pre-Christian expectation of the Messiah. All were fulfilled, according to classical Christian exegesis, in Jesus of Nazareth. The angelic visitor specifically announced to Mary concerning her coming son: "The Lord God will give him the throne of his father David, and he will reign over the house of Jacob forever" (Luke 1:32-33).

Though the whole of Israel was at times imbued with this spirit of expectation and moral accountability, the continuing history of Israel was filled with as many contingencies and ambiguities as that of other peoples. In time the hope of Israel would be borne by a remnant that lived in steady expectation, as in Zechariah, Anna, Elizabeth, Mary, and John the Baptist. Finally that remnant would, it seemed, narrow to a single individual, Jesus on the cross, despised and rejected by the world (Isa. 10:20-22; 53:3; Luke 18:31-33; Heb. 5:3). The promise of temporal blessings of land and seed to a special people of Israel was now able to be understood as anticipating a fuller spiritual blessing embodied in God's own personal coming.

The redemption of the world was accomplished after this lengthy preparation by the sending of the Son. "When the time had fully come, God sent his Son, born of a woman, born under law, to redeem those under law, that we might receive the full rights of sons" (Gal. 4:4-5). "What God promised our fathers he has fulfilled for us, their children, by raising up Jesus" (Acts 13:32-33).

Jesus summarized this complex history by telling such a simple, incisive parable that, as we learn later, it caused him to be arrested because it put the legitimacy of the prevailing religious elites in question. As God had planted Israel:

> A man planted a vineyard. He put a wall around it, dug a pit for the winepress and built a watchtower. Then he rented the vineyard to some farmers [priests and teachers] and went away on a journey. At harvest time he sent a servant to the tenants to collect from them some of the fruit of the vineyard. But they seized him, beat him and sent him away empty-handed. Then he sent another servant to them; they struck this man on the head and treated him shamefully. He sent still another, and that one they killed. He sent many others [the prophets]; some of them they beat, others they killed. He had one left to send, a son, whom he loved. He sent him last of all, saying, "They will respect my son." But the tenants said to one another, "This is the heir. Come, let's kill him, and the inheritance will be ours." So they took him and killed him, and threw him out of the vineyard. (Mark 12:1-8)[41]

The New Covenant of Grace Written on the Heart

The new covenant of which Jesus is sole mediator both fulfills and transcends the Mosaic form of the covenant (Heb. 8:6), for it is inaugurated by and grounded in God's own personal coming (John 1:17). Christ is the end of the Mosaic law in the sense that a legal condition is requisite to our being reconciled to God. Christ is the fulfillment of the Mosaic law in the sense that he himself obeyed the law completely (Rom. 7:1-4; 10:4; Gal. 3:4).

---

41. Irenaeus, *Ag. Her.* 4.58, AEG 5, pp. 8, 9; Origen, *Comm. on Matt.*, AEG 5, pp. 9ff.

Christ was made vulnerably human for our salvation[42] and died to repair the nature fractured through Adam and Eve.[43] Christ "died as a ransom to set them free from the sins committed under the first covenant" (Heb. 9:15). Neither by natural wit nor by legal striving could fallen humanity be finally restored to favor with God,[44] but only through the merits of the unique Mediator of the divine-human conflict.[45] The descendants of Abraham were "the first to hope in Christ" (Eph. 1:12). The blessing promised to Abraham was now being showered upon all (Gal. 3:14). Gentile believers were now invited to sit down with Abraham, Isaac, and Jacob, becoming joint recipients of their inheritance (Isa. 11:10; 42:1-17; 49:6-13; Jer. 16:19-21; Mal. 1:11).

In the new covenant the Holy Spirit is being poured out upon the church, and in fact upon all flesh (Joel 2:29). New life is given and empowered by God the Spirit, who will guide the faithful into all truth, convict the world of sin, and prepare for the judgment to come (Acts 1–2).

The new covenant expected by Jeremiah (31:31-34) was thus fulfilled in Jesus (Heb. 8:6-13), a covenant written on the heart, whose essential terms are: "I will be their God, and they will be my people" (Jer. 31:33; Heb. 8:10), and whose basic promise is forgiveness: "I will forgive their wickedness and will remember their sins no more" (Jer. 31:34; Heb. 8:12).

The promise of God from the earliest protoevangelium had been to bind the power of sin. Now this binding is coming to full fruition in the effectual calling of persons from sin to faith, confirmed by reliable sacramental signs that testify to the divine promise.[46]

These Last Days

With Christ's advent, the remaining history of the world until final judgment, however long or short it may be, is viewed comprehensively

---

42. Faith of Damasus, SCD §16, p. 10; cf. SCD §§9-10, 13, 40, 54.
43. Second Council of Orange, SCD §194, p. 79; cf. SCD §§794, 800.
44. Council of Trent, SCD §§793, 811.
45. Council of Florence, SCD §711, p. 228; cf. SCD §§790, 795, 809.
46. John 14:18; John Chrysostom, *Hom. on John*, 75, NPNF 1:14:274-75.

as these "last days" (Heb. 1:2). "He made known to us the mystery of his will according to his good pleasure, which he purposed in Christ, to be put into effect when the times will have reached their fulfillment" (Eph. 1:9-10). Christ has promised to remain with the faithful unto the end, looking toward the sanctification and restoration of all things, and to the fitting consummation of God's purpose in creating (Colossians 1).

In the death of Jesus, the atoning work is said to be historically and juridically a "finished" work (*teleō*, John 17:4; 19:30), though it awaits an extended process of reception and recognition as such. This is the revelation of a "mystery, which for ages past was kept hidden in God" (Eph. 3:9). "Even angels long to look into these things" (1 Pet. 1:12).

The inner meaning of Old Testament history is thus beheld in the light of the New. God set aside the promised land as an anticipation of the kingdom to come. The Old Testament economy is filled with types of promises of grace yet to be fulfilled by future unfoldings. These types are not merely abstract symbols, but real events and historical persons whom God chose and used to point silently to a completing reality yet to come. Adam, Eve, Noah, Abraham, Moses, David, and Jonah do not become "types" merely because scholars say they are, but because scripture and tradition have repeatedly designated them as those chosen vessels through which God has pointed to the culmination of the salvation event in Jesus Christ.[47]

From *klēsis* come the *ekklēsia*; from God's call come the called out people. As the people of Israel were called out, so are the new people of God called out of the world by the holiness of God and empowered to serve in the world by the grace of God. Grace is one of the most comprehensive terms of Christian teaching, gathering into a single word-picture a broad range of Christian teachings crucial to the Christian life: redemption, reconciliation, atonement, propitiation, predestination, calling, covenant, grace, conviction, repentance, forgiveness, justification, adoption, faith, conversion, regeneration, sanctification, and perseverance.

The whole range of the searching Spirit of grace is gloriously attested by Hildegard of Bingen:

---

47. Cyril of Alexandria, Letters 41, FC 76:168ff.; Gregory of Nyssa, FGG, 90ff.

Holy are you, cleansing the stench of wounds
O sacred breath O blazing
love O savor in the breast and balm
flooding the heart with
the fragrance of good,

O limpid mirror of God
who leads wanderers
home and hunts out the lost.[48]

---

48. Hildegard of Bingen, *Symphonia*, p. 149.

CHAPTER 11

THE CALL TO SALVATION

Grace requires decision. The offer of salvation is addressed to every discrete hearer, each subject self, in all human conditions. The inviter is the risen Lord, speaking through the Spirit. The Spirit works overtly through preaching, and inwardly in the heart to enable the hearing of the preached word. That calling is effectual which reaches its mark, when the hearer responds in faith to grace.

THE CALL

The electing love of God calls all humanity to saving grace. God's universal call is directed to the particularity of each personal human situation. The direct, external calling occurs through the Spirit and preaching of the Word. The inward call becomes effectual through the inner testimony of the Holy Spirit.

The Terms of Salvation

The terms of salvation are conditions of the personal appropriation of God's saving action—repentance and faith. They are the simple terms of the earliest Christian preaching: Repent and believe. The characteristic order of the apostolic teaching of the call to salvation is:

Repent
Be Baptized
For the Remission of Sins
Receive the Gift of the Holy Spirit

Having initiated the reversal called conversion, grace abides through the Spirit to continue as comforter, guide, witness, to bring every thought captive to the Son, and to bring all our redeemed powers to maturity in all spiritual graces.[1] Grace works to restrain, convict, regenerate, indwell, baptize, seal, and fill.[2] The study of salvation (soteriology) follows upon basic charismology by setting forth in due order the consequences of these outworkings.

The sequence is as follows: the restraint of sin, by which the Spirit provides time for repentance; the conviction of sin, by which the Spirit awakens the sinner to the awareness of sin; repentance, by which the Spirit leads the penitent to godly sorrow for sin, reform of behavior, reparation for harm done to others, revulsion against sin, and confession of sin; faith, by which the Spirit enables one to place personal trust in the Savior; regeneration, by which the Spirit quickens life spiritually so as to begin a new life born of God, born by adoption into the family of God; the indwelling of the Spirit, by which the Spirit comes to reside in the heart of the believer; baptism of the Spirit, by which the new person becomes dead to the old way and alive to the new; the sealing of the Holy Spirit, by which the Spirit confirms the living Word in the heart; assurance, by which the Holy Spirit witnesses inwardly to the spirit of the believer that one is a son or daughter of God, pardoned and adopted, enabling a firm conviction that one is reconciled to God; the filling of the believer by the Holy Spirit, by which the Spirit comes more and more fully to express the way of holiness in the life of the believer; and sanctification, by which the Spirit works to bring the regenerate spirit of the believer into full participation in the life of God through union with Christ.

The Order of Salvation

The order of salvation (*ordo salutis*) is the sequence of gracious acts by which salvation is prepared, enabled, conferred, sustained, and completed. It is the unfolding process by which God the Spirit awakens faith in the believer on behalf of the mission of the Son sent by the Father.

The order of salvation was summarized by Luther's Small Catechism: "The Holy Spirit has called me through the Gospel, enlightened me with his gifts, and sanctified and preserved me in true faith, just as he

---

1. Cyril of Jerusalem, *Catech. Lect.* 2–5, NPNF 2:7:8-33; cf. Merrill, ACE 164-68.
2. Owen, *Works* 4:8:352ff.; cf. Sperry, ST 6:103.

calls, gathers, enlightens, and sanctifies the whole Christian church on earth and preserves it in union with Jesus Christ in the one true faith."[3] Principal acts of the Spirit that belong to this sequence are: the call, illumination, repentance, faith, regeneration, conversion, union with Christ, and sanctification. This order begins necessarily with the call to salvation.

The Holy Spirit makes known the divine purpose for the salvation of humanity through proclamation. This part of Christian teaching is the doctrine of calling or vocation. Systematically viewed, this doctrine requires a discussion of:

The One who Calls	An Event of Calling	Those Called
The Inviter	The Invitation	Those Invited
Election	Vocation	The Church
Kaleo, to Call	*Klēsis*, Calling	*Klētos*, the Called

Those called are the *ekklēsia*, the community of those called out, breathed into life, and cleansed by the Spirit.[4] We focus first on the gracious One who calls, then the event of being called to faith, and finally the beloved community of those called.

At this point it is useful to recall the characteristic place of the doctrine of grace in the usual sequence of topics of systematic theology. Although charismology connects with all topics of theology, its special place is in pneumatology, since the Spirit is, among the triune persons, the applier and enabler of grace in our hearts. The location of charismology within systematics is seen in the following schema. After dealing with the Father who creates (creation, providence, and knowledge of God), the Son who reconciles (Christology), and the Spirit who consummates (pneumatology), systematic theology proceeds to ask how the grace of the triune God is beneficially applied to sinners.

---

3. CC 116.
4. Barth, CD 3/4:600ff.

DOCTRINAL LOCUS	SUBJECT OF INQUIRY
Charismology	The Grace of God
Soteriology	The Call to Salvation
Ecclesiology	The Called Community
Eschatology	The Destiny of Those Called

The Calling of Israel and the Calling of the Gentiles

In the Old Testament, the calling of Yahweh was limited to a particular people, who, as recipients of electing divine love, were through a complex history effectively called. In the New Testament, the calling of the triune God is universally addressed to all humanity, who, having been called by God's own coming, are elected by their own free confirmation and choice, an election foreknown from eternity by the all-wise eternal God.[5]

The gracious election of Israel is absolute, since "God's gifts and his call are irrevocable" (Rom. 11:29), even when resisted. Yahweh chose a lineage out of which the messianic Servant would arise, and having made that election did not swerve from it, even when the people were disobedient. Out of Abraham's seed came many who lived a holy life accountable to God, though many did not. The call of Abraham represents the anticipatory calling of God to all humanity through the promise of blessing to a particular people and the requirement of faith and obedience.[6]

The New Testament *ekklēsia*—the called community, the community of believers—are chosen not by absolute decree but in relation to their receptivity to the conditions of the call. By faith they are chosen "out of the world" (John 15:19). "God chose you to be saved through the sanctifying work of the Spirit and through belief in the truth" (2 Thess. 2:13).

---

5. Calvin, *Inst.* 3.21, 22; cf. Wm. Perkins, *A Golden Chain, the Work of Wm. Perkins* (Abingdon in Exeter: Sutton Courtenay Press, 1970), pp. 169ff.
6. Clement of Alexandria, *Stromata* 5.1, ANF 2:445-46; cf. Origen, *Hom. on Genesis* 3, FC 71:89-102.

The salutation of First Peter was addressed "To God's elect, strangers in the world, scattered throughout Pontus, Galatia, Cappadocia, Asia and Bithynia, who have been chosen according to the foreknowledge of God the Father," yet this election must be experientially confirmed "through the sanctifying work of the Spirit, *for obedience* to Jesus Christ" (1 Pet. 1:1, 2, ital. ad.). Election is for a setting apart, a sanctification through the Spirit, grounded not in any work or merit but in faith in God's atoning work.[7]

Those who accept the divine call are variously addressed as *ekklēsia*, the called out ones, the elect, those "called to be saints" (Rom. 1:6, 7), "those whom God has chosen" (Rom. 8:33), "God's chosen people" (Col. 3:12)—all who by grace are responsive to God's calling to belong to the household of faith "according to the foreknowledge of God the Father, through the sanctifying work of the Spirit" (1 Pet. 1:2).

Election always presupposes the call; but the call does not always issue in election.[8] When Jesus said, "Many are invited, but few are chosen" (Matt. 22:14), the implication was that the Good News is addressed to all, though only some answer responsively. He knew that some would "refuse to come to me to have life" (John 5:40).

Even those called effectively to faith may fall temporarily back into the temptations of the old life; hence, this injunction to the faithful: "Examine yourselves to see whether you are in the faith; test yourselves. Do you not realize that Christ Jesus is in you—unless, of course, you fail the test" (2 Cor. 13:5).

THE OFFER OF SALVATION

Those who freely accept the call and enter into the new family of God are designated "the called" (*klētois*, 1 Cor. 1:24). Evangelical preaching characteristically concludes with a summons to decision, symbolized in the tradition of revivalism as an altar call. At this point a response is pertinent: The gospel having been announced and its terms clarified, hearers are called to make a pivotal decision to receive the Good News.

---

7. Calvin, *Inst.* 3.22-24.
8. Pope, *Compend.* 3.345.

The offer of salvation occurs when the gospel is not only proclaimed, and its condition of repentance and faith clarified, and the offer of forgiveness made, but also its hearers commanded and called to believe. Hence proclamation, offer, and command must be united in any serious teaching of the call to hear and receive the gospel.[9]

The Gospel Call

The gospel call forms a bridge between preparatory (prevenient) grace and convincing (convicting) grace by actually inviting sinners to come and participate in the benefits of God's saving action. Calling is that act of the triune God by which all are invited to repent and believe the Good News of God's coming.[10] The gospel is "the power of God for the salvation of everyone who believes" (Rom. 1:16).

The Good News is that God's kingdom has been inaugurated by the ministry of Jesus. Its prototypical announcement in Luke's Gospel was addressed to the shepherds of Bethlehem: "I bring you good news of great joy that will be for all the people. Today in the town of David a Savior has been born to you; he is Christ the Lord" (Luke 2:10-11). The gospel is a message announcing God's coming and an invitation personally to receive the salvation offered by God. Gospel preaching announces that the time of fulfillment of the promised One expected by the prophets is now (Luke 3:9; Rom. 13:11).

The gospel call included not merely the simple announcement of God's Good News, but also the teaching necessary to make clear the plan of salvation, along with an urgent invitation to all hearers to repent and believe, warning of the consequences of neglect and disbelief. Hence preaching aims at a decision which cannot be self-initiated. Faith exists only in response to the convicting and justifying grace of God, for "no one can come to me unless the Father who sent me draws him" (John 6:44), and "no one can say, 'Jesus is Lord,' except by the Holy Spirit" (1 Cor. 12:3). The call to grace occurs by grace.[11]

The Inviter

The call issues out of eternity, before creation, from the eternal love of God who has "called us to a holy life—not because of anything we

---

9. Wesley, "The Way to the Kingdom," WJW 5:76-86; WJWB 1:217-32.
10. Calvin, *Inst.* 3.24; cf. Barth, CD 3/3:497ff.; 4/3:481ff.
11. John Chrysostom, *Baptismal Instructions*, ACW 31:173-74.

have done but because of his own purpose and grace" (2 Tim. 1:9). This primordial call in the fullness of time becomes explicit in history through the ministry of the Son.[12]

The call essentially takes the form of an invitation to come and receive: "'Come!' Whoever is thirsty, let him come; and whoever wishes, let him take the free gift of the water of life" (Rev. 22:17).[13]

The Inviter is Christ himself: "Come to me, all you who are weary and burdened, and I will give you rest. Take my yoke upon you and learn from me, for I am gentle and humble in heart, and you will find rest for your souls. For my yoke is easy and my burden is light" (Matt. 11:28-30). The invitation is addressed to all, embracing all classes, races, cultures, and languages.

The call of God assumes Christ's great commission to proclaim the gospel to all creatures (Matt. 28:18-20). For "how can they believe in the one of whom they have not heard? and how can they hear without someone preaching to them?" (Rom. 10:14).

The Variability of Perceptions of the Gospel

Since all hearers live within history amid some particular society, not abstracted from their own culture, the manner in which each hearer receives and processes the call will depend significantly on the historical conditions surrounding that person. To some the gospel is proclaimed in a way more perceptible than to others. This deepens the moral quandary for modern believers: What if all are not given a precisely equal chance to hear the gospel? Does this impugn the integrity or sincerity of God? This is one of many theological problems for which revelation does not always supply an easy or uncluttered answer, for "God gives His Word at one place and not at another," and "removes it from one place but lets it remain at another."[14] Paul celebrated the mystery of grace in this way: "Consider therefore the kindness and sternness of God: sternness to those who fell, but kindness to you, provided that you continue in his kindness" (Rom. 11:22). Faith does not itch every day to preempt secret things when so much is revealed: "The

---

12. Helvetic Consensus Formula, CC 316-19.
13. Macarius Chrysocephalus, "The Prodigal Son," in *Fragments*, ANF 2:581-84; cf. Kierkegaard, *TC*.
14. BOC 626.

secret things belong to the Lord our God, but the things revealed belong to us and to our children forever" (Deut. 29:29).

God's Singular Call Universally Addresses All Particular Conditions

The call is termed universal—*vocatio catholica*—because God's call to humanity is addressed to all at all times whether pre-evangelically through conscience or moral awareness or hope or according to the law written on the hearts of all (Rom. 1:19; 2:15; Acts 14:17), or more distinctly through the pure Word of God preached.

Even amid the history of sin, the world is always being variably and situationally drawn to grace by "the true light that gives light to every man," which "was coming into the world" (John 1:9). Wherever any glimpse of the truth is being grasped, there the Spirit of truth is guiding (John 16:13).

Because of the composite, finitely free nature of persons abiding in history, God's call to humanity can be personally addressed only in specific times and places. God's address is always located at some particular nexus of unfolding history. Because of the recalcitrance of sin, the process of human recognition of the divine love for humanity is typically slow, tardy, and gradual.[15] In principle, God's call is universally addressed to all humanity, yet within the conditions of history it only gradually appears as a concrete call to particular persons in particular times, representatively to all through some.

A prophetic prototype of the divine address is the call of Samuel as a boy during crisis times when "there were not many visions," when "the word of the Lord was rare" (1 Sam. 3:1). Three times the Lord called Samuel in the temple near the ark when the weak-eyed Eli was nearby. The third time Samuel said: "Speak, Lord, for your servant is listening" (1 Sam. 3:9). Thereafter, "The Lord was with Samuel as he grew up, and he let none of his words fall to the ground" (1 Sam. 3:19).

The Triune Premise of the Invitation

There is a triune premise in the Christian teaching of the call of God: The eternal One who calls is God the Father, who never leaves the world wholly without witness to divine mercy. The teachings of provi-

---

15. Arnobius, *Ag. Heathen* 1.54-65, ANF 6:428-33; cf. Pope, *Compend.* 3:336.

dence and prevenience assist Christianity in answering the moral complaints associated with variable and unequal circumstances of calling. The scandal is that the fall occurs precisely within, not above, history. While Eve's children scratch the ground, sweat to survive, bear children with difficulty, struggle with limitations, pain, and death, the whole order of nature and history is not without purpose but designed to provide time to elicit repentance and faith.[16]

The One who calls is God the Son, who in due time comes to announce God's kingdom, to call all to repentance and faith, and to offer pardon for all of humanity's sins.

The One by whom the Son effectively calls is God the Spirit, who makes the proclamation of the Good News capable of appropriation by attesting to it credibly in our hearts, working quietly to convict the world of sin, righteousness, and judgment to come (John 16:8).

These three are One. The Son said: "All that belongs to the Father is mine. That is why I said the Spirit will take from what is mine and make it known to you" (John 16:15). "We are witnesses of these things, and so is the Holy Spirit, whom God has given to those who obey him" (Acts 5:32).

EFFECTUAL CALLING

The invitation to faith has traditionally been distinguished in these three aspects: an *external* call (directly through pure preaching of the Word); an *inward* call (addressed to the heart through the Spirit); and an *effectual* call (wherein God's intent is fulfilled through grace awakening a fitting human response).

The Direct, External Calling of God the Spirit Through Preaching

The actual preaching of the gospel is sometimes termed the direct call, where the word of truth is publicly proclaimed and directly addressed to the sinner, with an invitation to repent and believe. The apostles were told: "As the Father has sent me, I am sending you" (John 20:21) to proclaim the gospel to every creature (Matt. 28:19). The call

---

16. Lactantius, *The Wrath of God*, FC 54:76ff.

of the Father comes through the heard Word concerning the Son, whose being heard is enabled by the Spirit working through human agency in the church (Rom. 10:14-17).

Though sometimes circuitous, the address of the Word is deliberate: "As the rain and the snow / come down from heaven" only later to yield "bread for the eater, / so is my word that goes out from my mouth: / It will not return to me empty, / but will accomplish what I desire / and achieve the purpose for which I sent it."[17]

The Inward Call

It was said of Lydia that "the Lord opened her heart to respond to Paul's message" (Acts 16:14). God's Spirit is inwardly present enabling the awakening of conscience, applying the truth to our hearts, and making effective the proclamation. Through an interior grace, the Spirit acts by a persuasive power to help enable the acceptance of the invitation to believe the gospel.

The gospel call which comes outwardly through the written and preached Word is heard through the inward testimony of the Spirit. This inward work does not disdain the importance of reason, rhetoric, moral awareness, aesthetic subtlety, disciplined study of scripture, ancient church teaching, or general lay consent. By these means the Holy Spirit strives with the human spirit, awakening, judging, and encouraging free response to convicting and justifying grace.[18]

The Effectual Call

The call to faith is not received by all in the same way. Some resist, some are indifferent. The hearts of some seem to be hardened upon hearing it. Some repent and believe. Jesus' parable of the seeds shows the variability of receptors (Matt. 13:3-27 and parallels). Not all who are called are subdued by grace.[19]

It is a point of intense irony that the call to repent and believe is addressed only to sinners. Jesus came to call not the righteous but sinners to repentance (Luke 5:32). The only readiness required is the

17. Isa. 55:10-11; cf. Juliana of Norwich, *RDL* 100-102.
18. Confession of Dositheus 12, CC 496.
19. Augustine, *Gift of Persev.* 9.21, NPNF 1:5:532-33; cf. *On Predestination of the Saints* 10.19, NPNF 1:5:493ff.

desire to flee the wrath to come (Matt. 3:7).[20] To "those living in darkness / and in the shadow of death," the light of God has shined, "to guide our feet into the path of peace" (Luke 1:79), precisely while we were "separate from Christ, excluded from citizenship in Israel and foreigners to the covenants of the promise, without hope and without God in the world" (Eph. 2:12).

The church's ministry wishes to furnish everything needed to enable an effective faithful response. If the seed falls upon hard ground and is rejected, it is then due not to the lack of preaching but to the resistance of the sinner who freely rejects God's offer of grace. Essential to God's inviting work is the premise that the Good News of God's own coming is being made clearly known, the offer of forgiveness stated meaningfully, and opportunity given to respond in faith. The divine command is regularly accompanied by the promise of grace that precedes obedience, and the blessing that follows obedience.[21]

The Westminster Confession brought the teaching of effectual calling to a refined statement: God has effectually called the elect

> by his Word and Spirit, out of that state of sin and death, in which they are by nature, to grace and salvation by Jesus Christ, enlightening their minds spiritually and savingly, to understand the things of God; taking away their heart of stone, and giving unto them an heart of flesh; renewing their wills, and by his almighty power determining them to that which is good; and effectually drawing them to Jesus Christ, yet so as they come most freely, being made willing by his grace.[22]

The Hour of Decision

In the hour in which decision is possible, one must decide. Indifference is a decision by default to reject the gospel. The decision is freely made. The person who hears the gospel call is entirely responsible for what is decided. Because of the brevity of life, one who neglects an opportunity at hand may not have another.[23]

Those who harden their hearts when the invitation is offered may have a harder time responding the next time the opportunity nears.

20. Wesley, *General Rules*, WJW 8:269.
21. Pope, *Compend*. 3.344, 345.
22. CC 206.
23. Tertullian, *Ag. Marcion* 4.28, AEG 4.80.

Those who imagine that they can delay may find life called away just when the storehouses are full (Luke 12:13-21).

At the moment of decision, the choice is simply to obey or to disobey—repent and believe or by not repenting disbelieve. It is a choice finally made in the presence of God. One's education, heredity, former habituation, character, oedipal relations, and neurotic tendencies may to some degree shape the conditions under which the choice is made, but finally the choice is radically clear-cut: Turn toward or away from the revealed mercy of God.[24] No one is saved without such a decision. No one is lost until the mercy of God in Christ is offered and rejected.

Every human being, even if twisted by pride and sensuality, by grace is given from time to time some capacity for contrition. When that gift is given, it must be exercised to the utmost; otherwise, the opportunity will wither and fade.

> Come, all ye souls by sin oppressed,
> Ye restless wand'rers after rest,
> Ye poor, and maimed, and halt, and blind,
> In Christ a hearty welcome find.
>
> Sent by my Lord, on you I call;
> The invitation is to all:
> Come, all the world! come, sinner, thou;
> All things in Christ are ready now.[25]

---

24. Baxter, *PW* 4.411, 412.
25. C. Wesley, "Come, Sinners, to the Gospel Feast," *PS* 111.

CONCLUSION:

THE ORTHODOX EVANGELICAL-CATHOLIC DOCTRINE OF GRACE

Grace is the favor shown by God to sinners. It is the divine goodwill offered to those who neither inherently deserve nor can ever hope to earn it. It is the divine disposition to work in our hearts, wills, and actions, so as to communicate effectively God's self-giving love for humanity.

Grace works through all the faculties of human consciousness: illumining the intellect, strengthening the will, and guiding the senses. Grace works with special power in the life of believers, first through awakening the radical need for illumination, then enabling the petition for illumination, then through illuminating the believer regarding the darkness of sin, moving sinners steadily toward the means of grace. Grace works precisely amid and through freedom both actually and habitually by going before willing, convicting the will, operating within the will, cooperating with the will, and following through by enabling the goodwill to persevere.

One does not acquire the disposition to receive grace without grace. One may not pray for grace without grace. By grace the sinner gradually learns to remove obstacles to the reception of grace.

Grace is necessary to enable the recovery of the fallen will, which cannot long persevere in good deeds without grace. The work of common grace is present in human history, reason, and moral awareness as restrainer of sin and providential caregiver in times of unusual historical crisis. Fallen humanity is never left without witness to grace. Whatever corruption it suffers remains incomplete. Even when rejected, grace does not cease to be sufficiently offered to all, and always within the range of the variable capacity of each.

What God gives is never ineptly given or wanting in sufficiency. The deficiency lies in recalcitrant responses to grace. God antecedently wills that all should be saved, but not without their own free acceptance of salvation. Consequent to that exercise of freedom, God promises unmerited saving mercies to the faithful and fairness to the unfaithful. God does not will woodenly without reference to the variability of human willing.

God's foreknowing does not rob human freedom of its efficacy. Though God's foreknowing of evil is steeped in mystery, the power of evil is once for all bound and conquered on the cross. Faith receives but does not merit election. Election is made sure by faith. Those called are responsible for their response or lack of response to grace. Only those are eternally separated from God's holiness who are by their own will self-alienated and self-condemned.

Grace is not merely an idea but a history. It is only when these ideas are related to a concrete history of the work of grace that they take on plausibility and power. The palpable, discernible, developmental outworking of grace in actual salvation history is the central narrative concern of the biblical teaching of grace.

The divine-human covenant is made known in an actual history of grace. Faith is the condition of receiving the blessings of covenant. All history in due time becomes embraced within the history of grace. From the dawn of human history, the covenant is gradually revealed through a history of sacrifice, which is finally ratified in the events to which the New Testament witnesses. Whatever diverse forms it may take, the divine-human covenant is one covenant, pretemporally anticipated in the covenant between Father and Son through the Spirit, and worked out through a history of covenant destined to be consummated on the last day.

Even in the general history of religions we see a widespread preparation for grace leading toward God's own coming. The history of the covenant people exists within the history of religions, and as a clarification and judgment of the history of religions. Abraham is the prototype of faith for the covenant people, who are his seed. The covenant promises are most fully understood and grasped from the vantage point of their fulfillment. In Moses the covenant takes the form of law, and in David the form of governance. In time only a remnant is left of the faithful people.

With the cross and resurrection and the indwelling of the Spirit, the history of the revelation of grace has reached its fulfillment, calling hearers to full responsiveness in the historical time that remains until the Son shall return in final judgment.

Grace requires decision. In the hour in which decision is possible, one must decide. Indifference is a decision by default to reject the gospel. Because of the brevity of life, one who neglects an opportunity at hand may not have another.